THE SEAWORTHY
Offshore
Sailboat

A GUIDE TO ESSENTIAL FEATURES, GEAR, AND HANDLING

JOHN VIGOR

CAMDEN, MAINE • NEW YORK • SAN FRANCISCO • WASHINGTON, D.C. • AUCKLAND
BOGOTÁ • CARACAS • LISBON • LONDON • MADRID • MEXICO CITY • MILAN
MONTREAL • NEW DELHI • SAN JUAN • SINGAPORE • SYDNEY • TOKYO • TORONTO

To June, my best friend, my love.

International Marine
A Division of The McGraw-Hill Companies

4 6 8 10 9 7 5 3

Copyright ©1999, 2001 John Vigor

All rights reserved. The publisher takes no responsibility for the use of any of the materials or methods described in this book, nor for the products thereof. The name "International Marine" and the International Marine logo are trademarks of The McGraw-Hill Companies. Printed in the United States of America.

The Library of Congress has cataloged the cloth edition as follows:

Vigor, John.
    The seaworthy offshore sailboat : a guide to essential features, gear, and handling / John Vigor.
       p.   cm.
    Includes bibliographical references and index.
    ISBN 0-07-134328-8
    1. Yachts—Design and construction. 2. Sailboats—Design and construction. 3. Yachting—Handbooks, manuals, etc. 4. Sailing—Handbooks, manuals, etc. I. Title.
    VM331.V54 1999
    623.8'22—dc21
                                          98-51698
                                              CIP

Paperback ISBN 0-07-137616-X

Questions regarding the content of this book should be addressed to:
International Marine
P.O. Box 220, Camden, ME 04843
www.internationalmarine.com

Questions regarding the ordering of this book should be addressed to:
The McGraw-Hill Companies
Customer Service Department
P.O. Box 547, Blacklick, OH 43004
Retail customers: 1-800-262-4729
Bookstores: 1-800-722-4726

This book is printed on 60-lb. Finch.

Printed by R.R Donnelley & Sons, Crawfordsville, IN
Design by Eugenie S. Delaney
Illustrations by Jim Sollers
Production by Publisher's Design & Production Services and Dan Kirchoff
Edited by Jonathan Eaton, Cynthia Flanagan Goss, and Scott Kirkman

Clorox, Dacron, Gore-Tex, Hypalon, Teflon, Terylene, Velcro, and WD-40 are registered trademarks.

Contents

Acknowledgments iv
Introduction v

Part 1. Defining the Capable Boat 1
1. SEAWORTHINESS 2
2. TEST *YOUR* BOAT 16
3. THE ESSENTIALS 22
   The Hull 22
   The Bulkheads 25
   The Deck 26
   The Cockpit 27
   The Rudder 28
   The Keel 29

Part 2. Fitting Out 31
4. SPARS AND RIGGING 32
5. GROUND TACKLE 43
6. DECK, COCKPIT, AND SUPERSTRUCTURE 55
7. ENGINE AND PROPELLER 65
8. SAFETY EQUIPMENT 75
9. NAVIGATION GEAR 97
10. ELECTRICITY 114
11. THE GALLEY 121
12. CREATURE COMFORTS 139
13. SELF-STEERING GEAR 151
14. WHAT ABOUT YOU? 162
15. THE PAPER CHASE 177

Part 3. Theory and Practice 185
16. SURVIVING HEAVY WEATHER 186
17. ANCHORING IN PRACTICE 204
18. GASTRO-NAVIGATION 209
19. THE BLACK BOX THEORY 214

Appendix 1. *OVERTURE*'S ATLANTIC ADVENTURE 217
Appendix 2. BEEFING UP A CATALINA 27 221

Bibliography 227
Index 228

Acknowledgments

Where credit is due, it is mostly given in the text. But there are at least three sources who are worthy of special acknowledgment.

My thanks go to Patrick Childress, who generously shared with me his work list for the conversion of his Catalina 27, *Juggernaut*.

Also, I must acknowledge the contribution of Dave and Jean Parsons, whose courage, seamanship, and skillful handling of *Overture* saved their lives when they were overwhelmed by a storm in the Bay of Biscay.

Finally, I'd like to thank Jonathan Eaton, Editorial Director of International Marine, for his valuable guidance, patience, and professionalism.

Introduction

That splendid voyager and author Eric Hiscock maintained that remarkably few vessels used for ocean voyages were actually built for that purpose. He said a study showed that most of the small boats that had crossed oceans were old, or at least secondhand. They were, in fact, just whatever would-be voyagers happened to possess "at the time they decided to cross an ocean or two."

Or else they were just as much boat as they could afford. The majority of long-distance cruisers, Hiscock noted in chapter 1 of *Voyaging Under Sail*, had difficulty making ends meet.

> "Yet a large proportion of them succeeded in doing what they set out to do, which emphasizes once again the truth of the saying: 'It's not the ships but the men in them.'
>
> "Nevertheless, a suitable vessel suitably rigged and fitted does increase the chance of success, and will undoubtedly make the voyage less hazardous and more enjoyable . . ."

But what is "a suitable vessel suitably rigged and fitted"? You must have pondered that question if, like most of us, you've occasionally found yourself dreaming of sailing over the horizon. You must have wondered if your standard production sailboat is sound enough to cross an ocean, or if your proven cruising design has all the gear necessary for a successful passage to foreign shores.

That deep-seated urge to sail over the horizon and keep going can be very strong. It even affects those who don't yet have boats of their own. Every day, some potential buyer looking at a boat somewhere is assured that she's capable of sailing around the world. If you're that someone,

and you're not an experienced deep-sea sailor, treat the information with reserve. There is a great deal of emotion and misinformation bound up with buying boats. It's very difficult to get good advice and trustworthy facts, even if you pay for them. But if you're going to trust your life to a boat on a wild ocean, and perhaps the lives of your family and friends too, you badly need that advice and those facts.

That's where this book comes in. It will tell you, without pulling any punches, if your present boat (or the one you've got your eye on) is ready to take on the sea. And if she's not, it will tell you what you have to do to put her right. There is no mumbo-jumbo here, just proven facts and the old-fashioned, tested principles of safe boat design and handling. This a simple book for practical sailors, expressed in down-to-earth terms.

Most boats built today are standard production boats, many of which could be classified as coastal cruisers. They are greatly influenced by racing designs but are modified for greater luxury and more accommodations. They have many of the basic elements of ocean seaworthiness, but not all those elements. And the ones they do have are often not sufficient.

In these pages you will find simple, understandable explanations of the most important elements of seaworthiness—what naval architect and research scientist C. A. Marchaj calls "The Forgotten Factor" in modern boat design. And just so we know exactly what we're talking about, you'll find a simple definition of that much abused word *seaworthiness*, as it applies to small sailboats.

Incidentally, one of our basic requirements for seaworthiness is a boat's ability to recover from an upside-down position, because scientific tests have shown that any small monohull can be capsized when struck broadside by a breaking wave with a height of 55 percent or more of the yacht's overall length. So even a seaworthy boat can turn upside down if conditions are bad enough. But she won't stay that way long enough to sink.

To help you determine whether your present boat is inherently fit for long-distance voyaging, there is a unique quiz in chapter 2 that touches on all the important elements of seaworthiness, not forgetting you yourself. After you've evaluated your boat's potential, you can find out in successive chapters how to alter and strengthen her, if necessary. And, in the fitting-out section, you'll discover what equipment is *essential* for ocean voyaging. It may surprise you to know how little that really amounts to.

All the simple tables, graphs, and rules of thumb you need are sprinkled throughout the text in condensed form, where you need them.

In keeping with the practical theme of this book, the detailed descriptions of the gear and equipment your boat should carry are divided into two categories: essential gear and luxury gear. This will help you to tailor your own requirements, and to keep costs down, without sacrificing any elements of seaworthiness.

Part 3 and the appendices in this book are worthy of special mention, because they progress from the theoretical requirements of the ocean-going yacht to the everyday practice of boat handling and living aboard.

Part 3 opens with a comprehensive section on how to survive heavy weather. A full exposition of Vigor's Black Box Theory, which explains why some boats survive storms and some don't, is also included. Two chapters deal with very important facets of the cruising life: anchoring, and gastro-navigation (yes, gastro, not astro—from a woman who has actually been there, cooked that, and got the T-shirt).

The two appendices include, first, a startling true story of how *not* to do it—a story of an extraordinary voyage in an unsuitable boat by a plucky but inexperienced couple during the wrong season. Their voyage resulted in the loss of the rudder and the mast and three roll-overs—but luckily no loss of life. In the second you will find practical instructions on how to prepare America's most popular 27-footer, the Catalina 27, for a world circumnavigation, from a man who actually did it.

Throughout the text, I have recommended certain books as sources for further information. Details on all the books mentioned are included in the bibliography (page 227).

According to estimates in yachting magazines and cruising newsletters, about 2,000 to 3,000 small U.S.-registered sailboats are voyaging around the world at any one time. If that's your dream—if you, too, are itching to see what's on the other side of the horizon—this book will show you how to make it come true.

NOTE: Because retail prices change so quickly, the actual cost of many of the items of equipment mentioned would be out of date in short order. To overcome this problem, the cost is referred to in beers. In the interests of political correctness, it should be noted that these are fiscal beers, not alcoholic beers. This artifice permits direct arithmetical comparisons between the prices of equipment mentioned in the text without using actual dollar amounts that would soon be out of date. Any convenient unit of comparison would have sufficed; but for reasons of no consequence here, the currency selected was fiscal beer.

The advantage of the fiscal beer monetary system is plain. At any date in the future, you need only to enquire after the current retail price of a bottle of beer served in a restaurant or a yacht club bar, and simple multiplication will give you a pretty good idea of the current price of the equipment mentioned in this book. By way of comparison, the monetary value of a fiscal beer at the time of writing was fixed at $2.50.

PART 1

Defining the Capable Boat

CHAPTER 1

Seaworthiness

Most mass-produced sailboats are based on the coastal cruiser philosophy. Their design and construction is governed by the theory that they will not stray far from a safe port and that their owners will seldom want to be at sea for more than a couple of nights. This philosophy calls for a light, fast, stiff, weatherly boat with spacious accommodations, plenty of auxiliary power, and sufficient crewmembers to handle her.

An ocean cruiser, on the other hand, must look after herself and her shorthanded crew in all types of weather for extended periods of time far from land. This calls for sturdier construction, stronger spars and rigging, more stowage, less need for weatherliness, and more need for seakindliness. In short, an oceangoing sailboat needs to be more seaworthy than a coastal cruiser.

That statement would border on the banal were it not for the fact that seaworthiness is poorly understood and difficult to define. If seawor-

Typical Differences Between Coastal and Ocean Cruisers	
Coastal Cruiser	**Ocean Cruiser**
Taller, narrower rig	Often lower, wider sail plan
Average-strength rigging	Heavier standing rigging
Often single lower shrouds	Double lower shrouds
Fin keel	Longer keel
Spade rudder	Rudder hung from keel or skeg
Low or no bridgedeck	Solid, full-height bridgedeck
Large cockpit, small drains	Smaller cockpit, larger drains
Large portlights	Smaller portlights
Poor ventilation	Good ventilation
Minimal chocks and cleats	More, bigger chocks and cleats
No bow anchor rollers	Bow anchor rollers
Single row of reef points	More reef points
Maximum number of berths	Fewer berths
High freeboard and/or high cabin trunk	Lower freeboard and cabin trunk
Minimal navigation station	Bigger navigation station
Small fuel and water tanks	Larger fuel and water tanks
Little stowage	More stowage
Plenty of crew	Mostly shorthanded

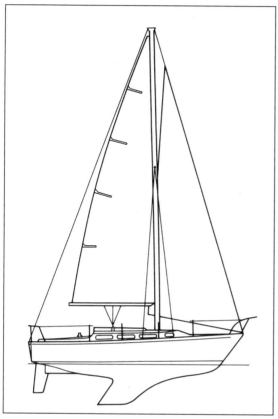

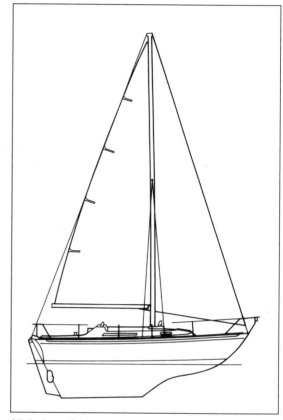

Catalina 30

Nicholson 31

thiness were merely the ability to stay afloat in the worst conditions of wave and weather, then a corked bottle, an empty eggshell, or a scrap piece of plastic foam all would qualify as supremely seaworthy.

Unfortunately, that's not a practical definition for our purposes, although it does illustrate that seaworthiness has more to do with design and construction than with size. It is a fact that a good big boat is more seaworthy than a good small boat, but size alone is not a reliable indication of seaworthiness. Many very small boats, including at least one less than 6 feet (1.83 m) long, have crossed oceans. But without going to that extreme, it is safe to say that boats of 20 feet (6 m) in overall length have proved themselves seaworthy enough to sail around the world.

There are two more important characteristics of a seaworthy boat: the ability, even in extremely heavy weather, to maneuver clear of dangers such as rocks and shorelines; and habitability, the ability to accommodate human beings. And there is a very desirable third characteristic: the ability of a sailboat to right herself quickly from the upside-down position and to continue her voyage.

There is no guarantee that even the largest yachts are immune from capsize, since (according to tests carried out at Southampton University, England) they can be turned turtle by a breaking wave with a height equal to 55 percent of their overall length. Thus, a 35-foot (10.7-m) boat would be capsized through 180 degrees by a 20-foot (6-m) wave, which could be generated by a 40-knot wind blowing for about 40 hours. Even a

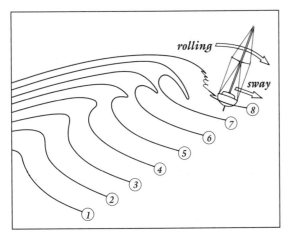

Development of a plunging breaker. Because of the rapid change in the steepness of the wave, a small boat caught between stages 2 and 7 would have little or no chance of avoiding capsize.

breaking wave with a height equalling only 35 percent of the boat's length (a 12-foot wave for a 35-footer or a 3.7-meter wave for a 10.7-meter boat) will roll her 130 degrees—from which position she may recover or turn turtle. And a 12-foot (3.7-meter) wave can be generated by a 24-knot wind blowing for 24 hours. Even large ocean liners and tankers have fallen victim to freak waves off the South African Wild Coast, between Durban and East London, where the swift-flowing Agulhas Current rears up in frenzy when confronted by southwesterly gales.

It is prudent, in any discussion of seaworthiness, to take it for granted that a boat may be rolled upside down at some stage. The chances of this happening depend on the size of the yacht, where she is sailed, the experience of her crew, and the time of the year. Along the well-used trade wind routes during the recommended times of passage, the likelihood of capsize is extremely small. Around Cape Horn in winter, it is infinitely greater.

A seaworthy boat, therefore, is one that is:

- Able to recover from the inverted position

without serious damage to her hull, deck, rig, rudder, or interior, and without shipping substantial amounts of water.
- Strong enough to look after herself while hove-to or lying ahull.
- Seakindly—that is, free of violent, extravagant, jerky rolling and pounding.
- Well balanced, docile on the helm, and easily handled under sail at all times.
- Agile downwind, to maneuver out of the way of plunging breakers.
- Able to beat to windward, or at least hold her ground, in all but the heaviest conditions.
- Habitable—able to carry ample crew with good headroom and comfort, plus water and supplies, for extended periods.
- Capable of good average speeds on long passages.

No boat can fulfill all these requirements to perfection, since many are mutually exclusive. For instance, the long keel that makes a boat hold her course well also makes her less maneuverable. The widely spread-out sail plan that helps with helm balance also makes her less efficient to windward. Everything in boat design is a matter of trade-offs. One desirable feature must be sacrificed for another. But the most successful designs spring from a kind of mysterious resonance that occurs when sacrifices, judiciously made, add up to a net gain.

The requirement for a boat to be self-righting from a capsize would also disqualify most multihulls, because they are just as stable upside down as they are standing the right way up. Although some multihulls may be able to regain their feet by methods such as flooding one hull or inflating a masthead float, this is often more difficult than it sounds—especially under the conditions likely to cause a capsize. In their favor, it can be said that, without a heavy ballast keel, multihulls will not sink; but they will not be capable of going anywhere. Even if their crews are capable of finding shelter on board, they will be totally dependent on outside help for rescue.

A properly designed and built monohull yacht, however, is capable of righting herself and continuing toward land under her own power, even if that power is a jury rig. Many have done it, some more than once. Again, the likelihood of a multihull's capsizing is small if she is in the right places at the right times: There are many well-documented accounts of catamarans and trimarans weathering prolonged storms without damage.

In the end, it boils down to making choices. Does the lack of heeling and the inherent positive flotation of a multihull compensate for the risk of remaining upside down after a capsize? Many people think so, and who can say they are wrong?

How Design Affects Seaworthiness

The yacht designer's vocabulary is full of moments, righting arms, lines of buoyancy, centers of gravity, and so forth. But simply put, two things counterbalance the overturning force of the sails: beam and keel weight.

Wide beam gives a boat *initial* stability—it's hard to get her started heeling.

Keel weight gives a boat *ultimate* stability, the ability to right herself from a 180-degree capsize. Keel weight starts to work only after the boat has begun to heel, and its maximum efficiency occurs when the keel is sticking straight out sideways. The deeper the keel and the farther it sticks out, the more effective it is.

Incidentally, the pressure of the wind in the

THINK INVERTED

Cruising yachts should be designed for *minimum stability upside down*, in the opinion of British expert John Lacey, former honorary naval architect of the Royal Naval Sailing Association (RNSA). Lacey, a member of the Royal Corps of Naval Constructors, said in the fall 1982 issue of the *RNSA Journal* that until the disaster of the 1979 Fastnet Race, few people had explored the stability characteristics of yachts sailing on coastal waters beyond a 90-degree knockdown.

But on the night of August 13, 1979, that complacency changed. Sixty-three yachts each experienced at least one knockdown that went substantially farther than 90 degrees. Many did not right themselves quickly and remained upside down for significant periods.

Lacey said the influence of the International Offshore Rule (IOR) had radically changed the shape of yacht hulls by greatly increasing the proportion of beam to length.

"Increase of beam gives great sail carrying power without additional ballast," he pointed out.

"It also provides the benefit of greatly increased accommodation in a given length."

But the shape of such a hull made it very stable when inverted: To bring the boat upright again would require about half of the energy needed to capsize the yacht in the first place.

"Since the initial capsize may have been caused by a once-in-a-lifetime freak wave, one could be waiting a long time for a wave big enough to overcome this inverted stability."

By way of contrast, Lacey calculated that a narrower cruising hull with a lower center of gravity, like a Nicholson 32, would require only one-tenth of the capsize energy to recover from a 180-degree capsize.

Beamy, shallow-bodied boats, he said, "may increase the size of the wave needed to initiate capsize, but in the end the sea will still win if the wave is awkward enough. It therefore seems in my opinion that we should tackle the problem from the other end, and design yachts for minimum stability when upside down."

Reasonable Beam

To talk about narrow beam and excess beam is meaningless unless we know what normal or reasonable beam is. For purposes of comparison, it is usually related to length on the waterline (LWL). In ancient times, ships were generally about three times as long as they were broad.

The longer a boat's waterline length, the less beam she needs, proportionately, because a hull's stability, its resistance to being overturned, varies as the fourth power of the waterline length.

In other words, all else being equal, if you double (× 2) the waterline length, the stability increases

16 times (2 × 2 × 2 × 2). At the same time, the heeling moment of wind pressure on the sails varies only as the cube of the waterline length. For example, if you double (× 2) the waterline length, the heeling forces increase only 8 times (2 × 2 × 2) for the same amount of breeze. This is why a boat only a few feet longer than yours is able to carry much more sail with proportionately less beam.

Small sailboats need a waterline-length-to-beam ratio of less than 3 to 1 to stay on their feet in moderate winds. The smaller the boat, the greater the beam, until you end up with a circular coracle. In addition, there is a modern tendency toward

Pearson Triton 28

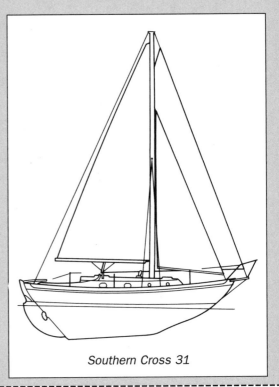

Southern Cross 31

sails, even the sudden blast of an unexpected squall, is unlikely to cause a 180-degree capsize. The sails spill wind as they become more horizontal, and the rig puts up great resistance to further heeling as it hits the water surface.

The usual cause of a 180-degree capsize is

wave action. If the boat continues to turn upside down, the ballast keel's efficiency (what the designers call its *righting moment*) tapers off until it is sticking straight up in the air, at which point it has no righting effect whatsoever.

If, however, your boat's beam is reasonably

beamier boats that is driven by a demand for interior space rather than seaworthiness.

The waterline length-to-beam ratios of three well-known "traditional" deep-sea designs indicate what has proven to be acceptable in practice:

- Pearson Triton 28 (designed by Carl Alberg): LWL 20 feet, 6 inches (6.25 m); beam 8 feet, 3 inches (2.51 m) (ratio 2.48 to 1)
- Southern Cross 31 (Tom Gillmer): LWL 25 feet (7.62 m); beam 9 feet, 6 inches (2.89 m) (2.63 to 1)
- Valiant 40 (Bob Perry): LWL 34 feet (10.36 m); beam 12 feet, 4 inches (3.76 m) (2.76 to 1)

While the amount of beam is an important element of a deep-sea design, it is not the be-all and end-all of seaworthiness. Its role is modified by other design elements so that a range of ratios becomes acceptable for any one waterline length. That is why beamier coastal cruisers—such as Frank Butler's Catalina 27, which has a ratio of 2.46 to 1 on a waterline length of 21 feet, 9 inches (6.63 m)—are still capable of sailing around the world after suitable modification.

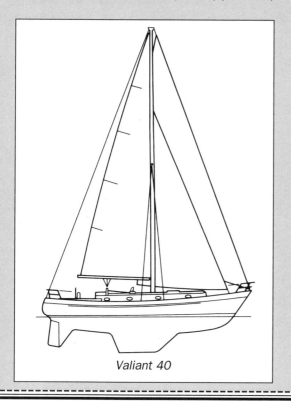

Valiant 40

Catalina 27

narrow and your keel is quite deep, any oncoming wave at this stage will tend to tilt the boat. The keel will then gain some righting moment: It will want to fall into the water and lever the boat upright again.

But if your boat has a very wide beam, oncoming waves will have to tilt the inverted hull much further before the keel exerts enough righting moment.

You may have seen some news footage of singlehanded Vendée Globe 60-footers drifting upside down in the stormy Southern Ocean with their keels sticking up in the air—and seeming to stay that way permanently. Such boats have an excess of beam that gives them the ability to plane at high speeds; it also provides enormous resistance to a capsize from wind forces alone. But this property makes them inherently unseaworthy, if you count in the possibility of capsize by wave action. Extreme designs like these sacrifice ultimate stability to speed, and they rely on the skill of their crews to keep them upright. But singlehanded crews have to sleep now and then, no matter how skilled they are, and they can't watch out for every rogue wave.

There are, naturally, other factors besides beam and keel weight that affect seaworthiness. Before we assess your boat's seaworthiness and determine what she might need for an ocean crossing, we must look at these other factors briefly. Here, expressed in nontechnical terms, are definitions of some of the most important elements of yacht design and how they affect performance and seaworthiness.

WIDE BEAM

Gives greater initial stability.

Gives more interior room.

Gives more deck space.

Contributes to a jerky, tiresome movement at sea.

Enables a boat to carry more sail with a shallower draft.

Gives a wider, safer base for mast-support shrouds.

If carried down low into the water, slows the boat down by making bigger waves and offering more resistance to the water.

Excess beam makes it more difficult to recover from a 180-degree capsize before the boat fills with water.

NARROW BEAM

Gives less initial stability.

Slips through the water more easily.

Contributes to a slower, easier motion at sea, but a greater range of roll downwind.

Usually means a deeper hull is required for the same volume of accommodations.

Often means more heeling for the same windspeed.

Cramps decks and accommodations below.

Provides a narrower, less efficient base for shrouds.

Results in quicker, more positive recovery from a full capsize.

CABIN TRUNK

A cabin trunk, or coach roof, provides light, ventilation, and standing headroom in the cabin.

A wide cabin trunk restricts the width of side decks and makes access to the foredeck more difficult.

A high cabin trunk creates wind resistance and detracts from windward performance.

COCKPIT

A cockpit provides shelter and seating for the deck crew. While it is pleasant to be able to stretch out full-length on a cockpit seat on a hot tropical night, a cockpit of that length can be dangerous. The less water the cockpit contains after a wave sweeps over the stern, the safer it will be.

It must be self-draining through at least two drains that are each a minimum of $1\frac{1}{2}$ inches (38 mm) in diameter, and all hatches must be dogged and made leakproof. How fast should the cockpit drain? As fast as possible—preferably before the next wave sweeps over the lowered stern.

The larger the volume of the cockpit in relation to the displacement weight of the boat, the faster it needs to drain. That's why some true cruising boats have very small cockpits—often no more than footwells. The problem then is that they provide little shelter for the crew from wind and waves.

A strong bridge deck at the height of the cockpit seats should separate the cockpit from the accommodations below, otherwise disastrous amounts of water will surge into the cabin after a pooping.

FREEBOARD

High freeboard provides a greater range of stability.

Too much freeboard adversely affects sailing ability, particularly to windward.

High freeboard means a lower cabin trunk for the
same headroom.

Flare, the outward projection of the topsides
from the waterline to the deck, promotes
drier decks and provides increasing buoyancy
as the boat heels.

Tumblehome, the inward inclination of the upper
topsides, gives the hull great longitudinal
stiffness.

HATCH OPENINGS

Hatch sizes should be kept to a minimum. The
absolute minimum size for a person to get
through is 22 × 22 inches (560 × 560 mm).

The normal size for an access hatch is 24 × 24
inches (610 × 610 mm).

Large hatch openings weaken the deck or cabintop structure, unless properly braced, and
invite disaster if the cover is broken or lost in
a storm.

The washboards, or dropboards, that seal off the
companionway beneath the main sliding
hatch must have some arrangement to lock
them in place at sea. Otherwise, they can be
lost in a capsize.

HULL SHAPE

Hard bilges (sharply rounded edges where the
keel joins the hull) contribute to initial stability, or form stability.

Slacker (or softer) bilges have less wetted area to
cause friction and resistance, make for less jerky
motion at sea, and provide more headroom
and more stowage space for the same beam.

INERTIA

Capsizes are largely, but not entirely, the result of
a contest between wave impact (which is try-

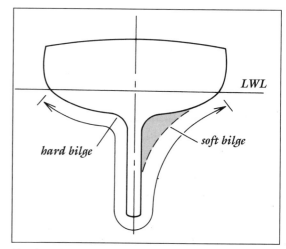

Hard and soft bilges

ing to knock the boat down) and her inertia
(which resists this action).

The deeper, heavier, and longer a boat, the more
inertia she possesses.

In fact, heavy-displacement boats may have five
times greater roll moment of inertia (that is,
resistance to wave-impact capsize) than ultra-
light displacement boats *of the same length*,
according to renowned research scientist and
naval architect Tony Marchaj.

If you have trouble understanding the physical property called inertia it will help to know it
has two opposite effects. Matter that is at rest
wants to stay at rest: It will resist suddenly being
moved. And the more the matter weighs (or, the
greater the mass), the more it resists. That's why
it's hard to make a boat with a heavy mast roll
suddenly: The mast resists quick movement.

The opposite effect shows itself when matter
is already moving. Then it wants to keep moving
at the same speed and in the same direction, and
it will resist any sudden changes.

This is not to say that a mast with great inertia will prevent rolling altogether. A steady force
will always start the mast moving. What inertia

prevents is *sudden* movement, so that a wave breaking against the side of a heavy-displacement boat with a heavy mast will not immediately throw her over on her beam ends as it might a light-displacement boat.

Of course, there are limits to how much inertia you can induce with a heavy mast, and there are penalties to be paid. Inertia will slow down the jerky, frenzied rolling of a boat running in the trade winds and let her tick slowly from side to side like the pendulum on an old grandfather clock. But if she falls into a rhythm with the swells that amplifies the distance of her roll, you will end up with that sickening feeling that she's going to keep rolling over forever and will never recover.

So, as in everything to do with yachts, you have to find the happy medium.

Incidentally, a mast with too much inertia is detrimental to windward work. When the boat is pitched forward on the back of a wave, her mast will tend to keep pushing the bow down for a while after the new wave has arrived, and she will tend to *hobbyhorse*, or plug away in the same hole, instead of riding buoyantly up and over the seas. For similar reasons, racing boats always try to keep heavy weights away from the ends of the hull.

But there is always a need for compromise, a need to find a safe balance between buoyancy in the ends of a boat and the weight of gear stowed there. Too much weight, as we have seen, results in detrimental inertia and reduces spare buoyancy. Too little weight results in a jerky see-saw motion that is unkind to the rig and crew, and interferes with the steady drive of the sails.

KEEL DEPTH AND SHAPE

The keel has two main functions: to stop the boat from being blown sideways by the force of the wind in the sails, and to counterbalance the overturning force of the sails. A third function is to provide resistance to any sud-

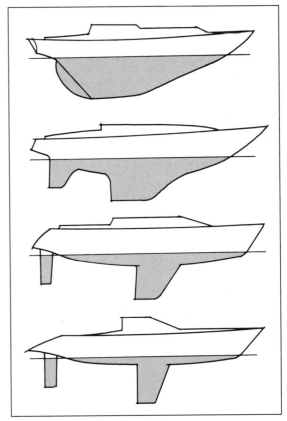

The evolution of the "traditional" keel (top) to the modern keel (bottom). Note the reduced underwater area of modern boats.

den sideways overturning force from a breaking wave.

A narrow, deep, fin keel is more hydrodynamically efficient than a wide, shallow keel of the same area, especially when going to windward.

A fin keel, to be efficient, must be moving forward through the water to gain *hydrodynamic lift*, which counteracts sideways movement. If it is stalled (if the boat is hove-to, for instance) the boat will quickly drift sideways.

A full-length "cruising" or "traditional" keel depends more for efficiency on sheer lateral area than on hydrodynamic lift. It acts more like a barn door and less like an airplane wing. While it is less efficient to windward, it is better at stopping drift to leeward when it's stalled.

A long keel provides a level surface for a boat to rest on when she dries out. It also protects the propeller and rudder from entanglement with kelp, crab-pot lines, and other underwater obstructions.

A fin keel, or modern keel, makes a boat highly maneuverable but dependent on constant helming to stay on course.

A long keel keeps a boat on course for extended periods without attention to the helm and improves performance under autopilot or wind-vane self-steering gear.

A fin keel has less surface area, and therefore creates less drag than a full-length keel.

A long keel provides the strongest support for the rudder.

Keel/Centerboard Combinations

Sailboats designed to operate in shallow waters, or to be beached frequently, often have pivoting centerboards or fixed daggerboards instead of fixed ballast keels.

Such boats usually carry more than average beam, since their initial stability is their total stability. They have little or no tendency to right themselves from a 180-degree capsize, and they therefore fail to fit our definition of seaworthy.

But there are some boats in which the centerboard is housed in a stub keel of such a weight that it alone would provide sufficient ballast to right the vessel after a capsize. The seaworthiness of such a boat is very difficult to evaluate, but its ultimate stability—the ability to return the boat from a fully inverted position—must obviously be greater than that of an unballasted centerboarder.

But when the mass of the ballast is so close to the center of buoyancy, it lacks the *arm* (or leverage) of ballast fixed at the end of a deep keel. Anyone contemplating an ocean voyage with a keel/centerboarder would be wise to consult a qualified naval architect about the boat's ultimate stability.

You should also ensure that the centerboard cannot crash through its housing in the event of a full capsize. If a heavy metal centerboard were fully extended at the time of the capsize, but not held firmly in place, it would cause considerable damage to the interior of the boat and could possibly plunge through the cabintop with disastrous results.

OVERHANGS

The amount of hull that overhangs the water, at stern or bow, affects seaworthiness.

Long overhangs look elegant and lengthen the waterline when the boat heels, thus increasing her potential top speed (see Waterline Length, below).

Excessively long overhangs cause pounding at the bow and slamming at the stern. In quartering seas, a long stern overhang hit by an overtaking swell may slew a fast-moving boat around into a dangerous broaching position.

Long overhangs work well in calm water, but short overhangs—even absolutely plumb bows and sterns—are safer at sea.

RUDDER SHAPE AND FASTENING

A deep, skinny rudder, like a deep skinny keel, is more efficient than a wide, shallow one.

The farther aft the rudder is placed, the greater its turning leverage will be.

A *semi-balanced* spade rudder, one with about 15 to 17 percent of its area forward of the pivoting axis, gives a lighter helm and a quicker response. But it stalls at a smaller angle of attack, and it tends to take a "lead," making the boat wander off course if left unattended for more than a few seconds.

An *unbalanced* rudder hung from a skeg or a full keel will not stall as readily, and it tends to center itself when left alone.

The International Dragon One-Design's long over-hangs contribute more to speed and elegance than to seaworthiness.

The Falmouth Cutter, designed by Lyle Hess for ocean cruising, has almost no overhangs.

A rudder hung from a skeg or a keel is stronger than a spade rudder that depends entirely on its projecting stock for strength, and is better protected when the boat runs aground or dries out.

SAIL PLANS

The Bermudian, or Marconi, rig is simpler and less susceptible to chafe than the older gaff rig; but it requires a taller mast and more complicated staying.

The Bermudian rig is closer-winded, but its sail area is carried higher up, which promotes more heeling.

The sail area on a gaff-rigged boat is lower and spread out more fore and aft. The shorter mast can be more efficiently supported by shrouds and stays, so it is less likely to be lost in a capsize. The gaff rig is very powerful off the wind, and the lower sail plan's center of effort causes less heeling.

The sloop rig, with one mainsail and one foresail, is most efficient to windward, but ocean cruisers tend to choose rigs with sail sizes that are convenient for one person to handle. So while a sloop rig might suit a small boat, a bigger boat might need a cutter or ketch rig with smaller individual sails.

A mainsail of about 350 square feet (32 sq m) is about the maximum one person would want to handle with any regularity. Most people would prefer to handle less. John Hanna's famous double-ended Carol cruisers, nearly 37 feet (11.3 m) on deck and displacing 18 tons (16,300 kg), carried gaff mainsails of 370 square feet (34 sq m). Eric

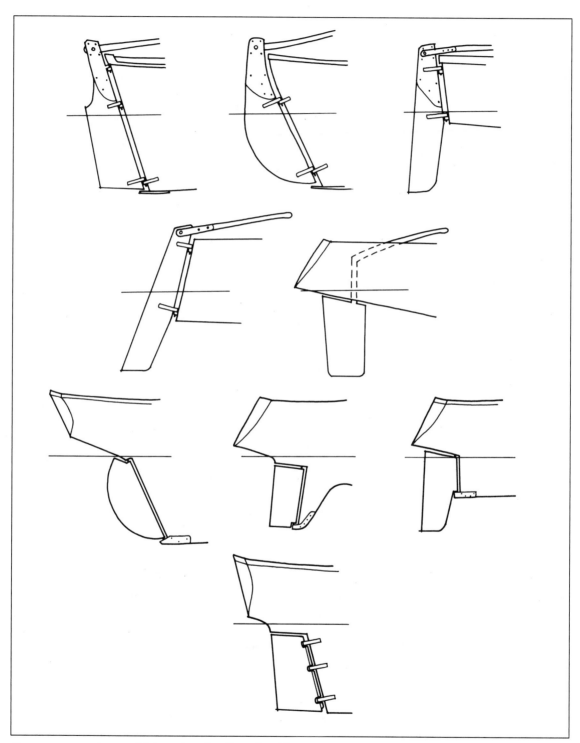

Some common types of inboard and outboard rudders

Hiscock's *Wanderer III*, a 30-foot (9.1-m) sloop displacing 7 tons (6,400 kg), carried a Bermudian mainsail of 280 square feet (26 sq m).

The cutter rig, with a forestaysail and a jib, is useful where large foresail areas need to be broken up, but is slightly less efficient to windward than the sloop rig.

The ketch rig is rightly popular among cruisers, because it divides the total sail area into easily managed portions. The two masts of the ketch rig offer certain advantages, but the windage on their standing rigging makes the ketch less weatherly than the cutter.

The yawl rig is rarely found on ocean cruisers, because it amounts to a sloop or a cutter with a very small and comparatively inefficient mizzen sail tucked way aft in an often inaccessible position. The mizzen mast does, however, offer the opportunity to fly a powerful mizzen staysail on a broad reach—and this rig certainly has its proponents. Shallow-hulled yachts might also find the mizzen useful to keep the boat pointed into the seas when lying to a sea anchor from the bow.

As long as sail areas are manageable, all of these rigs—plus the schooner rig, which is normally confined to larger boats—have proved to be perfectly seaworthy.

STANDING RIGGING

In theory, the stays, shrouds, and chainplates that support the mast should be strong enough to withstand a 180-degree capsize under full sail. In practice, that's unlikely—and probably unnecessary—because few boats would be carrying full sail in a storm.

The masthead rig is safest and simplest, with shrouds, forestays, and a standing backstay leading to the top of the mast.

Two lower shrouds on each side, from the spreaders to the deck, one leading forward and one leading aft, are the best support for the middle of the mast.

Inner forestays, or baby stays, should be backed up by running backstays.

The farther outboard the shrouds are from the mast, the less strain they will be under.

STERN SHAPE

There is no evidence that a boat with a transom stern or short counter stern is any less seaworthy than a double-ender or a boat with a canoe stern. There are occasions, however, when a pointed stern might prove advantageous. The most obvious one is when a boat is running under bare poles before a bad storm and streaming a drogue to slow her down. Waves breaking against a lifeboat stern would certainly inflict less damage than they would against a flat transom.

A transom stern gives maximum buoyancy aft and maximum stowage space below.

Disproportionately long stern overhangs, such as those found on 30-Square Meters and other lightly built racing sloops, are dangerous for sea work because of the leverage they afford an overtaking wave. Such craft are too easily swept into a vulnerable broaching attitude because their inboard rudders cannot overcome the powerful turning moment generated by the long stern.

WATERLINE LENGTH

Among displacement boats (vessels that are not capable of planing) there is a simple rule: the longer the boat, the faster she can go. The maximum speed of a displacement boat is governed almost entirely by the length of her waterline. The speed in knots is 1.34 times the square root of the waterline length in feet ($1.34 \times \sqrt{LWL}$) or 2.43 times the square root of the waterline length in meters ($2.43 \times \sqrt{LWL}$).

WEATHER HELM

Imagine a boat shaped like an old-fashioned flat iron—almost triangular in shape, pointed in front and wide at the back. Now think what happens when that boat heels under sail. The bow end sinks slightly because it has little buoyancy; the stern end rises much more because it has excess buoyancy.

Now that the stern has less grip on the water than the bow has, the stern tends to be blown downwind through the water and the boat weathercocks into the wind, pivoting from the bow. This is called *griping*.

If you wish to keep the boat going straight on her course, you have to counteract this griping tendency by pulling the tiller to the weather side of the boat; the boat is said to have weather helm.

Small amounts of weather helm, 3 or 4 degrees, are advantageous. They help a boat climb to windward and they ensure that the boat will round up into the wind and stop if you fall overboard.

Excessive weather helm is unseaworthy because it makes a boat hard-headed and almost unmanageable in any strength of wind. Furthermore, with the hard-over rudder acting as a brake, it slows the boat down drastically.

Designers of oceangoing cruisers try to balance the ends of a boat by keeping the *submerged* areas fore and aft roughly equal at all stages of heel. This results in a boat that is easily balanced by varying the areas of sail fore and aft of the mast. Such a boat obeys the helm easily and quickly in all conditions without excessive strain on the rudder. It is a great safety feature.

CHAPTER 2

Test *Your* Boat

Is your boat fit to cross an ocean? The following test indicates seaworthiness in sailboats from 25 to 40 feet (7.6 to 12.2 m) on deck with fixed keels, average draft, and no extreme design characteristics.

This test is an *indication*, rather than a definitive verification, because seaworthiness is many different things to many different boats. In the end, the only practical arbiter of seaworthiness is the sea itself. But we can at least judge a boat by certain characteristics that have proved seaworthy in the past—and equally by characteristics that have proved disastrous. This test is based on both negative and positive aspects of boat design and construction. It also takes into account one of the most important requirements for survival on the open ocean—the seaworthiness of the skipper, whose personal skill and experience may well compensate for a vessel's lack of inherent seaworthiness.

Hull

Choose the shape most like the one on your boat. Ignore the questions that do not apply to your boat, then tally your score (the number in parentheses).

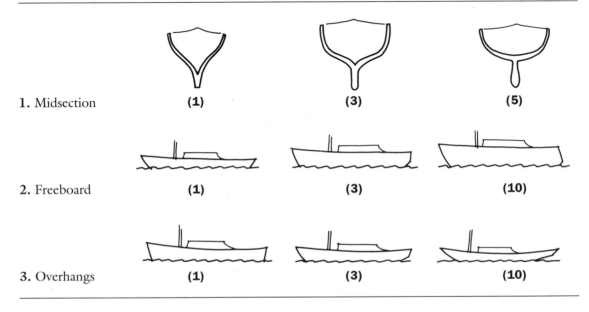

1. Midsection	**(1)**	**(3)**	**(5)**
2. Freeboard	**(1)**	**(3)**	**(10)**
3. Overhangs	**(1)**	**(3)**	**(10)**

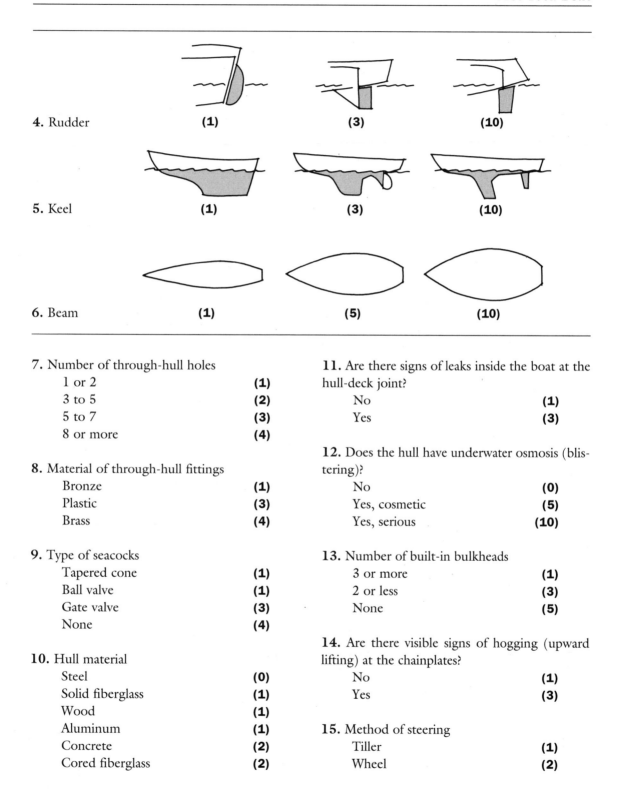

4. Rudder   **(1)**   **(3)**   **(10)**

5. Keel   **(1)**   **(3)**   **(10)**

6. Beam   **(1)**   **(5)**   **(10)**

7. Number of through-hull holes

1 or 2	**(1)**
3 to 5	**(2)**
5 to 7	**(3)**
8 or more	**(4)**

8. Material of through-hull fittings

Bronze	**(1)**
Plastic	**(3)**
Brass	**(4)**

9. Type of seacocks

Tapered cone	**(1)**
Ball valve	**(1)**
Gate valve	**(3)**
None	**(4)**

10. Hull material

Steel	**(0)**
Solid fiberglass	**(1)**
Wood	**(1)**
Aluminum	**(1)**
Concrete	**(2)**
Cored fiberglass	**(2)**

11. Are there signs of leaks inside the boat at the hull-deck joint?

No	**(1)**
Yes	**(3)**

12. Does the hull have underwater osmosis (blistering)?

No	**(0)**
Yes, cosmetic	**(5)**
Yes, serious	**(10)**

13. Number of built-in bulkheads

3 or more	**(1)**
2 or less	**(3)**
None	**(5)**

14. Are there visible signs of hogging (upward lifting) at the chainplates?

No	**(1)**
Yes	**(3)**

15. Method of steering

Tiller	**(1)**
Wheel	**(2)**

16. If you have a wheel, is there an emergency tiller?

Yes	**(0)**
No	**(3)**

Deck

17. Does the deck feel sound and solid underfoot and when tapped with a screwdriver handle?

Yes	**(1)**
No	**(3)**

18. Are there leaks or brown streaks inside the hull at any through-deck fastenings?

No	**(1)**
Yes	**(2)**

19. Do through-deck fastenings have backing plates?

Yes	**(1)**
No	**(3)**

20. Is there an anchor windlass?

Yes	**(1)**
No	**(2)**

21. Are there ample, large chocks and cleats for shore lines?

Yes	**(1)**
No	**(2)**

22. Is there a Sampson post or extra-strong fore-deck cleat for the anchor rode or for a towline?

Yes	**(1)**
No	**(2)**

23. What shape is the forward edge of the cabin trunk?

Squared off	**(1)**
Sloping	**(3)**

24. How high are the bulwarks or toerail?

8 inches (203 mm)	**(1)**
4 to 8 inches (102 to 203 mm)	**(2)**
None	**(5)**

25. Are the hatches and skylights:

Small and few?	**(1)**
Small and many?	**(2)**
Big and few?	**(4)**
Big and many?	**(5)**

26. How many bow rollers are there for the anchor rodes?

Two	**(1)**
One	**(2)**
None	**(5)**

27. What supports the main-boom end?

Permanent gallows	**(1)**
Topping lift	**(1)**
Spring clip attached to the backstay	**(4)**
Nothing	**(5)**

28. What self-steering gear is there?

Wind-vane gear	**(1)**
Under-deck autopilot	**(1)**
Cockpit-mounted autopilot	**(3)**
None	**(5)**

29. Choose the cabin portlights that look most like yours.

(1)   **(3)**   **(5)**

30. Choose the cabin profile that looks most like yours.

(1)   **(3)**   **(5)**

31. Is there a spray dodger?

No	**(1)**
Yes, folding	**(1)**
Yes, fixed	**(2)**

Cockpit

32. Choose the cockpit size (volume) that seems closest to yours.

(1)	**(3)**	**(5)**

33. Is the cockpit completely watertight?

Yes	**(1)**
No	**(4)**

34. Is the cockpit self-draining?

Yes	**(1)**
No	**(5)**

35. Is there a bridge deck to stop water flowing into the accommodations below if the cockpit fills with water?

Yes	**(1)**
No	**(5)**

36. Apart from the sliding hatch, how does your main companionway close?

Washboards	**(1)**
Hinged doors	**(3)**
Both	**(3)**

Rigging

37. What is the lay-up of your standing rigging?

1 × 19 wire	**(1)**
7 × 7 wire	**(1)**
Solid rod	**(3)**

38. What material is your standing rigging made of?

316 stainless steel	**(1)**
Galvanized steel	**(1)**
302/304 stainless steel	**(2)**

39. How do the rigging wires terminate?

Norseman or Sta-Lok terminals	**(1)**
Wire splices	**(1)**
Poured sockets	**(1)**
Rolled swages	**(2)**
Talurit or Nicopress sleeves	**(3)**

40. Are there two-way toggles at both ends of all rigging wires?

Yes	**(1)**
No	**(2)**

41. Are there two lower shrouds on each side, rather than one?

Yes	**(1)**
No	**(2)**

42. What design are the rigging turnbuckles?

Open	**(1)**
Closed barrel	**(2)**

43. Is there a permanent backstay?

Yes	**(1)**
No	**(3)**

44. Is the mast:

Keel-stepped?	**(1)**
Deck-stepped?	**(2)**

Engine

45. What fuel does the engine use?

Diesel	**(1)**
Gasoline	**(2)**

46. How powerful is it?

4 hp or more per ton displacement	**(1)**
2 hp to 3 hp per ton	**(2)**
1 hp or less per ton	**(3)**

Safety

47. Construction of lifelines

Double lines	**(1)**
Single line	**(2)**
No lifelines	**(4)**

48. Is there a bow pulpit?
 Yes   **(1)**
 No   **(2)**

49. Is there a stern pulpit?
 Yes   **(1)**
 No   **(2)**

50. Are there steps or a ladder from the water to the deck/cockpit?
 Yes   **(1)**
 No   **(2)**

51. How does your boat handle under sail with the wind forward of the beam?
 Slight weather helm   **(1)**
 Balanced   **(2)**
 Bad weather helm   **(4)**
 Lee helm   **(5)**

Accommodations

52. How much headroom is there below?
 Full standing headroom
  throughout   **(1)**
 Full headroom in main cabin
  and galley   **(2)**
 Sitting headroom only   **(3)**

53. What kind of chart table is there?
 Permanent, dedicated table   **(1)**
 Foldaway occasional table   **(2)**
 Dual-purpose icebox lid/chart
  table   **(2)**
 None   **(4)**

54. Are the number of shelves and stowage drawers for charts and navigation books:
 Adequate?   **(1)**
 Inadequate?   **(2)**

55. Are there two berths or more, located away from the ends of the boat:

At least 6 feet, 4 inches (1.93 m) long? **(1)**
At least 6 feet (1.83 m) long?   **(4)**
None as long as 6 feet (1.83 m)? **(10)**

Personal Experience

56. You have the following sailing experience—choose one:
 Have skippered across
  an ocean   **(1)**
 Have crewed across an ocean   **(4)**
 Have skippered on coastal
  sailboat trips   **(6)**
 Have skippered dinghies
  extensively   **(7)**
 Have crewed on coastal sailboat
  trips   **(8)**
 Little or none   **(12)**

Tallying Results

Now add up your score. The range is from 60 points (most seaworthy) to 242 points (least seaworthy). Please note that this quiz is based on generalities, not specifics. Many other factors contribute to seaworthiness, including displacement, sail area, and centers of gravity and buoyancy. The age of the boat and the soundness of her initial construction also come into play.

Nevertheless, the results of this quiz will give you a general idea of your boat's overall seaworthiness so that you can better assess her ability to cross an ocean.

HOW TO INTERPRET YOUR SCORE

A score of 100 or less: Your boat has the ability, in theory at least, to cross an ocean. But check each chapter in the following pages to be sure she doesn't suffer from a major flaw. If you're in any doubt, consult a good surveyor.

A score of 101 to 130: Your boat can probably be made seaworthy enough to cross an ocean if you are prepared for some work and expense to bring her up to the standards detailed in this book. The first step is to get her surveyed professionally.

A score of 131 or more: Don't waste your money on a survey. Your present boat is not a likely can-didate for an ocean crossing. Either the design is unsuitable, or the boat's too badly neglected. If it's truly your ambition to sail over the horizon, it would be safer and probably more economical to sell your present boat, buy a more suitable cruis-ing hull, and fit her out as this book suggests.

CHAPTER 3

The Essentials

Your boat may have passed the seaworthiness indicator test in the previous chapter. But before you begin the process of fitting out for an ocean voyage, you need an assurance that the four most important components of your boat are fit for the job. You should therefore make a detailed inspection of the hull, deck, cockpit, and rudder. And while we're at it, we'll also take a look at the bulkheads and the keel.

No boat is perfect. All are lacking in some respect or other but, equally, all are capable of improvement. Descriptions of the repairs or modifications suggested here are only included so you can judge their degree of difficulty. If you would like detailed instructions and feel capable of tackling these jobs yourself, the books recommended in this chapter will be useful (see Further Reading, page 30).

As always, however, if you are uncertain of your ability, consult a good surveyor and make certain he or she understands that you want to take the boat across an ocean. Then have a reliable boatyard make the improvements suggested. It will be money well spent.

The Hull

It is almost impossible to test the structural integrity of a fiberglass hull without cutting out samples and sending them to a laboratory for analysis. But your eyes and ears can tell you a great deal when you peek into dark corners inside the

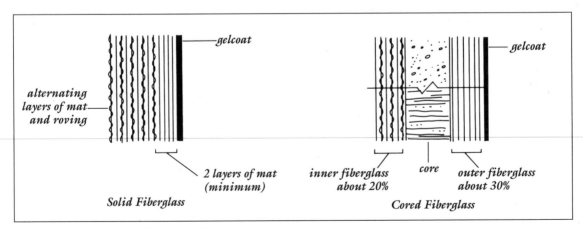

Types of fiberglass for hull construction

boat and tap the hull all over outside with a light ballpeen hammer or the handle of a screwdriver. Trouble is most likely in areas that are difficult for the boatbuilder to mold, so inspect deep down inside a narrow skeg or at the bottom of a hollow fin. If the workmanship is evidently good in these areas, it's likely to be first-class throughout.

WHAT'S DESIRABLE
A seagoing hull should be strong and absolutely watertight. A typical solid fiberglass hull needs two or more longitudinal stringers on each side for stiffness. Alternatively, hull stiffness may be derived from sandwich construction (two layers of fiberglass with a core in the middle), correctly designed interior furniture, or special structural fiberglass grids.

Structural bulkheads should be evenly spaced throughout the length of the hull to transfer mast and rigging loads and to prevent any tendency toward wringing.

The hull thickness should vary gradually, being thickest on the bottom and thinnest at the gunwales.

A fiberglass hull should have no air pockets or dry glass.

There should be no separation anywhere of the layers of fiberglass cloth and resin (the laminates).

Frames and stringers should be tapered at their ends and should not stop suddenly. Otherwise, they can develop *hard spots* where the hull is more likely to crack. Alternatively, they can be joined to bulkheads or struc-

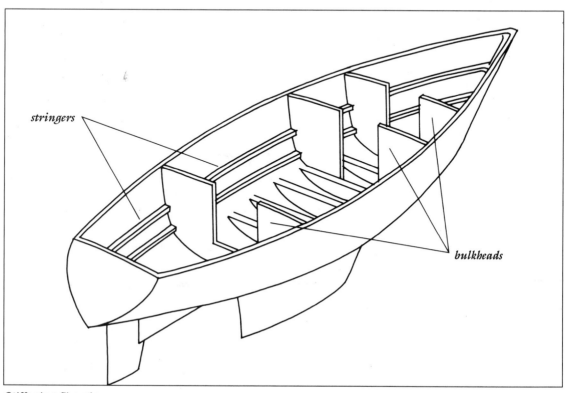

stringers

bulkheads

Stiffening fiberglass

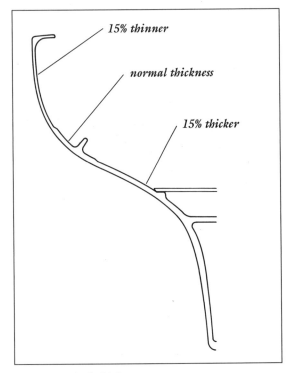

15% thinner

normal thickness

15% thicker

Fiberglass hull thicknesses

Recommended Hull Thickness

The rule of thumb for solid fiberglass hulls is that skin thickness in inches should equal 0.07 + (WL in feet ÷ 150) or skin thickness in millimeters should equal 1.8 + (WL in meters ÷ 1.8).

This thickness is for the middle of the topsides. The upper topsides may be 15 percent thinner. The bottom of the hull should be at least 15 percent thicker.

tural furniture that will dissipate the stress gradually.

The gelcoat should be free of chips, cracking, starring, and, preferably, crazing. Light crazing as a result of age is more of a cosmetic blemish than a structural fault, but it should be corrected before it deteriorates into cracks and admits water to the laminate.

WHAT TO WATCH OUT FOR

Flexing of the hull, known as *panting* (or *oilcanning*) in a seaway. Sometimes, if you watch from inside, you can see the side of the boat flexing in and out as waves hit it at sea, particularly at the topsides near the bow.

Lifting fiberglass tape in corners where structural members join.

Cracks that radiate from one point (star cracks).

Dry fiberglass mat visible beneath chipped-off gelcoat.

Osmosis (boat pox, or blistering) of the underwater hull. This may be cosmetic (small, shallow blisters) or structurally serious (many large, deep blisters that penetrate more than one-fifth of the laminate).

Separated laminations, or a skin separated from a core, indicated by a dull thud when tapping with a hammer. Good material will "ring," and the hammer will bounce back smartly.

HOW TO FIX IT

Hull flexing: Some authorities maintain that flexing is no indication that strength is inadequate; but continual flexing on a long voyage must lead to material fatigue. So add longitudinal stringers by fiberglassing over forms of plastic, wood, or foam inside the hull.

Lifting tape: Pull or cut away old tape, sand, fillet, and retape with epoxy resin.

Star cracks: These indicate excessive local stress points. They let in water that eventually causes delamination. Find out what is causing the cracks, strengthen the area mechanically or by adding extra layers of fiberglass, and fill the cracks with new gelcoat or painted epoxy resin.

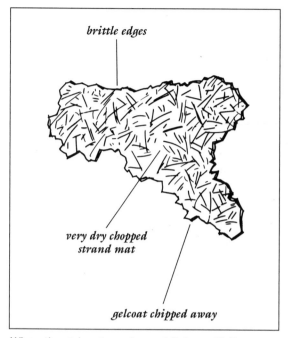

When the gelcoat cracks and flakes off, it some-times reveals a patch of chopped strand mat that has not been soaked by resin. Large areas of dry mat are weak and dangerous.

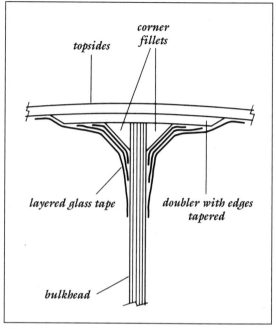

This is a bird's-eye view of how a first-class builder fits a bulkhead into a fiberglass hull. The doubler spreads the load over a wide area of the hull and topsides. The corner fillets avoid a weak right-angled bend in the fiberglass tape.

Dry mat: This is likely to be serious. It occurs when a builder wets more than one layer of fiberglass cloth at a time, but with insufficient resin for both layers; or because the resin started to gel too soon and could not wet out the glass strands. Other areas of the hull might also be affected. These areas must be cut out completely and the hole must be repaired with new glass and resin.

Osmosis: Small blisters can be drilled out, drained, allowed to dry, filled with thickened epoxy resin, sanded, and painted. Serious blistering is best dealt with by an experienced boatyard, because the gelcoat may need to be peeled off and replaced.

Separated laminations: On a solid hull, separated laminations should be cut out and replaced, in the same way as areas of dry mat. Separation of a fiberglass skin from a saturated balsa or foam core is serious and is usually fixed by cutting away one skin, replacing the core, and building up a new skin.

The Bulkheads

Bulkheads are usually made of plywood. It should be marine-grade plywood, which is the strongest and longest lasting, but often it is only exterior grade. Veteran cruiser and boatbuilder Larry Pardey says many of the repairs he has made in his professional career have involved replacing exterior-grade plywood whose core (often hemlock) has rotted.

Bulkheads are structural members that tie the sides of the boat together to prevent wringing movements and to spread stress loads over large areas of hull. They transfer thrust from the deck and mast step to the keel, and they transfer the upward pull of the shrouds to the hull. They often divide the hull into waterproof compartments, and they need to be strongly bonded to the hull with overlapping layers of fiberglass tape on both sides.

In high-quality construction, the right-angled joint where the bulkhead meets the hull is filled in with a triangular or rounded fillet, which eases the bend the fiberglass tape must take and strengthens the joint. This fillet may also provide a cushion between the edge of the bulkhead and the hull, avoiding a hard spot in the fiberglass hull that would be prone to cracking stresses.

WHAT TO WATCH OUT FOR
When looking at your bulkheads, watch out for:
Fiberglass peeling away from the edge of a bulkhead.
Glass missing on one side.

HOW TO FIX IT
Peeling fiberglass tape: Cut the tape back to where it is adhering well, remove all paint and grease, sand thoroughly, and add another layer of tape over everything.
Missing glass: Remove all paint and grease, sand well, fillet with epoxy mush and apply four layers of tape, starting with the thinnest strip and overlapping by an inch at each edge with subsequent strips.

The Deck
The deck should be strong, light, and watertight. Openings should be kept to a minimum and reinforced where they occur. Decks of fiberglass boats are usually cored with balsa or foam for stiffness and lightness. But they should be solid glass—or have built-in wooden pads—at the edges where they join the hull, or where highly stressed deck fittings are through-fastened. Solid fiberglass decks should be stiffened on the underside with beams of wood or fiberglass. Teak planks screwed down onto fiberglass decks look beautiful, but they add weight, maintenance costs, and the potential for hundreds of leaks.

WHAT TO WATCH OUT FOR
When looking at your deck, watch out for:
Flexing when you jump on the deck.
Delamination, indicated by dull thudding sounds when you tap with a hammer.
Cracks in the gelcoat.
Poor fit between the deck and the hull. Watch inside for daylight, which indicates there are openings. Squirt the joint with a hose from the outside and watch for dribbles inside.

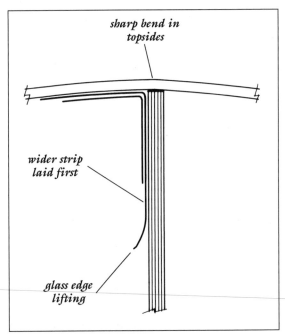

sharp bend in topsides

wider strip laid first

glass edge lifting

Watch out for these defects, especially high up on a bulkhead near the outside edge or deep in a narrow bilge space.

Be sure there are bolts, or machine screws, and nuts, mechanically fastening the hull to the deck, usually no more than 8 inches (200 mm) apart.

HOW TO FIX IT

Flexing: Add beams, or more layers of fiberglass, under the deck.

Delamination and/or saturated core: Fiberglass skins must adhere strongly to an inner core of foam, balsa, or plywood, otherwise there will be serious loss of strength. Delamination is a common problem, especially when holes have been drilled through the deck for fittings without sealing the edges; this allows water to enter the core. Small areas of delamination may be allowed to dry out and then injected with epoxy resin. Large areas must have one skin cut away (usually the bottom one) and a new core resined in place. A new bottom skin must then be built over the core. This is often a difficult repair, almost always expensive. Extensive delamination should disqualify a boat from sea service.

Gelcoat cracks: Small, individual cracks should be opened slightly in a V shape, then filled with new gelcoat paste. The cause of larger, more numerous cracks—usually stressed deck fittings—should be found and cured (by removal or reinforcement) before receiving the same treatment.

Ill-fitting deck-hull joint: This is almost impossible to cure without enormous expense, but injecting gaps with a polyurethane adhesive sealant such as 3M-5200 should keep the water out.

Lack of bolts: If there are no bolts, or machine screws, and nuts holding your deck to your hull, don't think of crossing an ocean. Self-tapping screws and/or rivets are not an acceptable substitute, even in combination with a flexible adhesive sealant such as polyurethane.

The Cockpit

The cockpit should be strong and watertight. It should give sufficient protection to the person at the helm without being so large as to compromise the safety of the boat if a wave from astern fills it with water. The cockpit should drain quickly through large scuppers and not allow water to enter the hull.

WHAT TO WATCH OUT FOR

Excessive size.

Flexing beneath your feet and parallel cracks where the floor meets the sides.

Leaking through the cockpit hatches.

Potential blockage of drain holes.

Leaking into the companionway.

HOW TO FIX IT

Excessive size: Partially fill the cockpit in with plywood and fiberglass cladding at one end or the other, possibly forming a bridge deck at the same time. Use the space for stowage of a liferaft or other gear. Use the top for a table. In an emergency, fill the cockpit with bags of sails and other bulky gear. Lash them down well, but keep the drains clear. What should you lash them to? Install padeyes well in advance and bolt them through the cockpit sides.

Flexing: This "hinge effect" is very common and indicates flimsy construction unsuitable for deep-sea work. The effect can be mitigated by a teak grating or a well-fitting floorboard to spread impact loads over a greater area, but the typical cure is to beef up the underside of the cockpit with beams or thickened fiberglass laminate, which is a messy, expensive job.

Leaking through hatches: Lay down a seal of closed-cell foam tape. Dog the hatches down tightly and be sure the catches can't release accidentally.

Blockage of drain holes: Drains can be blocked by

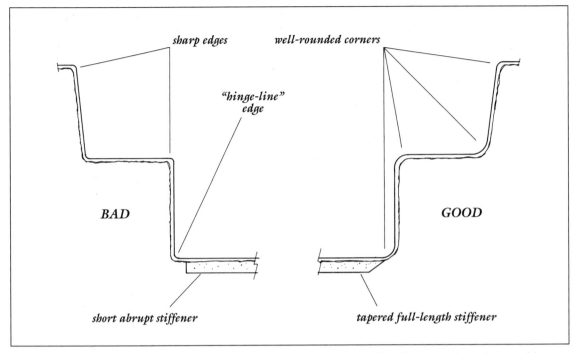

Rounded edges in fiberglass are stronger than abrupt angles, less likely to have air pockets or blow holes, and less likely to be damaged. Stiffeners should taper gradually to avoid hard spots.

rope ends, spilled food, and debris of many kinds. Avoid this dangerous situation by covering each hole with a stainless steel wire cage—and by constant vigilance.

Leaking into the companionway: This potential disaster is best avoided by having a substantial built-up bridge deck between the cockpit and the accommodations. A cockpit full of water flooding straight down below can sink a boat in seconds. If your cockpit coamings extend a long way above the cockpit seats, a substantial extra amount of water could be trapped above the level of the bridge deck, in which case you should investigate the possibility of installing hinged freeing ports in the coaming. They act as large one-way valves, allowing water to pass only from the inside out.

The Rudder

A boat's rudder is every bit as important as the steering wheel on an automobile. It must be strong enough to withstand the pounding of gale-driven waves, even when being driven astern through the water. It should be long and thin, for more effective turning power, and secured to the hull in the strongest possible fashion. It should be protected from collision by the keel, or by a skeg. It must be easily moved by a tiller or wheel.

WHAT TO WATCH OUT FOR

Worn pintles and gudgeons. Test by pushing the rudder hard when hauled out.

Water penetration. Listen for a swishing noise when you turn the rudder quickly.

Delamination. Many modern rudders have fiberglass skins bonded to a core of foam or plywood. Test for delamination by tapping the rudder all over.

Warping. Wooden rudders sometimes warp and cause constant weather or lee helm. Stand directly aft of the rudder and check it by eye or with a straightedge.

HOW TO FIX IT

Worn fittings: These can usually be fixed with washers, if the wear is in an up-and-down direction. But if sloppiness is from side to side, new pintles and/or gudgeons will probably be needed.

Water penetration: Drill as few $\frac{1}{4}$-inch (6-mm) holes as possible in strategic places and let the water drain out. Flush the rudder with fresh water, drain it, blow hot air through, and let it dry as long as possible. Fill the holes with hardwood dowels epoxied in place, or with thickened epoxy resin. Seal the ends of dowels with epoxy resin and then paint. Water often penetrates where the rudder shaft enters the rudder, so seal there, too, with a low-viscosity, flexible-drying, penetrating sealer.

Delamination: Small areas can be injected with epoxy resin after drying out. The outer skin must be removed from bigger areas, and the core must be allowed to dry out before building up the fiberglass skin again. Extensive areas of delamination should condemn a rudder because of the possibility of corrosion on the shaft and the internal web of metal strengtheners.

Warping: Sometimes a hollow in a wooden rudder can be faired with inset layers of fiberglass and resin, but all too often this problem is incurable because internal fastenings, such as drift bolts, have bent with the warping timber; in this case, the only answer is a new rudder. Marine plywood, laminated to the required thickness, faired, and sheathed with epoxied fiberglass, is a suitably strong and stable material for a rudder.

The Keel

The ballast keel works hard to keep the boat upright and to counteract leeway when the boat is in the water. It also takes the strain of accidental groundings and deliberate drying out.

Many modern keels are a hollow continuation of the hull skin, filled with lead or steel ballast that is epoxied in place and fiberglassed over.

Other fiberglass boats have a stub keel formed in one piece with the hull, to which a shaped lead or iron ballast keel is bolted. Wooden boats also have external keels of lead or iron bolted through interior floors to spread the load.

WHAT TO WATCH OUT FOR

On a wooden boat, watch out for opening seams and weeping, or signs of rust stains, along the garboard strake (the plank next to the keel).

On a fiberglass boat, watch out for linear stress cracks where the keel joins the hull. Small cracks are usual here and are almost inevitable because of constant tiny movements, but large cracks that might indicate substantial keel movement sideways should be regarded with suspicion.

Watch out for cracks in front of the keel and behind it that run from side to side. They could indicate that the keel has flexed aft during a hard grounding.

On the external lead ballast, watch out for gouges that might indicate a grounding. The gouges aren't serious, but they should warn you to look for other signs of damage that might have occurred at the same time, such as the detachment of internal bulkheads from a subsequent grounding and drying out on rock.

Check the keel bolts, if there are any, from inside the boat. Look for rust, powdering, fracture lines, and any other signs of deterioration.

HOW TO FIX IT

Ordinary stress cracks: Fill them with polysulphide and paint over them.

Gouges in a lead keel: Fill them with an epoxy sludge, sand fair, and paint.

Rusty keel bolts: You can have keel bolts examined by X-ray or ultrasound equipment, but it is very expensive. A cheaper way is to have a boatyard pull one out, if that's possible, or undo all the nuts and raise the boat off the keel to expose the length of the bolts. There is no other way to check the condition of the bolts. Stainless steel bolts may corrode as fast as mild steel if water gets in and oxygen is absent. Bronze or Monel bolts are likely to last the lifetime of the boat, but they can sometimes suffer from electrolytic corrosion.

Further Reading

There are very few boat repairs or modifications an amateur cannot do as well as a professional, given sufficient time and money. In fact many jobs, once started, turn out to be simpler than expected. Two books that are highly recommended for amateurs who would like to do professional repairs are *Spurr's Boatbook: Upgrading the Cruising Sailboat* by Daniel Spurr and *This Old Boat* by Don Casey.

THINK INVERTED

If your boat turns upside down:

- Will the cabintop be able to withstand the pressure?
- Will the portlights cave in?
- Will the rudder fall off?
- Will your companionway drop slides fall out?
- Will your deck-mounted liferaft inflate itself and/or disappear?
- Will your hatches and/or skylights break and let in water?
- Will your cockpit hatches open accidentally?
- Will your cockpit floorboard stay put?
- Will your ventilators let in disastrous amounts of water?

PART 2

Fitting Out

CHAPTER 4

Spars and Rigging

When you're fitting out your sailboat for deep-sea work, you'll need to inspect the spars and standing rigging with great care. Just about everyone can tell you what's needed in this department: sturdy masts and booms rigged strongly enough to withstand a 180-degree capsize. But not everybody knows how to judge whether a rig is that strong. The following notes should help. They list individual components in alphabetical order, including some that have little to do with strength but much to do with seaworthiness.

Baggywrinkle

It's not essential, but nothing typifies a long-distance cruiser more than some shaggy baggywrinkle placed in the rigging to prevent chafe. Today's rigging wires are so slick and smooth, however, and sail material is so much sturdier, that chafe is minimal. Still, if you crave the ancient look of yesteryear, make your own baggywrinkle.

Cut small stuff into scores of 4-inch (100-mm) lengths. String a thin line horizontally between two points, and, starting at one end of the line, attach each piece of small stuff to it. Do this by doubling the small stuff back upon itself and placing it behind the horizontal line. Then bring the two loose ends of the small stuff forward, over the line, and through the loop at its other end. Haul taut, and thread another piece on right next door. When you have several feet of tightly packed lengths of small stuff strung on your line, wind the line tightly around and around the stay and make it fast.

Booms

Check the dimensions of your boom against these minimums.

Simple round aluminum boom
Diameter: overall length ÷ 45
Wall thickness: diameter ÷ 26

Elliptical-section aluminum boom
Width (transverse section): length ÷ 50
Height (vertical section): width × 1.5
Wall thickness: width ÷ 26

Boom Brakes

Boom brakes are not essential, but they add to safety on board because they automatically control the speed of the boom's movement during a jibe. There are some pros and cons to consider.

Pros: Boom brakes also act as preventers and boom vangs.

Cons: They add expense, lines on deck, and complication.

Boom Gallows

Boom gallows are essential if you don't have a boom topping lift. When you drop the mainsail, this board (raised on edge) allows the end of the

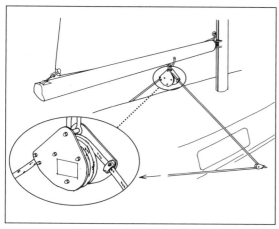

A boom brake is three controls in one: a vang, a preventer, and a way to ease the boom over gently for controlled jibing.

boom to fit into any one of three notches. Modern boom gallows may also be made from metal or fiberglass.

Pros: Boom gallows are simple and sturdy.

Cons: They add more weight up high, more wind resistance.

Boom Preventers

Boom preventers are essential when you are running at sea, and they are very simple to set up. Take a strong line from the end of the boom, run it forward through a block at the bow, and then back to the cockpit.

A preventer holds the boom rigidly forward, tensioned against the mainsheet, to prevent accidental jibes.

Pros: Boom preventers are cheap and simple.

Cons: You need to remember to uncleat the preventer before you do an intentional jibe.

Boom Topping Lifts

A boom topping lift is essential for reefing if you don't have a gallows or a rigid boom vang to hold the boom up when you lower the mainsail. Use

prestretched Dacron line that is strong enough to double for a main halyard if need be.

Pros: A topping lift stops the boom from accidentally falling and keeps it adjusted to any height.

Cons: They can cause some wind resistance and chafe on the mainsail leech, unless you use elastic cord to take up the slack.

Boom Vangs

A boom vang is essential to stop the boom from skying when you are running downwind (if you don't have a boom brake) and for controlling draft in the mainsail.

Pros: Vangs made from a four-part tackle are simple and effective; mechanical vangs with springs or pneumatic or hydraulic systems do away with the need for a topping lift.

Cons: All vangs place a fair amount of strain on the boom; mechanical vangs are expensive.

Chainplates and Tangs

To avoid metal fatigue, chainplates and mast tangs must line up with the wires they anchor. Each chainplate should be capable of accepting the displacement weight of the boat on its own. They should comfortably withstand loads 30 to 50 percent greater than those imposed by the rigging wire.

The table on page 34 shows how to gauge the strength of a stainless steel chainplate or tang. It is for chainplates of stainless steel or silicon bronze. These dimensions produce chainplates or tangs about 33 percent stronger than the compatibly sized, stainless steel, 1×19 rigging wire shown in the table.

Halyards Led Aft

It seems to be fashionable to lead halyards, downhauls, and all control lines aft to the cockpit, but it is not essential. Many experienced cruisers prefer not to do this, since you have to go on deck to tame most sails anyway.

Sizing Chainplates and Tangs					
Wire Diameter	Breaking Strength	Clevis Pin (A)	Radius (B)	Offset (C)	Thickness (D)
1/8 in. 3 mm	2,100 lb. 760 kg	1/4 in. 6.5 mm	3/8 in. 9.5 mm	1/16 in. 2 mm	1/8 in. 3 mm
5/32 in. 4 mm	3,300 lb. 1,350 kg	5/16 in. 8 mm	7/16 in. 11 mm	1/16 in. 2 mm	3/16 in. 5 mm
3/16 in. 5 mm	4,700 lb. 2,100 kg	3/8 in. 9.5 mm	1/2 in. 13 mm	1/8 in. 3 mm	3/16 in. 5 mm
7/32 in.	6,300 lb.	7/16 in.	9/16 in.	1/8 in.	1/4 in.
1/4 in. 6 mm	8,200 lb. 3,000 kg	1/2 in. 12 mm	11/16 in. 17 mm	1/8 in. 3 mm	1/4 in. 6.5 mm
9/32 in. 7 mm	10,300 lb. 4,150 kg	1/2 in. 14 mm	11/16 in. 17 mm	1/8 in. 3 mm	5/16 in. 8 mm
5/16 in. 8 mm	12,500 lb. 5,400 kg	5/8 in. 16 mm	13/16 in. 21 mm	3/16 in. 5 mm	5/16 in. 8 mm
3/8 in. 9 mm	17,600 lb. 6,400 kg	5/8 in. 18 mm	7/8 in. 22 mm	3/16 in. 5 mm	7/16 in. 10 mm
7/16 in. 10 mm	23,400 lb. 8,400 kg	3/4 in. 20 mm	1 in. 25 mm	3/16 in. 5 mm	1/2 in. 12 mm
1/2 in. 12 mm	29,700 lb. 12,200 kg	7/8 in. 22 mm	1 3/16 in. 30 mm	1/4 in. 6 mm	1/2 in. 12 mm
9/16 in. 14 mm	37,000 lb. 16,600 kg	7/8 in. 23 mm	1 1/4 in. 32 mm	1/4 in. 6 mm	5/8 in. 16 mm
5/8 in. 16 mm	46,800 lb. 21,700 kg	1 in. 25 mm	1 3/8 in. 35 mm	1/4 in. 6 mm	11/16 in. 17 mm
3/4 in. 19 mm	59,700 lb. 27,000 kg	1 1/4 in. 32 mm	1 5/8 in. 41 mm	1/4 in. 6 mm	3/4 in. 20 mm
7/8 in. 22 mm	76,700 lb. 34,500 kg	1 1/2 in. 38 mm	1 3/4 in. 44 mm	5/16 in. 8 mm	7/8 in. 22 mm

Pros: All controls are in one safe place.

Cons: Yards of spare line all over the place; leading halyards aft causes more expense, more turning blocks, more rope clutches, more chafe, and heavier strains on lines, blocks, and deck fittings.

Inner Forestay

An inner forestay is not essential, but it is useful for adding sail area to a sloop or for rigging a storm jib farther inboard. This forestay is usually fastened to the deck with a quick-release fitting and a turnbuckle so it can be removed and stowed alongside the shrouds when not needed.

Pros: In combination with running backstays, an inner forestay strengthens the mast. It also aids boat control in heavy weather by bringing aft the center of effort of the foretriangle, thus better balancing the thrust of the mainsail, whose center of effort moves forward as it is reefed. In heavy weather, this forestay allows a more efficient foresail to be used for windward work while the genoa staysail is kept tightly furled.

Cons: An inner forestay needs a strong anchor point on deck and a separate mast tang, and it needs to be opposed by running backstays; adds more windage; stowage when not in use can sometimes be awkward.

Masts

Check your aluminum mast against these rules of thumb.

Keel-stepped masts with single spreaders

Width (transverse section): length from the masthead to the deck ÷ 90

Fore-and-aft section: width × 1.4

Wall thickness: width ÷ 35

Double-Spreader Rigs

For masts with two sets of spreaders, calculate all sizes as you would for a single-spreader rig (above). Then reduce only the mast width (transverse section) by 10 to 15 percent. The fore-and-aft section should be the same as for a single-spreader rig.

Deck-stepped masts

Use the rule of thumb for keel-stepped masts (above), but divide mast length by 85 (instead of 90) to find mast width (transverse section). Then follow through as before.

Mast Boots

The mast boot, or coat, stops water gushing through the mast partners, and it is essential when the mast penetrates the deck. Most mast boots will perish after a few years in sunlight, so check the condition of yours. Self-bonding mast-boot tape and universal mast boots are available from chandlers, as is a new liquid mast-wedge replacement system that is poured in place to form a custom-made, watertight chock.

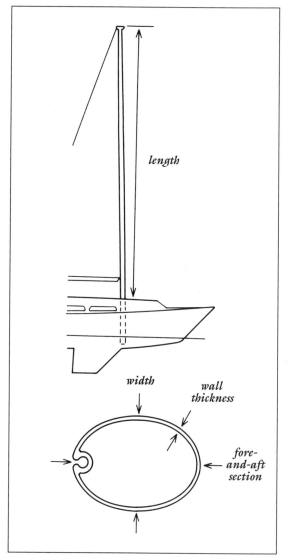

Keel-stepped mast

Mast Noise

You can be driven crazy by the nonstop noise of wires slapping against the inside of a mast. Electrical feed wires for navigation lights, spreader lights, and masthead instruments should be contained inside a special conduit, but they often aren't. It's possible, but not easy, to retrofit a plastic pipe for a conduit. If there are no internal halyards, you can fill the mast with plastic foam peanuts. Some people remove the wires, bundle them together, and put them back with pieces of springy wire bound around them, leaving the ends of the wires sticking out so that they're slightly wider than the inside of the mast. But only the conduit really works properly. Don Casey tells how to fit one in his book, *This Old Boat*.

Mast Steps

Mast steps are not essential, but they are a good alternative to the bosun's chair. They make going up the mast much easier, and maybe safer.

Pros: Mast steps are ready for immediate use; more convenient for working on fittings, especially at the masthead.

Cons: They are expensive, often entangle halyards, and add windage.

Mast Vibration

Sometimes a bare mast will sway back and forth alarmingly in a moderate wind from the side; the action can become severely amplified when its natural frequency coincides with the frequency of vibration. If this happens to you, tighten any loose stays, then tighten the shrouds a little. If that doesn't work, turn the boat so that the wind strikes more from fore or aft. A narrow (4-inch or 100-mm) strip of stiff, heavy canvas hoisted in the luff groove will quiet things down, as will increased tension on an inner forestay. If you're desperate, stretch a Dacron line from the bow, once or twice around the mast (as high as possible), then aft to a winch, and haul it really taut.

Mast Wedges

Check that the softwood wedges or hard rubber pads that fill the gap between the mast and the deck partners are firmly in place. Constant movement at sea tends to force them up and out; it's a nasty job to replace them out there because you have to take the mast boot off to get at them (see

also the previous reference to liquid mast wedges in the discussion on mast boots, page 35).

Masthead VHF Antenna

A masthead VHF antenna is not essential, but they are almost universally used and having one is a good idea. Some stick-in-the-muds won't have them, though, because they prevent the flying of a traditional club burgee from the masthead.

Pros: A masthead antenna provides greater range for your VHF transceiver than does a deck-mounted antenna; small and out of the way.

Cons: It adds a little more weight aloft; causes sneers from stick-in-the-muds.

Masthead Lights

Masthead lights are essential, as long as you understand what they are. Despite their name, they're not placed at the masthead but on the forward side of the mast, usually near the lower spreaders.

A boat under power must show a white light in a forward direction through a horizontal arc of 225 degrees. If she's longer than 12 meters (39 feet, 5 inches) but less than 20 meters (65 feet, 7 inches), the masthead light must be not less than 2.5 meters (8 feet, 2 inches) above the gunwales. If she's less than 12 meters (39 feet, 5 inches) in length, the masthead light must be carried at least 1 meter (3 feet, 3 inches) higher than the sidelights.

Navigation Lights

Under sail: According to Rule 25 of the International Regulations for Preventing Collisions at Sea, a sailing vessel under way, powered by sail only, *shall* exhibit (i) sidelights; (ii) a stern light.

But a sailing vessel less than 12 meters (39 feet, 5 inches) in length *may* combine these three lights in one lantern carried at or near the top of the mast "where it can best be seen."

A sailing vessel of any size *may*, in addition to the sidelights and stern light carried at or near deck level (mentioned above, in the first paragraph), exhibit two all-round lights in a vertical line at or near the top of the mast. The top light *must* be red and the lower light green. But these optional lights *shall not* be used in combination with the combined lantern mentioned in the preceding paragraph.

Under power: Rule 23 says a power-driven vessel (including a sailing vessel under sail and power, or power alone) of less than 50 meters (164 feet) under way *shall* exhibit: a masthead light forward; sidelights; and a stern light. The exception is for a vessel less than 7 meters (23 feet) in length whose maximum speed does not exceed 7 knots. She *may* instead exhibit one all-round white light; but she *shall, if practicable,* also exhibit sidelights.

Incidentally, Rule 21 states that sidelights on vessels less than 20 meters (65 feet, 7 inches) in length may be combined in one lantern carried on the fore-and-aft centerline.

At anchor: Rule 30 indicates that a vessel of less than 50 meters (164 feet) in length *may* exhibit one all-round white light where it can best be seen, instead of the two all-round white lights required of larger vessels.

Note that the masthead tricolor lantern uses only one bulb and is therefore economical. But it is illegal under power because you can't place a masthead light above the sidelights. So you still need lower sidelights, a masthead light, and a stern light to cover all situations. Some masthead lanterns (those perched on the truck, as opposed to regular masthead lights) carry two or three decks, combining a tricolor lantern, an anchor light, and sometimes a strobe light. The use of a strobe light is controversial. It's an emergency signal in some places, and it's a normal navigation light for some craft in inland waters. But when you're in trouble, the rules allow you to attract attention by any means you can, and there are sometimes situations in heavy weather at sea when a small yacht desperately needs to be

Visible Distances of Navigation Lights

For vessels 12 to 50 meters (39 feet, 5 inches, to 164 feet) long:
Masthead light, 5 miles (exception—a vessel under 20 meters or 65 feet, 7 inches, 3 miles); Sidelights and sternlight, 2 miles; anchor light, 2 miles

For vessels less than 12 meters (39 feet, 5 inches) long:
Masthead light, 2 miles; sidelights, 1 mile; stern light, 2 miles; anchor light, 2 miles

For vessels under sail or oars, less than 7 meters (23 feet) long:
Masthead light is not required; but if carried, 2 miles; sidelights are not required; but if carried, 1 mile; a stern light is not required; but if carried, 2 miles. Alternative: electric torch or lighted lantern, no distance specified. An anchor light is not required; but if carried, 2 miles.

For vessels under power, less than 7 meters (23 feet) long:
The same requirements as for vessels less than 12 meters (39 feet, 5 inches) long apply, except when the maximum speed does not exceed 7 knots. (In this case, a single, all-round white light shall be shown, visible for 2 miles.) An anchor light is not required; but if carried, 2 miles.

noticed. So strobe and be damned—but be aware of the consequences.

Boatbuilders and sparmakers love to place anchor lights at the masthead, but experience has shown such lights to be almost invisible at close quarters. If someone on an approaching boat happens to be looking high overhead, instead of in front, he or she will probably mistake the light for a star. The proper place for an anchor light is a few feet off the deck, or about a third of the way up the forestay. If you don't want to be run into during the night, that's where you'll put it.

By the way, navigation lights don't need to be electrical. As long as they're visible for the stipulated distance (see sidebar on page 37), you can use kerosene lamps.

Reefing Gear

Reefing is a bit like taming lions: You either get good at it in a hurry, or you don't live to tell the tale. If you want to take your boat over the horizon, you'll need to know how to reef quickly and competently. You'll need to get so good at it that you'll be able to reef automatically in pitch darkness. What you don't need is a lot of failure-prone gimmicks to help you reef.

You'll see plenty of advertisements for exotic reefing systems that have been thoroughly sea-tested by sailing Supermen in heroic round-the-world races. There are systems that cunningly wind a mainsail into a hollow mast and others that craftily wind it inside a hollow boom. But the system best tested of all, and the one most suited to those of us who cruise closer to the bottom of the food chain, is good old-fashioned slab reef-

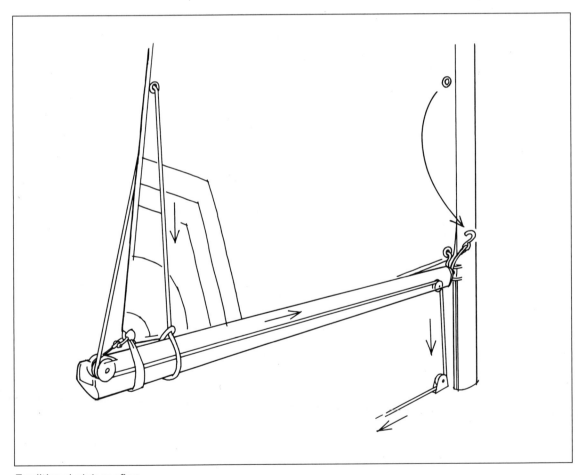

Traditional slab reefing

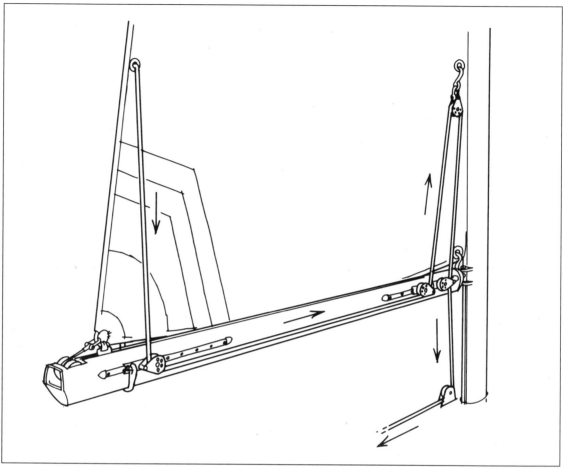

Single-line slab reefing

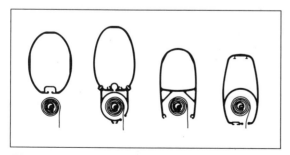

Bird's-eye views of four popular systems for roller furling the mainsail in or behind the mast

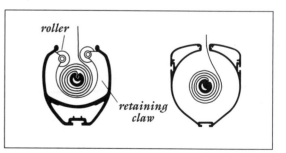

Cross-sections of two systems for furling the mainsail inside the boom

ing, or jiffy reefing. It calls for nothing more than a few lines, a few blocks, a couple of hooks, and a few hours of practice.

A sophisticated mainsail reefer/furler for which you've paid a lot of money isn't supposed to go wrong a thousand miles offshore at 0200 when the wind suddenly pipes up. But it can. And what if it does? Can you fix it? Immediately? If not, stick to slab reefing.

It's advisable to have three rows of reef points, with the third reef leaving an area about the same as that of a storm trysail. Few yachts carry dedicated trysails now, because modern cruising-weight Dacron mainsails can withstand gale-force winds when reefed.

To calculate the area of the third reef (or trysail) take the length of the full mainsail luff in feet (or meters), and multiply it by itself; then multiply the result by 0.05. For example, if the mainsail luff equals 36 feet, the third reef area is: 36 × 36 = 1,296 × 0.05 = 64.8 square feet (say 65). (Or, in metric equivalents, 10.97 m × 10.97 m = 120.34 sq m × 0.05 = 6 sq m.)

Rigging Wires

Shrouds hold the mast up sideways. Stays hold it up fore and aft.

On an ocean cruiser, the shrouds on one side of the boat should together be capable of supporting at least 1.4 times the boat's displacement—that is, the weight of the boat and crew with all stores, water, and gear aboard.

If you have double lower shrouds, use only one shroud in this calculation. The second lower should be the same size as the first, but it's presumed that only one lower at a time carries the load.

The headstay and backstay should be the size of the heaviest shroud or one size larger. On a cruising boat, however, it's handy to have all shrouds and stays the same size.

They should be made of 1 × 19 (one strand of 19 wires) stainless steel type 302/304, or the

more corrosion-resistant type 316. An alternative is 7 × 7 (seven strands of seven wires) galvanized plow steel wire, whose main advantages are that the ends can be spliced and that it gives fair warning before it breaks.

To establish the breaking strength of your rigging simply, measure its diameter, ascertain the material it's made from and its lay-up, and check the accompanying tables.

Breaking Strength of 1 x 19 Stainless Steel Wire			
Diameter of Wire		**Breaking Strength**	
in.	**mm**	**lbs.**	**kg**
1/8	3.2	2,100	953
5/32	3.9	3,300	1,497
3/16	4.8	4,700	2,132
7/32	5.6	6,300	2,858
1/4	6.3	8,200	3,719
9/32	7.1	10,300	4,672
5/16	7.9	12,500	5,670
3/8	9.5	17,600	7,983
7/16	11.1	23,400	10,614
1/2	12.7	29,700	13,472
9/16	14.3	37,000	16,783
5/8	15.9	46,800	21,228

Breaking Strength of 7 x 7 Galvanized Plow Steel Wire			
Diameter of Wire		**Breaking Strength**	
in.	**mm**	**lbs.**	**kg**
3/32	2.4	705	322
1/8	3.2	1,160	530
5/32	3.9	2,500	1,140
3/16	4.8	3,950	1,810
1/4	6.3	5,650	2,580
9/32	7.1	7,700	3,520
5/16	7.9	10,100	4,610
13/32	10	15,700	7,180
15/32	12	22,600	10,300

Please note that the figures in the table on the breaking strength of 1 × 19 wire are for type 302/304 commercial grade wire—the product most commonly used for standing rigging. Type 316 stainless steel wire, recommended for tropical use because of its increased resistance to corrosion, is approximately 15 percent weaker.

Rigging wires terminate in several ways: splices, rolled swages, eyes made with compressed oval copper sleeves (such as Talurit and Nicopress), poured sockets, and screw-on, reusable cone terminals (such as Sta-Lok and Norseman).

Splices are usually found in 7 × 7 galvanized wire. They are usually parcelled and served, so you'll need to remove the marline to check them. If they're given the occasional dressings of slush that they need, they'll last decades.

You should check rolled swages for cracks and for fatigue of the wire where it emerges from the swage. If you feel prickly wires ("meathooks") there—or on any other rigging wire, for that matter—the wire must be condemned.

Watch for electrolytic corrosion on Talurit and Nicopress sleeves, as well as ordinary oxidation of the copper and hairline cracks. These sleeves should not be trusted for standing rigging, except on very small sailboats.

You're not likely to encounter poured sockets these days, except on very large boats, but if you do, see if the zinc has oxidized and/or cracked, and check the socket for hairline cracks.

Cone terminals made by Sta-Lok, Norseman, and other companies are expensive, but they can be reused many times on 1 × 19 stainless steel wire, needing only the replacement of a small wedge each time. They are highly recommended for cruising boats because they are easily installed with just two wrenches, and they retain 100 percent of the wire's strength. They are impervious to corrosion. They cannot, however, be used with galvanized wire.

Temporary or emergency eyes can be made by doubling back the wire and fastening it with wire clamps (sometimes called bulldog grips) of the correct size. Two bolts and nuts tighten them down. But be sure to place the saddle part of the clamp on the standing wire that takes the strain, and the hoop on the doubled-over end.

Running Backstays

Unless you have a racing rig with a bendy mast, every stay on the forward side of the spar must be backed up by another aft of the mast. So if you have an inner forestay that does not go to the top of the mast, you will also need to rig two running backstays to counteract its forward pull, one for each jibe.

Rope Clutches

Rope clutches are toothed clamps operated by rotating cams attached to short levers. A line fed through the clutch may be clamped tight under strain and released again at will. Rope clutches are not essential, and are best suited to racing boats. When control lines are all led aft to the cockpit, it's usual to place the clutches on the cabin trunk on either side of the companionway. But cruising boats manage very well without them.

Pros: Rope clutches make it possible for one winch to control several lines.

Cons: They add expense, complication, rope chafe.

Spreaders

Simple struts under compression, spreaders must be angled correctly to bisect exactly the angle the stays make as they pass around the tips of the spreaders. That means the tip of the spreader where it touches the shroud should be higher than the root of the spreader where it rests in the socket against the mast.

If there is no built-in means of keeping the spreaders locked to the stays, use wire clamps top

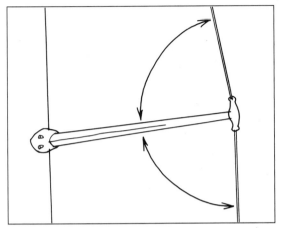

Spreaders should exactly bisect the angle formed by the shrouds at their tips. The roots of single spreaders should be located 50 to 52 percent of the distance upward from the deck to the masthead. For double spreaders, the lower spreaders should be located from 37 to 39 percent of the distance upward from the deck to the masthead, and the upper spreaders 68 to 70 percent of that distance.

and bottom to stop their moving up or down and wire the tips securely to the stays. Disaster will surely follow if a stay comes free of its spreader tip. Cover the tips with plastic spreader boots, trimmed to leave a gap in their underparts for water evaporation. Corrosion and rot is hastened by wrapping the tips with plastic tape. Check all over for rot if your spreaders are wooden; check the mast fitting for corrosion or fatigue if they're metal.

Turnbuckles

Standard, open-body bronze or stainless steel turnbuckles should have screws twice the diameter of the wire they're attached to.

The opening at the turnbuckle jaws should be twice the diameter of the wire.

All turnbuckles should have toggles where they join their chainplates, to give them the universal-joint action needed to avoid bending and metal fatigue.

THINK INVERTED

If the boat turns upside down:

- Will the cabintop be able to withstand the pressure?
- Will the mast remain standing? Do you know the weak points of your rig?
- Do you have a plan to free a toppled mast from alongside, where it may batter the hull? Can you get an undamaged portion back on deck again? Can you unscrew the turnbuckles? Will you try to release cotter and clevis pins? What if they're under great tension?

Have you ever tried cutting a stay with your bolt cutters on a slippery, viciously rolling deck with nothing to hang on to?

- Do you know what you'll use for a jury rig?
- Will you have enough spare rigging wire, terminal fittings, and so forth for a jury rig?
- Will you lose your SSB radio antenna?
- Will your EPIRB automatically start working— whether you want it to or not?

CHAPTER 5

Ground Tackle

On the far side of that horizon you're planning to sail over are lands where you'll want to drop anchor. There are many kinds of anchors, but anchoring is a very imprecise science. Human beings have more assurance of success when docking a shuttle at a space station than when anchoring a small boat. About the only thing that is certain about anchors is that no one anchor works perfectly all the time. Some set better in hard bottoms, some in soft. Some will foul their stocks if the anchor line drags across them, and some won't. Some are quick to reset themselves when the wind direction changes; others hate to be disturbed. Some stow better on deck or in bow rollers than others do.

Scores of anchor tests have been conducted by navies, anchor manufacturers, oil-rig design-

ers, and yachting magazines. None has achieved consensus. None has revealed a magic anchor that stands stock and crown above the rest in holding power, setting ability, structural strength, ease of handling, simplicity, cost, or anything else.

The most popular anchors, therefore, are general-purpose models. They are rarely the best in any given situation, but they perform adequately over a wide range of bottom conditions.

Thus the serious cruiser should carry at least three anchors, each of a different type, of which two will be available for immediate use.

Incidentally, it was the custom in the days when most yachts carried only fisherman anchors to refer to the yacht's main anchor as the bower. The secondary anchor, usually two-thirds the

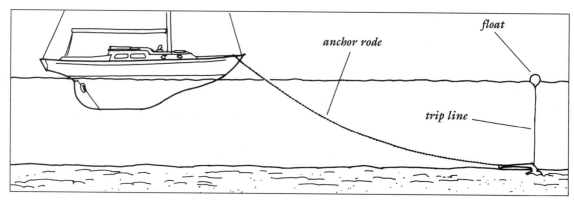

An all-chain rode with a scope of 3 to 1—too little for safety. The trip line is handy if your anchor becomes fouled and you can't raise it in the normal way.

weight of the bower, was known as the kedge, and it was the one used to kedge a yacht off a sandbank. But modern anchors depend for their holding power as much on improved design as on weight, and the boundaries between bower and kedge have become blurred. In fact, there's no reason why today's bower shouldn't weigh less than the kedge.

Anchor Types and Characteristics

Anchors basically fall into three types, with variations: the fisherman, the plow, and the lightweight pivoting fluke. An anchor's holding ability is determined largely by the surface area it presents to the bottom after it has dug in. If you allot the traditional fisherman, with its small flukes, a holding power of 1 unit, then the plows are 2 to 3 times more effective; and the lightweight pivoting anchors, with their large flat flukes, are about 5 or 6 times more effective. But that's only *after* they have dug into good holding ground.

Holding power is not everything by which to judge an anchor. Penetrating ability is important, too, as is the ability to penetrate again—to reset—after a wind or tide change. Penetration is aided by heaviness, sharply pointed flukes, and an anchor line that pulls more or less parallel to the seabed rather than upward toward the boat.

FISHERMAN TYPES (HERRESHOFF, LUKE)

For adequate holding power in sand, mud, or clay bottoms, the traditional fisherman or yachts-

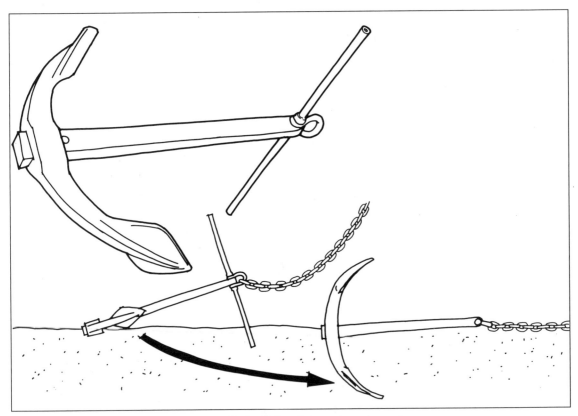

The fisherman-type anchor rolls over to dig its flukes into rock and weed.

man's anchor, such as a Herreshoff or a Luke, must be very large. For example, you'd need a 100-pound (45-kg) fisherman to equal the holding power of a 35-pound (16-kg) plow anchor.

Nevertheless, many cruising boats follow the rule of thumb and carry a fisherman anchor weighing 2 pounds for every 1 foot (3 kg/m) of their waterline length. If this anchor is intended as a storm anchor, it should be two sizes larger than normal, disassembled, and stowed down below.

Although the fisherman can easily be fouled by the rode after a wind or tide shift, and even though it is difficult to drop and recover without damaging the topsides, it has one great advantage: It holds better than any other anchor on rocky bottoms or in coral. In fact, the fisherman will work where other anchors won't hold at all. It also performs as well as—or even better than—the others in bottoms comprised of pebbles or shingle. Furthermore, it can usually be relied upon to penetrate sea grass or weeds.

PLOW TYPES (CQR, DELTA, BRUCE)

Despite the differences in their appearances and prices, all plow-type anchors behave with remarkable similarity. Generally, the firmer the bottom, the better they perform. They're very popular with cruising sailors because they perform *adequately* almost all the time.

Plow types are the norm by which other anchors are judged. They perform well in sand, gravel, rocks, and coral, and not so well in clay and thick grass. They also hold poorly in soft mud.

The *CQR* has a swiveling shank that is said to help the anchor hold when a pull comes from the side, but that's not easily proved. There is no doubt, though, that its hand-forged construction makes it very strong. It stows well in a bow roller, but with difficulty anywhere else. As with all anchors, you should attach a buoyed trip line to the crown when you anchor among rocks or on a bottom fouled with old tree trunks, cables, or

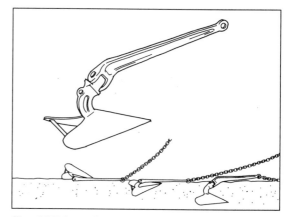

The CQR is a plow-type anchor much favored by cruisers for its ability to reset itself after changes in wind direction.

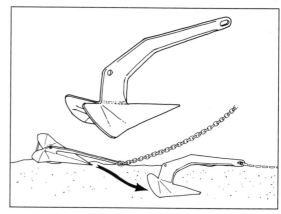

The Delta, another plow, lacks the hinged neck of the CQR. Also popular with cruisers, it will launch itself from a bow roller.

other debris. It has been noted that the performance of the CQR is definitely improved when it's attached to a length of chain at least the length of the boat.

The *Delta* is a newer design than the CQR, and it lacks the pivoting hinge. It appears to perform as well as the CQR, and it is cheaper. It has a weighted plow tip that makes it roll over into the dig-in position immediately after it hits bot-

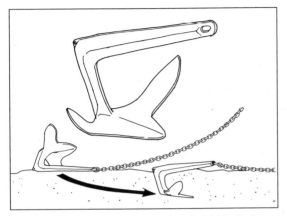

The *Bruce*, originally designed to hold North Sea oil platforms in place, has the ability to reset itself very quickly—usually within two shank lengths.

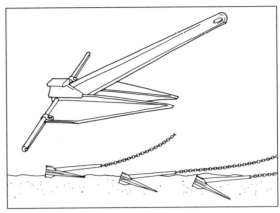

The Danforth-type anchor has large flukes that give it the greatest holding power for its weight—especially in soft clay, sand, and mud.

tom. It stows well in a roller and launches itself without any help when you release the rode. One set of tests showed it to be better than any other anchor at resetting itself after a pull from a new direction had caused it to break out.

The *Bruce* was designed to hold North Sea oil rigs in place. It is actually more of a winged scoop than a plow, although it shares the plow's general characteristics. This is another anchor cruisers swear by. It's simple and very rugged. Once again, it only stows well in a bow roller, although a small one will snuggle quite comfortably over a corner of a stern pulpit. Various tests have shown the Bruce to be much better than the CQR—and much worse.

It's probable that there's not much difference in average performance between any of the three plow types. You simply need to get to know your anchor so you can judge when to trust it.

LIGHTWEIGHT PIVOTING FLUKES (DANFORTH, PERFORMANCE, FORTRESS)

No other anchor boasts as much holding power for its weight as the type generically known as the

Danforth. These lightweights have large fluke areas that generate tremendous resistance to being pulled through soft bottoms. No anchor type performs better in soft clay, sand, or mud. Their performance is markedly inferior, however, in hard clay, gravel, or rock, and frequently they won't work at all when weeds cover the bottom, because they don't have the weight to penetrate them. The angle that their flukes make with the stock is carefully controlled for optimum penetration and holding power, but quality control varies among manufacturers, so it's possible to get one that doesn't work well at all. On some makes, you can alter the angle of the flukes so they open further, the better to deal with soft mud. One problem is that, despite their light weight, they must be exceptionally strong to endure the strains imposed by high winds and swells; sometimes, their strength doesn't match their holding power. They can't be stowed on anchor rollers, but their lightness and flat shape make them easy to handle and stow on deck, in an anchor locker, on a pulpit, or below.

The *Danforth*, the granddaddy of the lightweights, comes in standard and high-tensile versions. In addition, there are Deepset models of these two versions, which have thinner shanks and are said to be able to penetrate deeper. Although the high-tensile model costs more, most cruisers prefer it to the standard model because of its superior strength. Apart from the Performance and the Fortress (mentioned below), the Danforth has many imitators, but too few tests have been done to tell how their performances compare with it.

The *Performance* anchor looks very much like a Danforth. It was developed by the West Marine chain of boating stores to strict engineering specifications and has proved to be very successful. *Practical Sailor* magazine rated it the best all-round of seven anchors tested by the Safety at Sea Committee of the Sailing Foundation in Puget Sound in 1995, with a CQR second, and a Fortress in third place.

The *Fortress's* holding power is much the same as the other Danforth types for a given physical size, but because it's made of aluminum, it's lighter. In fact, it's so light it will plane if you drag it at a little less than 3 knots. One that was deployed off the stern of a boat in the Columbia River by naval architect Robert Smith planed to the surface in a current of 1.5 knots. Its rode was 25 feet (7.6 m) of ⅜-inch (10-mm) rope with no chain. So, while the Fortress is lighter, easier to handle, and just as able as the other lightweights to cope with large forces, it's harder to get it to set. In fact, it will hardly set at all if there is even the slightest suggestion of seaweed or grass on the bottom.

HOLDING POWER

Practical Sailor magazine ranked the holding power of some well-known anchors after plotting and analyzing the results of nine tests, including some conducted on behalf of the U.S. Navy and the British Royal National Lifeboat Institution.

These were anchors of approximately comparable physical size, not weight. But *Practical*

Sailor stated that if weight alone had been considered, the results would have been almost identical—except that the Fortress would have had a considerably higher ranking because of its lightweight aluminum construction.

The results of the tests may be paraphrased as follows. If the holding power of a traditional fisherman anchor is assessed at 100 percent, then:
A folding grapnel scores 60 percent.
The CQR plow anchor scores 240 percent.
The Danforth plow and the Bruce score 250 percent.
The Delta scores 270 percent.
The Danforth Standard and Danforth Deepset (standard version) score 520 percent.
The Danforth Deepset (high-tensile version) scores 540 percent.
The Danforth Hi-Tensile scores 550 percent.
The Fortress scores 560 percent.

RECOMMENDATIONS
For serious cruising you need three anchors.

For a storm anchor choose a fisherman, a Herreshoff (if you can find one), or a Luke. An everyday, working fisherman should weigh 2 pounds for every 1 foot (or 3 kg per meter) of your boat's waterline length, but your storm anchor must be two sizes bigger. Stow it in pieces down below.

For your working anchors select a lightweight pivoting fluke (preferably a Danforth or a Performance) and a plow (a CQR, a Delta, or a Bruce).

Incidentally, there is not much use for a patent folding grapnel anchor aboard a cruising yacht, although a small one works well for a dinghy anchor and may also prove useful when you need to drag for a sunken line or lift a fouled anchor rode.

Sizes of Anchors and Rodes by Boat Length
The following table lists conservative minimum sizes for plow-type anchors on boats of medium

to light displacement under normal conditions. But be aware that experienced cruisers seldom recommend the use of plow anchors weighing less than 25 pounds (11 kg), because of the difficulty they have in penetrating some bottoms.

If your boat has a heavy displacement, greater than normal windage, or frequently is anchored in areas subject to storms, choose an anchor and rode one size bigger.

Pivoting fluke anchors of the Danforth type need be only half the weight of a plow anchor for the same holding power.

Traditional fisherman-type anchors should be 2.5 times the weight of a plow for the same holding power, or at least 2 pounds for every foot of waterline (3 kg per meter).

Storm anchors of any kind should be two sizes bigger.

Chafe on Anchor Lines

A boat with a bowsprit is likely to chafe her anchor rode on the bobstay if the roller is at the stemhead. Use guys or preventers to eliminate contact if possible.

Roller jaws should be flared and smoothed to lessen chafe on nylon lines, which are very vulnerable when they stretch under tension.

Chocks and fairleads also are sources of chafe. They, too, must be very smooth. If possible, use plastic tubing to reduce chafe. Consider whether it would be advantageous to lead your rode through a chock after the anchor is set, rather than leaving it in the roller.

Better yet, if you have a nylon rode coming aboard, make up a short length of chain with a shackled loop in one end that can be dropped over your anchor bitts, windlass, or deck cleat. Permanently splice an 18-inch tail of nylon rope in the other end. Now lead the chain from the anchor bitts, through the roller or chock, and attach the tail to the anchor rode with a rolling hitch. Ease out a foot or two of nylon rode and make it fast again. All the chafe will be taken by the chain.

Sizing Plow Anchors and Rode			
Boat Length	**Plow Anchor**	**Rope Diameter**	**Chain Diameter**
Up to 21 ft. Up to 6.4 m	11 lb. 5 kg	$7/16$ in. 11 mm	$3/16$ in. 5 mm
22–25 ft. 6.7–7.5 m	22 lb. 10 kg	$1/2$ in. 13 mm	$1/4$ in. 6 mm
26–30 ft. 8.0–9.0 m	25 lb. 11 kg	$9/16$ in. 14 mm	$1/4$ in. 6 mm
31–40 ft. 9.4–12.0 m	35 lb. 16 kg	$9/16$ in. 14 mm	$5/16$ in. 8 mm
41–45 ft. 12–14.0 m	44 lb. 20 kg	$5/8$ in. 16 mm	$3/8$ in. 10 mm
46–50 ft. 14–15.0 m	55 lb. 25 kg	$3/4$ in. 19 mm	$3/8$ in. 10 mm

Chain Stoppers

Strangely enough, comparatively few cruisers use chain stoppers on the anchor line, but stoppers should be regarded as essential, whether you have a windlass or not. A pawl-action chain stopper stops the rode from running back out of the roller and takes all the tension as the boat rises on a swell. It prevents the chain from jumping off a windlass barrel, and it reduces the incidence of hernia among us purists who weigh anchor by hand.

Marine discount stores carry stoppers, but you can have a simple pawl fabricated to your own design if necessary. A pawl will work with a rope rode, too, but should only be used in an emergency since it may damage the fibers by compressing them.

Eric Hiscock maintained that a chain pawl made it feasible to do away with a windlass altogether when using a 35-pound (16-kg) anchor and 5/16-inch (8-mm) chain, particularly if an engine were used to ease the boat up to her anchor or if you jiggled her up to it under the mainsail.

In fact, an old rule of thumb states that it's possible for a person of average strength and fitness to raise and bring aboard a 60-pound (27-kg) Danforth or plow anchor without any special gear. Nevertheless, it's heavy work, and in boats exceeding 5 or 6 tons of displacement, some mechanical assistance is generally considered necessary.

Foredeck Wells

Foredeck wells are not essential, but they are very shipshape and handy if their lids are substantial and well hinged. They often house a windlass and/or mooring bitts as well as a working anchor. They leave the foredeck clear of obstructions while under way. Because they ship water in a seaway, they must be well drained—out through the hull, not into the bilge—and the deck pipe that leads the chain below must stand up high, clear of the bottom of the well.

Mooring Bitts, Sampson Post, Cleats

These are essential for securing the inboard end of the anchor rode. Substantial bitts, or a traditional Sampson post anchored in the keel and attached to a bulkhead, are best. A windlass, if large enough and correctly bolted down, also will suffice. Deck cleats must be through-bolted, not screwed, onto large backing plates.

Rodes: Chain and Nylon

Because nylon anchor lines are easily chafed by coral, rocks, and all kinds of underwater obstructions, it is essential that at least that part of the anchor rode in contact with the sea bottom should be chain.

But most experienced cruisers go one step further and carry one, if not two, all-chain rodes. The pros and cons of using an all-chain rode follow.

Pros: In crowded anchorages, you can often get away with a scope of 3 to 1; chafe is not a problem; the rode is self-stowing and does not tangle.

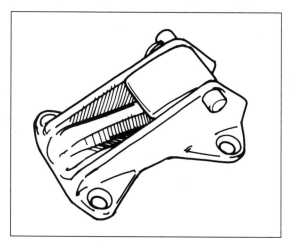

This sturdy chain stopper is fastened down to the deck with four bolts. It will relieve the windlass of the strain of the anchor rode.

Cons: It adds expense; weight near the bow is detrimental to performance; it will eventually rust and need to be regalvanized.

Three-strand nylon rodes with a length of chain at least the length of the boat attached to the anchor are more often used by weekend cruisers and day sailers.

Pros: A nylon rode is cheaper than chain, lightweight, and it doesn't rust; can be spliced and knotted; prevents snatching and shock loading of deck fixtures by stretching.

Cons: It needs greater scope and is susceptible to chafe from rocks or coral; easily severed by a turning propeller and degraded by sunlight; doesn't stow as easily; may tangle.

All-chain rodes may snub viciously in gale conditions in shallow water. They can seriously damage the anchor or the fitting to which the rode is made fast on the foredeck. A 20- to 30-foot (6- to 9-m) length of three-strand nylon line made fast to the anchor chain with a rolling hitch or a chain hook and brought aft to a mooring cleat or Sampson post, will ease the strain by stretching and absorbing the shock.

Be aware, though, that too thick a line will not stretch, and so will defeat the object of the exercise. Never use polyester line (Dacron, Terylene) for anchor rodes because it does not stretch enough.

A little-used method of reducing snubbing in an all-chain rode is to slide a heavy weight part of the way down the chain, suspended from a large shackle or a special roller. This, too, absorbs sudden jerks on the chain and is effective in reasonably deep water, but almost useless in shallow water. A 20-foot (6-m) length of nylon will work as well in deep water and is better in shallow water.

Depth Markers

Depth markers are essential so you know how much anchor line you have out. One popular sys-

Types of Chain

Proof-coil chain has long links and is made from low-carbon steel.

BBB chain is also made from low-carbon steel, but it has shorter, more precisely made links that work better with windlasses.

High-test chain is made from high-carbon steel, which makes it stronger, but more brittle and prone to rust faster.

All three chain types are supplied galvanized, but hot-dip galvanizing is superior to zinc electroplating.

Most cruisers use BBB chain because, unlike high-test, it will stretch and deform under excessive load to give warning before it breaks.

By the way, it is important to match the chain exactly to the windlass. The easiest way, when you're buying new chain, is to remove the windlass barrel with the chain gipsy on it and take it with you to the store.

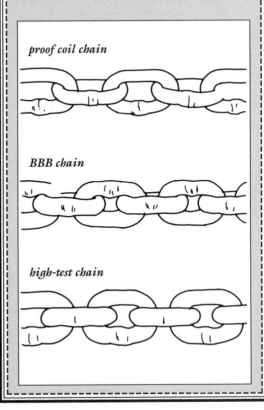

proof coil chain

BBB chain

high-test chain

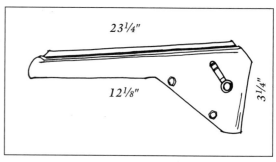

Many bow rollers are integral with specially fabricated stemhead chainplates, but you can also retrofit a manufactured roller. This one, designed for the Bruce anchor, fastens down with five bolts and measures nearly 24 inches (610 mm) overall.

tem uses small pieces of canvas, about 8 inches by 1½ inches (200 mm by 40 mm), that are marked with waterproof black ink and knotted through chain or tucked through the strands of a nylon line at appropriate intervals. Mark them in fathoms, meters, or feet—whatever takes your fancy. You can also buy ready-made fluorescent plastic markers to tuck into a nylon rode.

Another method is to paint several links of the chain every 5 fathoms or so. Use different colors, or differing numbers of bands, to indicate depths. If you're a traditionalist, use the old leadline marking system of leather bootlace, red bunting, blue serge, feathers with holes in them, and lines with knots.

Rollers

Rollers are essential: Weighing an anchor without a roller guide for the rode is hard and desperate labor.

Rollers must be very firmly bolted down to resist substantial sideways pulls by the rode, but they must also protrude far enough forward from the stem head to prevent the rode from chafing on the bows.

Strong, long-lasting rollers are made from stainless steel with rollers of polished bronze or a special plastic material that resists wear, distortion, and damage by sunlight.

Twin rollers are handy for setting and recovering the lines when it's necessary to lie to two anchors in a V ahead.

All rollers should have a removable pin that will prevent the rode from jumping out when the boat pitches.

If you stow your anchor on a roller, be sure the shaft doesn't interfere with a roller furler on the forestay. If it does, the furler must be raised, and the sail recut if necessary.

Stowing Anchors

It's essential that anchors be stowed so they can't break free and launch themselves into the ocean with 40 fathoms of chain attached.

Anchors stowed on rollers should be held in place by a pin through the two roller side plates. Drill a hole through the anchor to accept the pin, if the shaft lies too high in the roller, but be sure the pin will never bend. If it does, you might not be able to release the anchor in a hurry.

Plow anchors should also be hauled back tightly against the roller for more security. Lashing the anchor to the pulpit is a last resort:

Waves breaking against the anchor can place a great strain on that fitting.

Anchors stowed on deck should be stowed in specially shaped chocks that are securely bolted through the deck.

On a long ocean passage, the anchors are best removed from the bow altogether. They should be securely stowed low down toward the middle of the boat.

The Bitter End

Secure the bitter end (the inboard end) of a chain anchor rode with a nylon line long enough to reach the foredeck, in case you ever have to cut it and slip your cable.

The nylon line should be made fast to a very substantial fitting in the chain locker, such as an eye through a bulkhead or the base of a Sampson post.

If you ever have a runaway anchor and chain, the nylon will absorb much of the shock when it fetches up. A chain made fast directly to a bolt through the stem could simply blast a hole through the bow: It has happened before.

Trip Line and Buoy

A trip line and buoy is essential if you are forced to anchor in rocky or foul ground.

Secure to the crown of your anchor a light line a little longer than the maximum depth of water in which you are anchoring. Buoy the end of the line, then send it overboard with the anchor and rode.

If your anchor fouls, bring the buoy aboard and haul on the trip line. In theory, the anchor should come straight out. In practice, very little about anchors is certain.

Buoying the anchor is also a handy indication to newcomers of its exact location.

Windlasses

A windlass is not absolutely essential in boats of about 30 feet (9.1 m) in length or less; but a windlass does save a lot of back-breaking work. A windlass is essential in bigger boats, unless you can use mast or sheet winches, or you prefer to rely on handybillies and tackles.

Strictly speaking, a windlass is a winch with a horizontal barrel. A capstan has a vertical barrel. But it's the modern style to refer to them both as windlasses. They have either a horizontal axis or a vertical axis.

As we learned when discussing chain stoppers earlier in this chapter, a simple pawl may make a windlass unnecessary on your boat.

Windlasses may be powered by hand or by electricity, and most can handle rope as well as chain. There are hydraulic windlasses, too, but their use is mostly restricted to larger and more complicated vessels. You don't need one.

One thing needs to be clearly understood: Windlasses are not designed to pull the boat up to the anchor in 30 knots of wind and 3-foot (1-m) swells. Neither are they intended to break out a 45-pound (20-kg) CQR embedded 3 feet (1 m) in hard clay. Windlasses are simply designed to lift an anchor and rode that is not under tension.

In practice, it's so tempting to let the windlass do the work of pulling the boat up to the anchor, and unsticking it, that almost everybody does it. To allow for at least some of the extra strain, windlass manufacturers mostly recommend that the pulling power of the windlass should equal three times the weight of the anchor and rode.

MANUAL WINDLASSES

Horizontal-barreled manual windlasses are operated by pushing a long handle backward and forward. They have maximum pulls varying from about 500 to 1,000 pounds (220 to 450 kg).

Pros: These windlasses are light, simple to repair, easily installed on deck or in a well, and you need only human power to run them.

Cons: They are prone to corrosion and slow in action; they won't work if you lose the handle.

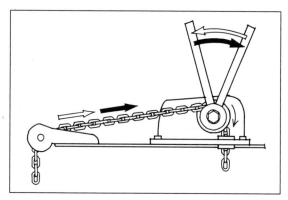

Horizontal-barreled manual windlass

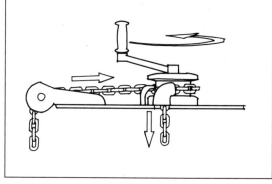

Vertical-barreled manual windlass

Vertical-barreled manual windlasses look like metal mushrooms sprouting from the foredeck. They use a standard winch handle.

Pros: These windlasses are compact, comparatively cheap, light, and easily installed. They take rode through a 180-degree bend for greater security on the barrel.

Cons: You must kneel, stoop, or curtsy to operate them; need a large clear area to swing the handle; power is limited to about 500 pounds (220 kg). They are fairly slow in operation and may not be self-stowing with rope.

ELECTRIC WINDLASSES

Horizontal-barreled electric winches have their motors right alongside the barrel on deck.

Pros: They require simple installation and allow fast operation and push-button weighing and lowering.

Cons: They are more expensive; rode wrap around the barrel is usually only slightly more than 90 degrees. They are subject to corrosion and need big cables to supply large amperage at 12 volts.

Vertical-barreled electric winches have their motors mounted below deck.

Pros: There is less machinery to clutter the foredeck and better protection for motor; almost

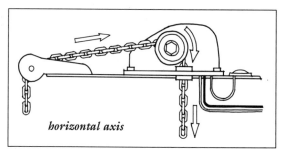

horizontal axis

Horizontal-barreled electric windlass

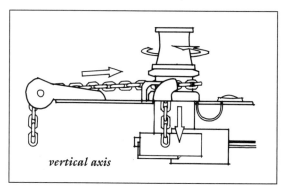

vertical axis

Vertical-barreled electric windlass

180-degree rode wrap; fast, push-button weighing and lowering.

Cons: They add expense and require thick wiring that can handle amperage loads in excess of 130 amps at 12 volts.

Windage

A boat's windage, as much as its displacement, determines the size of anchor rode it needs. The American Boat and Yacht Council (ABYC) recommends that your chain be strong enough to withstand five times the normal horizontal load on the boat.

To estimate that horizontal load, multiply bow height in feet by maximum beam in feet. To that figure, add another $\frac{2}{3}$ to account for spars, standing rigging, and deck gear. Also add the frontal area of anything else that might be sticking up, such as a raised dodger.

Now double the resulting figure, to account for the effects of yawing in the wind, and enter the table below at the figure closest to your number of square feet. You can now read off the pull, in pounds, that your anchor must resist in winds of various speeds. For metric users, multiply square meters by 10.76 to get square feet; and multiply pounds by 4.45 to get newtons. (Note that the power of the wind quadruples as its speed doubles.)

Size It Right

Many cruisers spend a large percentage of the time at anchor. According to one of the most experienced cruising couples in the world, Lin and Larry Pardey, the average yacht on a world cruise spends 85 percent of the time at anchor (10 percent of the time is spent at sea; 5 percent is spent tied to docks). Hence the need for good ground tackle that is properly sized.

Here's a good rule of thumb: Don't use anchor chain or nylon any thicker than you need. The larger diameter may hinder the anchor's ability to set and bury itself. The nylon rode is designed to stretch and absorb sudden loading shocks on the anchor and mooring bitts or Sampson post. If it's too thick, it can't do its job.

Wind Pressure in Pounds According to Wind Speed				
Area (sq ft)	Wind Speed			
	30 Knots	60 Knots	80 Knots	100 Knots
1	3	13	22	32
50	150	630	1,115	1,600
150	450	1,890	3,345	4,860
200	600	2,520	4,460	6,480

THINK INVERTED

If your boat turns upside down:

- What happens to your anchor chain?
- Is your storm anchor securely stowed down below, or will it break loose and crash through the cabin roof?
- Will your plow anchor escape from the bow roller, taking the chain with it?

CHAPTER 6

Deck, Cockpit, and Superstructure

I t shouldn't be necessary to point out that the deck, cockpit, and cabin trunk of your boat must be watertight. Unfortunately, it *is* necessary. Too many people go to sea with cockpits that leak into the bilges, or skylights that leak into the cabin.

Boats that have covered thousands of ocean miles without problems suddenly find themselves in big trouble when a bad storm comes along and forces water through leaky cockpit locker lids. It happened to the 40-foot (12-m) yawl *Mary T* during the Queen's Birthday storm off New Zealand in 1994. Until the crew discovered the source of the leaks and made temporary repairs, *Mary T* was taking on more water than her pumps could cope with. She was lucky to survive.

Wherever you get an opening, a joint, or a through-fastening, there is a chance of a leak: And minor leaks become gushers under the pressure of storm-driven waves.

Inspect the upper surfaces of your boat for leaks. Try to imagine water under pressure coming from all angles, not just downward, and see where it might force its way through.

When you go to sea, your decks should be clear for safety's sake. Nautical nomads often clutter their lifelines with bikes, surfboards, rusty fuel cans, and ancient generators. They convince themselves that it adds an air of romance. But in fact all it adds is windage and top-heaviness that detract from performance and stability. In the interests of seaworthiness you must be able to pass along the side decks unhindered with sailbags, anchors, or any other equipment you might need in an emergency. Remember: There are times when you can move along those side decks only on all fours, towing a sailbag behind you. You don't need a pedal or a handlebar up your anorak then.

As far as cabin trunks go, the best superstructure is low and sturdy. The higher it is, the more vulnerable.

Most decks and cabintops are built of fiberglass with a core of balsa wood or plastic foam for lightness and stiffness, so they should be painted a fairly light color. Too much heat softens foam, makes balsa brittle and crumbly, and burns the soles of your feet.

Bimini Tops

Bimini tops are essential to provide shade in the cockpit in the tropics—unless you're prepared to slather yourself with sunscreen every few hours. Biminis come with their own fold-down frames. But if you have a boom gallows, you can form a Bimini extension from the companionway dodger to the gallows (see the section on dodgers, page 59). Use a material that matches the dodger and has some weight in it—probably an acrylic such as Sunbrella—so it won't rattle and flutter in every little breeze and drive you crazy.

If you run with twin jibs in the trades, you

can fashion yourself a cockpit shade with a rectangle of canvas slung over the main boom or over a line taken from the mast to the backstay.

Boarding Ladder

If you don't have a sugar-scoop stern, a boarding ladder is essential. Getting back on board wearing sailing gear is no picnic.

The best ladders are rigid and have at least two rungs under water.

A stainless steel ladder hinged low on the transom will fold up neatly alongside or into the stern pulpit.

By the way, round rungs less than an inch (25 mm) in diameter are hell on bare feet. Portable ladders—roll-up plastic rungs strung between spacers on Dacron lines—are better than nothing, but they are difficult to use.

Cabin Trunk

The cabin trunk is a type of of lid with sides, placed over a hole in the deck. Without the trunk, the deck would be much stronger. But the trunk exists to provide headroom, light, and ventilation down below.

The higher the sides of the trunk, the greater the area they present to the wind. So when you're trying to sail against the wind, the cabin trunk is holding you back. It's also vulnerable to waves breaking over the boat. But most damage to a cabin trunk occurs when a boat is flung sideways by a wave and the leeward side of the trunk slams into the sea.

Portlights or deadlights in a cabin trunk or doghouse must be strong, watertight, and preferably small. If yours are large, and therefore vulnerable—anything larger than about 6 to 8 inches (150 to 200 mm) across—you should make storm covers of ½-inch (12-mm) plywood, ⅛-inch (3-mm) aluminum, or ⅜-inch (10-mm) Lexan. You'll need a special frame (or retainers) tapped for wing nuts so you can fit them quickly when the weather turns nasty.

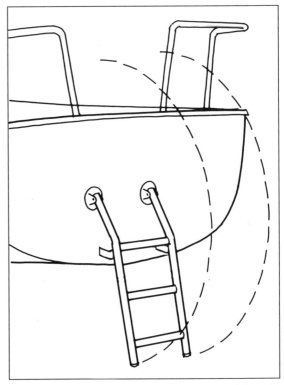

This transom-mounted boarding ladder is hinged, so it will swing up when not in use.

A flush-decked boat lacks a cabin trunk. It may also therefore lack headroom, light, and ventilation—particularly if it is a small boat. But it will almost certainly be stronger than a boat with a cabin trunk.

Chain Locker Pipe

The pipe that leads the anchor chain from the windlass and down to the chain locker is a potential source of leaks. Some chain pipes come with fancy covers that fit around a link of chain; but you can also plug the pipe with a piece of cloth or soft foam rubber. Also make sure that the top of the pipe stands well proud of the deck, or of the bottom of the anchor well. Otherwise, it can admit copious quantities of water.

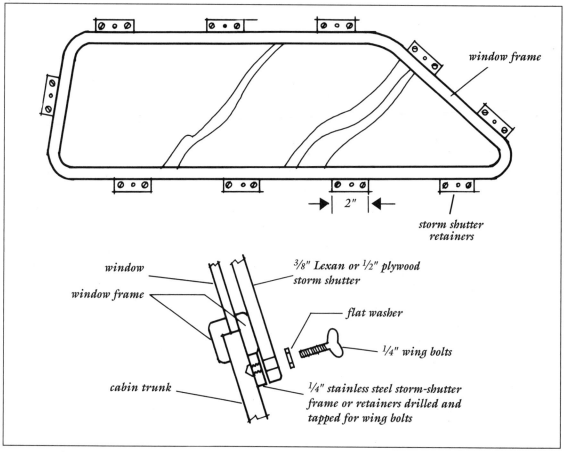

window frame

2"

storm shutter retainers

window

window frame

3/8" Lexan or 1/2" plywood storm shutter

flat washer

1/4" wing bolts

cabin trunk

1/4" stainless steel storm-shutter frame or retainers drilled and tapped for wing bolts

Storm covers should be about an inch bigger all around than the ports they protect. Stainless steel retainers, bolted permanently in place alongside the window frame, are predrilled and tapped to accept 1/4-inch (6.4-mm) wing bolts. Instead of separate retainers, you could fit a continuous outer frame.

Cockpit Bilge Pump

It's essential to fit a manual bilge pump in the cockpit. Two manual bilge pumps should be carried in addition to any powered pumps you might have. One of those manual pumps must be so positioned you can work it from the helm. The other (usually bigger) manual pump should be positioned so that you can pump it from below with the companionway hatch tightly closed. Mount it in the bilge so someone can work the handle while sitting on a bunk or the cabin sole.

Both should be good diaphragm pumps that will not easily clog. Each should be fitted with a strum box or strainer.

Cockpit Drains

A so-called self-bailing cockpit filled with water by a breaking wave takes an unconscionable amount of time to empty itself. The advice often offered in cheerful consolation is that the boat will be rolling so wildly at this time that half the water in the cockpit will be spilled out over the

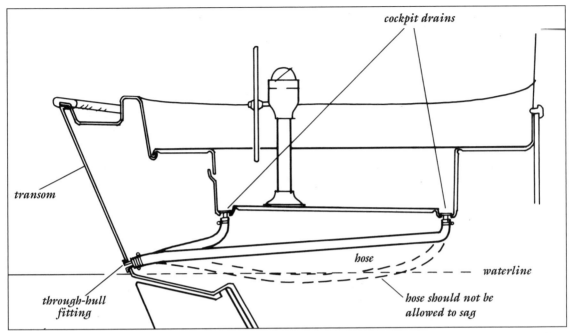

No seacocks are necessary if you make your cockpit drains discharge through the transom, above the waterline.

coamings anyway—leaving you with only the other half to panic about.

The cockpit that empties itself fastest is the racing-style one that lacks a transom; the next fastest is the cockpit that has large opening ports right through the transom.

If you have cockpit drains that empty downward through the hull, they will usually be located at the forward end of the cockpit. They should be at least 1¼ inches (30 mm) in diameter, preferably 1½ inches (40 mm), and they should have bronze through-hulls and proper seacocks. You can buy guards, or strainers, to fit over the tops of the drains to keep rope ends and other undesirable things out of them. (For a description of how one solo circumnavigator made extra drains for his Catalina 27, see Appendix 2, page 224.)

The hoses connecting the cockpit floor to the seacocks are particularly vulnerable. When the seacocks are open, which they normally are, the hoses are the only things keeping the sea out of the boat. Squeeze them now and then, and replace them if they feel sticky or suspiciously soft and rubbery.

Cockpit Lockers

Do whatever is necessary to prevent your cockpit lockers from leaking. You'll be very glad you did when you hit your first storm on the other side of the horizon.

If necessary, glue a rubber gasket around the inside perimeter of the lid and install a lever-action fitting that will force the lid down tightly onto the gasket.

Make sure your lockers can't possibly open accidentally at sea.

Incidentally, whether your lids have gaskets or not, seat lockers need deep draining gutters at their fore and aft edges so water won't overflow into them when the boat is heeled.

Cockpit Size

Many coastal cruisers have cockpits that would be regarded as too large for safety on an ocean-going boat.

You can reduce the volume of the footwell by closing off one end or the other with a simple box made of plywood and fiberglass. A watertight, lockable lid will provide handy access to a liferaft in a valise or anything else you need to stow.

You can also make the footwell narrower with plywood fiberglassed to the sides. In an emergency you can partially fill this space with bags of sails, well lashed down, or anything else light but bulky.

Crew Overboard Pole

A crew overboard pole is not essential—until you're the one who falls overboard. This is a racing boat requirement that not all cruisers follow, but it's a very good idea. This is just a blank fishing pole, buoyed and weighted with lead to float upright, with a red or yellow flag on top and an automatic-switching, battery-operated light attached. A horseshoe lifebuoy should also be attached. The whole caboodle is flung over the stern as soon as the "Crew Overboard!" cry is heard, and the person in the water should try to swim to it.

Dodger

A dodger is not essential, if you don't mind getting hit in the face by every little dollop of cold spray that comes along, but it's a great comfort if you're not a practicing Spartan or a nautical masochist. A dodger provides shelter from wind, rain, and sun for the crew on lookout duty. It also stops rain falling below when the companionway sliding hatch is open.

Solid stainless steel tubing, firmly braced open by turnbuckles, is the best foundation for a dodger. Acrylic material is the best choice for the fabric covering. Clear plastic windows should be as small as possible while still giving you a clear view forward and to the sides. It may be difficult to make them small, but it will be easier if you remember that the plastic is the weakest part and will stretch most and distort soonest.

An extension aft to the boom gallows, or to a special frame, creates a very practical bimini top to shade most of the cockpit.

Dodgers should fold down flat in a neat forward semicircle, and there should be some way to fasten them down very securely. If they work loose, and open up partially, waves can fill them and rip them off. At sea in very heavy weather, and even at anchor in a hurricane, you need to reduce your windage, even if it does rob you of comfort. That's why a permanent, hard-topped dodger is not a good idea on a small oceangoing boat.

If you're planning to add a dodger for the first time, make sure it won't interfere with the handles of the cockpit winches.

Dorade Boxes

Ventilators such as Dorade boxes are often presumed to be totally waterproof, but they're not if the whole fitting is submerged. Waves flooding

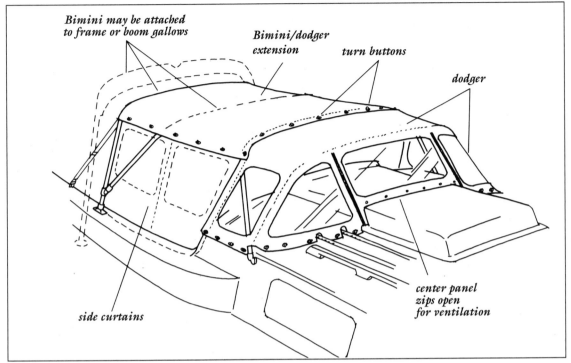

Bimini may be attached to frame or boom gallows

Bimini/dodger extension

turn buttons

dodger

side curtains

center panel zips open for ventilation

A sturdy companionway dodger provides good protection from sun, wind, rain, and spray. A Bimini awning, extended aft from the dodger, is a blessing in the trade winds.

over the deck will find their way below through water-trap ventilators in dangerous amounts. If you capsize, you might as well have 4-inch-diameter (100-mm-diameter) holes through your hull.

So you must be able to close off every ventilator vent from inside the boat, usually by screwing a round deck plate into the interior fitting. Failing this, you'll have to remove the ventilator cowls on deck and plug the main hole and the small drain holes as best you can.

Many boats also have straight-through ventilators serving the engine compartment. There is not usually any provision for closing them off, but they will admit dangerous volumes of water in really bad weather, so give some thought to how you will plug them when the time comes. Some cowls can be removed and replaced with flush-fitting deck plates. You may be able to

secure a canvas or plastic bag over others. But a few will not respond to any treatment more resourceful than a sponge or a sock stuffed down the opening. Just be sure to do it.

Drop Slides

On small oceangoing boats, the companionway entrance from the cockpit is usually closed off with two or three drop slides, or washboards. On bigger boats where the companionway is more protected, or on daysailers, two hinged doors are often used for convenience; but they are weaker than drop slides.

A surprising amount of water jets through the cracks between drop slides when a wave slams against them. The best slides are rabbeted or otherwise fashioned with an overlap that keeps most of this water out, and they are fitted with barrel

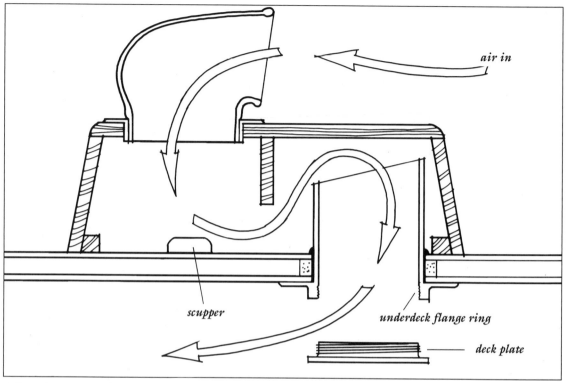

air in

scupper

underdeck flange ring

deck plate

A Dorade-type ventilator box admits only air. Water, stopped by a baffle, drains out of the box through small scuppers on each side. The vent can be closed from down below by screwing a deck plate into the underdeck flange ring.

bolts or small lashings so that they will not be lost if the boat capsizes.

Gunwales, Bulwarks

When you're working on deck, a surprising amount of irreplaceable gear jumps out of your hands and rolls overboard. Toerails prevent this to a certain extent, but gunwales 4 inches (10 cm) high, or higher, do it a lot better.

Gunwales also stop people going overboard by providing a better foothold on the leeward deck, especially when it's under water. And, as boating author Dan Spurr has pointed out, "One can't begin to appreciate the sense of security good bulwarks provide until sitting on the foredeck in a gale, trying to change jibs."

On many boats, it's practical to retrofit wooden gunwales fastened to braces bolted through the side decks. Spurr tells how in *Spurr's Boatbook: Upgrading the Cruising Sailboat.*

Harness Clip-On Points

Large eyebolts securely fastened through a deck or bulkhead provide safe clip-on points for your personal safety harness. Each bolt should be backed up by a large tapered plate inside to spread the shock load.

It's often tempting to clip onto a lifeline wire or stanchion, but neither is meant to take the strain of a crewmember falling overboard, as some tragedies have demonstrated.

Jacklines running fore and aft are a good

solution, and avoid your having to clip on and off as you move forward. They should run from a strong point on the foredeck, either side of the cabin trunk, to the cockpit aft. Jacklines of nylon webbing are very strong and lie flat underfoot.

In theory, it's a good idea to keep your tether so short that you can't possibly fall overboard. Even if you are saved by a long tether, it can be extremely difficult to get back aboard. Round-the-world singlehander Yukio Hasebe lost his boat and nearly his life when he fell overboard and was dragged alongside for hours, battered and bleeding, until the vessel hit a reef off Australia.

But a longer tether is often needed for work at the mast or on the foredeck, so some sailors carry two tethers: one long (about 6 feet or 1.8 meter) and one short (about 3 feet or 1 meter). They use the shorter one wherever possible. By clipping on and off alternately, you need never be untethered. But the weight and clutter is such that many people prefer a single long tether and hope they never fall overboard (see the section on jacklines, chapter 8, page 82, for more information).

Lifelines

Many boats have sailed around the world without lifelines. They never used to be considered essential; but public opinion has changed, and few people would want to do without them now.

Stanchions that support lifelines must be firmly through-bolted onto large backing plates. The best kind of stanchions are also bolted to gunwales or specially made vertical brackets.

The top lifeline wire should be as high as possible, though practical considerations generally limit its height to about 26 inches (660 mm), which should reach to mid-thigh on most people.

It's better to have no lifelines than ones that are too low or insecurely fastened. Too low a lifeline could catapult you overboard.

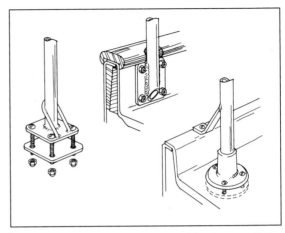

Lifelines need very secure stanchion bases. If the base is fastened to a vertical support, as well as being bolted through the deck, it will be much stronger.

Lifeline wire should be plain stainless steel: Plastic-covered wire hides corrosion.

Netting, or simple diamond-mesh knotted line, between the toerail and the upper lifeline on the foredeck helps greatly to prevent headsails from blowing overboard in windy conditions. Many family cruisers carry netting all the way aft as well—the better to confine small humans and animals.

Portlights

Large areas of brittle glass or relatively weak acrylic plastic are often the most vulnerable part of a cabin trunk. It's safer, therefore, to have two small ports than one large one.

Portlights must be able to withstand tremendous impact forces if the boat is thrown bodily to leeward by a large wave. Storm shutters (covered earlier in the section on cabin trunks, page 56) take a lot of pressure off them.

Pulpits

A foredeck pulpit is probably more necessary than a stern pulpit because of the danger of your falling overboard from the foredeck while changing headsails.

Pulpits should be strong and well bolted through the deck onto large backing plates. If they flex alarmingly when you lean against them, take them off and have a metal shop weld braces in the corners. You can also add a second row of tubing if they have only one; be sure you can pass your anchor through the space between the bottom row and the foredeck, if you need to.

A stern pulpit can incorporate a hinged boarding ladder, which is a wonderful safety feature. It's also a place where many people succumb to the temptation to hang an outboard motor, a charcoal barbecue, a spare anchor, and sundry other heavy objects, each of which adds its own feeling of frenzy to a boat's simple lines. Aesthetics aside, this gear can also detract from the boat's stability.

Skidproofing

Nonslip patterns molded into the fiberglass gelcoat of the deck and cabintop have improved over the years, but you should be sure to test your own decks for skidproofing—both in bare feet and in sneakers.

Basically, there are two ways to improve matters. You can paint the decks with a nonskid paint that has small particles of grit mixed in it, or with ordinary paint that is strewn with sand before it dries. Or you can glue down patches of rubberized nonskid overlay, such as Treadmaster M. Don Casey gives detailed instructions in his book, *This Old Boat.*

Large hatch covers can be slick and hazardous, so apply a couple of strips of self-adhesive nonskid tape across the full width. The companionway ladder can use the same treatment if its steps become slippery in wet weather.

Ventilation

There may be days at a stretch on an ocean crossing when the weather is uncomfortably warm, yet it's too rough to open a port or crack an overhead hatch. That's when you need good ventilation down below.

If your boat isn't fitted with ventilators that separate water from the flow of air, it should be. You can buy Dorade box kits, made of teak, from boat stores and fit them yourself (see more on Dorades, page 59).

Incidentally, no matter what size boat you have, it is almost always worthwhile to fit a 4-inch (100-mm) diameter ventilator rather than a 3-inch (75-mm) ventilator. If you recall that the area of a circle is π times the radius squared, you'll realize that a 4-inch (100-mm) vent admits almost twice as much air as a 3-inch (75-mm) vent. (The actual ratio is about 50 to 28.)

Air flow is important to prevent mildew and rot down below, as well as to dilute any carbon monoxide fumes from engine exhaust or cooking stoves.

If you hinge your forehatch at its forward edge—so that it will close itself if a wave comes

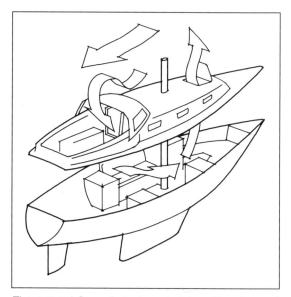

The natural flow of air down below, with a forward hatch that is hinged along its forward edge, is from the stern toward the bow.

over the bow—you will find that the flow of air through the boat when you're at anchor with the hatch propped open is from aft forward. In fact, wind from most directions swirls around the dodger and enters the companionway, making its way through the boat from there to the fore-hatch. If you use electric fans, direct them so they encourage this natural circulation.

THINK INVERTED

If your boat turns upside down:

- Where will water enter?
- Will the skylights or hatch covers break under the pressure of supporting the boat?
- Will you be trapped in the cockpit, or is your tether long enough to let you float free but still remain attached to the boat?

- Is there a quick-release snap hook or carabiner right there at your chest, so you can reach it to free yourself if you're dragged under water?
- Will you lose your bilge pump handle?
- Will your cockpit floorboard float away?

CHAPTER 7

Engine and Propeller

You can sail around the world without an engine. Many sailors have done so, and some experienced cruisers still do. After all, an oceangoing boat doesn't need the power a coastal cruiser does to get home on time after a weekend jaunt.

But the point is probably moot. Your boat likely already has an engine. The question is: Is it suitable?

Frankly, it hardly matters whether it is or not. Most of us are stuck with the engine we own because it's so expensive to replace, and as long as it keeps running—even if it's underpowered or uses enough fuel for a battleship—we're not likely to do anything about it except curse it once in a while.

In theory, these are your choices:
- Replace your engine with a new or used one.
- Throw it out.
- Replace it with an outboard.
- Put up with it.

There is a modern fashion for replacing gasoline engines with diesels, but this is not always the wisest move. Gas engines are cheaper, lighter (or more powerful for the same weight), easier to repair and service, quieter, and much smoother-running. They have much to commend them, especially modern engines with fuel injection and electronic ignition. As for the dangers of carrying gasoline fuel, they're no greater than the dangers

of cooking and heating with bottled gas (probably less, in fact, if you take reasonable precautions). And most boats with diesel engines store gasoline for their outboard motors anyway.

If you do decide to exchange your old engine for a new diesel, get the most powerful one that will fit the space, if you can afford it. In other words, take advantage of today's lighter, more compact, more powerful diesels. Aim for 3 or 4 horsepower for each ton of boat weight. If you're determined to have a dirty, smelly engine, it might as well be a *powerful,* dirty, smelly engine.

Some smaller boats with inboard engines, up to about 27 feet (8.23 m) overall, may be better off with outboards when they go ocean cruising. The gain in valuable interior space will be quite considerable, and the lighter outboard will provide sufficient power and range for maneuvering in an anchorage or marina, or for entering a pass through a coral reef. Without the drag of a fixed propeller, your sailing performance will improve. Don't expect an outboard to be of much assistance in really heavy weather, though, because the propeller will spend too much time out of the water, even if the outboard has a long shaft. Furthermore, you won't be able to generate much electrical power with this type of engine because most outboard alternators lack muscle.

Four-stroke gasoline outboard motors are probably the most suitable, although they weigh more than two-strokes, because they deliver

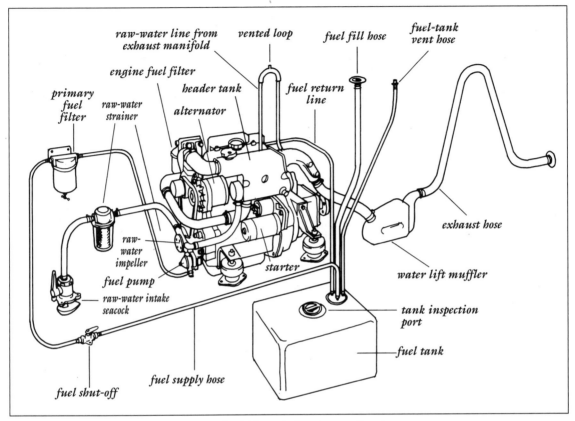

The essential elements of an auxiliary diesel installation in a sailboat

almost double the mileage of two-strokes. They are more expensive than two-strokes, however, and their valve trains make them more complicated.

Diesel outboards are available, but they are heavier and more expensive. They make economic sense only if you run them for long hours every day of the year, as commercial fishermen do.

If you decide to do without an engine altogether, you'll gain numerous skills. You'll learn to take the utmost advantage of light winds. You'll learn how to maneuver your boat under human power, or with warps, and to scull or row her at a knot or so in a calm. You'll learn to anchor when the tide turns contrary, and you'll find yourself getting up in moonlight to catch the ebb. You'll

discover that a dinghy and a small outboard, lashed alongside your quarter like a tug, will take you almost anywhere you want to go in port or in a sheltered anchorage. And you'll probably become very skilled at scrounging tows from passing powerboats.

Engine Life Expectancy

As a very general rule of thumb, the average marine gasoline engine runs for 1,500 hours, and the average marine diesel for 5,000 hours, before needing a major overhaul.

The typical gasoline engine on a boat gets about 1,000 hours of trouble-free operation. During the next 500 hours, minor troubles become increasingly likely. And they turn into major troubles as the 1,500-hour mark approaches.

Incidentally, gasoline engines in land-based automobiles run for an average of 2,900 hours before needing an overhaul at 100,000 miles. The difference in longevity reflects the fact that boat engines work harder and more intermittently under atrocious conditions of salt air, damp bilges, hot surroundings, too little fresh air, and pure neglect.

Diesel engines often deliver 8,000 hours of hard work before requiring a major overhaul—and in theory, they should last the life of the boat.

The average boat owner who uses the boat on weekends and for a short vacation cruise logs 200 engine hours a year, so it would take 40 years to do 8,000 hours. In practice, however, short running times, the difficulty of routine servicing, and harsh operating conditions doom yacht diesels to the wrecker's yard long before their 40 years are up.

Engine Mounts

All engines, but especially vibration-prone diesels, need to be mounted on heavy beds that spread the load over as much of the bottom of the boat as possible.

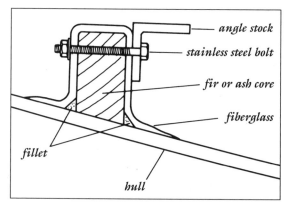

Properly mounted engines are fitted to heavy steel or aluminum angle stock through-bolted to the engine beds or stringers.

The longitudinal beds, or stringers, may be of solid wood or of fiberglass over a core of wood or foam. They should have heavy steel or aluminum angle stock bolted through the side of the stringer, leaving a flat horizontal surface on the outside of the stringer through which to bolt the engine mounts. A minimum of four bolts should fasten the angle stock to the stringer. Each bolt should have a minimum diameter, in inches, of the engine weight in pounds divided by 4,000. (Or a minimum diameter, in millimeters, of engine weight in kilograms divided by 70.) But no bolt should be smaller than $\frac{3}{8}$ inch (10 mm).

A safe standard for wooden and fiberglass hulls is to make the width of the stringers a minimum of $\frac{1}{40}$ of the boat's overall beam. The depth should be the same except at the engine itself: There it should be increased by 50 percent, using gradual tapers at either end.

Fuel Biocides

A little water and a lot of diesel fuel make a fine breeding ground for certain microscopic creatures in the vegetable kingdom. The sludge they create soon blocks filters and stops the fuel from reaching the engine.

It's not possible to keep all water out of a fuel tank; it will condense there if it doesn't run in through the filler or breather pipes. Sometimes, when you fill up, your friendly neighborhood fuel dock will supply you with a generous helping of the water that is sloshing around in its own diesel tanks.

So the first thing to do is to add a biocide when you fill up, to prevent microorganisms from breeding in your tank. Then you must use in-line filters to remove the water and dirt from the fuel before it gets to your engine.

Fuel Filters

The importance of water separators and clean fuel filters can hardly be exaggerated. The primary cause of failure, poor performance, and starting difficulty is problems with the fuel. On a diesel engine particularly, frequent inspection and changes of filters will do more than anything else to stave off engine failure.

If you fit two primary filters connected by Y-valves, you'll be able to switch filters while the engine is running. Install the biggest filters practical. Ones the size of those you see on 18-wheelers are easy to work with.

If you find dark globules in your filters, or notice the smell of rotten eggs, you probably already have an advanced case of microbial infestation.

Empty your fuel tank and have it professionally cleaned with pressurized steam. Fill it with new fuel to which you've added hefty amounts of biocide. Leave it for at least 24 hours and then fire up the engine, but be prepared for several filter changes until you've caught all those millions of little corpses. Then add biocide on a regular basis.

Incidentally, slavishly follow your engine manufacturer's recommendations about fuel filters: no second-guessing. Most manufacturers specify a 30-micron element for the primary filters and a 10- or 12-micron element for the secondary filter. Don't imagine your engine manufacturer

wouldn't have specified a 2-micron filter if it were needed.

Change filters religiously at the stated intervals, or—if you're in any doubt—after a maximum of 300 hours of engine running.

Gas vs. Diesel Engines

Gas and diesel engines each have their own virtues. The accompanying table lists the advantages of each.

Engine Virtues	
Gas	**Diesel**
Cheaper	Precision made
Quieter	More reliable
Smoother	Longer lasting
Better power/ weight ratio	Far more miles per gallon
Lighter	Safer fuel

Hour Meter

Regard an engine hour meter as an essential tool if you don't keep an accurate engine log and conscientiously write down the number of hours you run your engine. Otherwise, you'll never know when oil changes and routine maintenance are due.

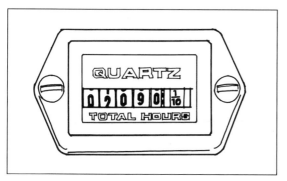

An engine hour meter lets you know when servicing is due.

An hour meter switches on and off automatically with the starter key, and it is easy to install.

Learn to Bleed

Never let a diesel tank run dry or close the tank shut-off valve while the engine is running: You'll suck air into the fuel system.

Air can also enter the fuel line while you're changing a filter, and then the engine won't work. If you're planning to go over the horizon, you must learn to purge the system of air, or bleed it.

Some diesels are allegedly self-bleeding, but even if you own one of these you should know the principle involved and be able to do it yourself.

Your engine manual will tell you how, but basically it's a case of loosening fuel line fittings upstream, where the air bubble migrates to, so the system can burp it out.

It's a messy business because fuel will dribble out while you're doing this, and you need to mop it up with cloths, but it's vital that you learn this skill.

Maintenance

The amount of maintenance given a sailboat auxiliary engine is in direct proportion to the space available and the ease of working on it. If your engine isn't easy to service, it's likely to be neglected and its life will be shortened.

Many engines are jammed into tiny hellholes beneath the cockpit, but access to some is aided by a removable engine box, a cockpit hatch, or ports in a sideberth bulkhead.

Do whatever you can to make it easier to get to important points on the engine, such as the oil dipstick, the alternator, the belts, the water pump, the sacrificial zinc, and so forth.

Install a fluorescent shoplight or a bright tungsten light in the engine box. It's amazing what a difference this makes and what confidence it inspires when you can see what you're doing.

Noise Suppression

Engine noise is wearying, especially for crew trying to sleep down below, but modern methods of noise suppression using foam and a lead-foil substitute are very effective.

You can buy a single-layer engine noise suppression kit or separate sheets of very effective, double-layer barrier material from marine discount stores.

Simply cut them to size and stick them to the inside of your engine compartment with spray adhesive.

Power Needs

The old rule of thumb was that an auxiliary engine should be powerful enough to give a bare-masted sailboat a speed of at least 2 knots against a Force 5 wind (17 to 21 knots) with the weather shore at least 2 miles distant. That's probably an engine with about 2 horsepower (1.5 kW) for every ton of boat weight, which would be judged not quite sufficient for today's needs.

With modern engines producing more power from lighter and less bulky machinery, it makes sense to aim for 3 to 4 horsepower (2 to 3 kW) per ton of displacement. This is not for extra top speed, but so you can maintain a reasonable speed against strong winds and choppy seas.

On the other hand, the engine can be as small as you like if you really know how to sail. Eric and Susan Hiscock took *Wanderer III* around the world with a 4-hp (3-kW) Stuart Turner inboard two-stroke. Lin and Larry Pardey's wooden 29-footer *Taleisin* doesn't have an engine at all.

Propeller Shafts

The need for a heftier propeller shaft is a great deterrent to installing a more powerful engine. A larger shaft means a larger hole through the hull, a new stern tube, a new Cutless bearing, and a new stuffing box—just for starters.

But maybe your present shaft could handle a few extra horses and a larger propeller. The rule of thumb for shaft diameter in inches is this:

- For a Tobin bronze shaft, divide propeller diameter in inches by 14.5 for a two-bladed prop, or by 14.0 for a three-bladed prop.
- For a stainless steel shaft, do the calculations above and subtract 10 percent from the diameter.
- For a Monel shaft, divide prop diameter in inches by 18.1 for two blades, and by 17.5 for three blades.

Propellers

Cruising boats normally carry two-bladed or three-bladed fixed propellers. Folding propellers reduce drag, but they may not open at all if a barnacle grows in the wrong place. Adjustable-pitch props are wonderful when they work, which is not all the time; they are also expensive and prone to malfunction. Automatically feathering props also reduce drag, but their fine engineering makes them very expensive.

Your prop is correctly sized when your boat reaches its maximum hull speed in knots (the square root of the waterline length in feet, times 1.34) in deep, calm water at a little less than the engine designer's stated maximum revolutions per minute.

Too large a prop will give you a good, economical cruising speed in smooth going, but will prevent the engine from reaching full rpm—and therefore full power—in adverse conditions. You can cook the engine with a prop that's too large.

Too small a prop will allow the engine to reach top revs before the boat reaches its maximum hull speed. It's the equivalent of riding a bike along the flat in low gear—not very fast, and not very economical.

Some prop shops have loaners you can try out to see if they improve your boat's performance.

A change in diameter makes more difference to a prop's performance than a change in pitch. You can expect an increase in prop-shaft revolu-

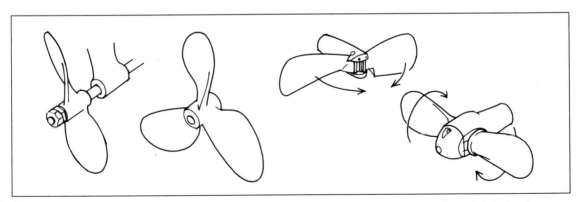

The most common types of propellers used on small auxiliary sailboats (from left to right): fixed two-bladed, fixed three-bladed, folding, and adjustable-pitch.

tions (not engine revolutions) of about 300 per minute for a decrease of 1 inch (25 mm) in prop diameter.

Correspondingly, you can expect an increase in prop-shaft revolutions of about 200 per minute for a reduction of 1 inch (25 mm) in pitch.

Most marine transmissions make the prop shaft turn more slowly than the engine does. Check your service manual for the reduction ratio.

Propshaft Locks

Some authorities assert that a fixed prop causes less drag when it is allowed to rotate freely. Other authorities of equal eminence say just the opposite, which leads the rest of us to conclude that it doesn't make any measurable difference.

So whether or not you lock the prop shaft while sailing depends on whether you are driven crazy by the continual whirring sound, or by the nagging suspicion that everything in the transmission is grinding itself to bits.

Not all transmissions receive lubrication when the shaft is freewheeling, however, so it's safer to lock the shaft. If you have a two-bladed prop on a full-keeled boat, you may be able to line the prop up vertically behind the keel and reduce its drag somewhat.

Range under Power

If you have developed the patience of the true sailor and are happy to spend some time drifting around in calms and light weather, you don't need a great range under power. But if you start fretting when the speed drops below 4 knots, and you can't wait to switch on the engine to make more ice cubes anyhow, you will need to carry a lot more fuel. Then, you'll need to find room for more fuel tanks, which will make the boat heavier and cause more drag, so that you use more fuel…

In round figures, a small diesel will run for about 50 hours on 25 gallons (95 liters) of fuel weighing 178 pounds (81 kg), which will give

the boat a range of 200 to 250 miles at 4 or 5 knots. This is plenty for the patient sailor.

You can check your own diesel engine's consumption: It will consume about 1 gallon (3.8 liters) per hour for every 18 hp (13 kW) of its capacity that you're using. So if you're running an 18-hp (13-kW) engine at half-power (thus using roughly 9 hp or 6.5 kW), it will consume about half a gallon (2 liters) an hour. And if you're running a 36-hp (27-kW) engine at full speed, it will use about 2 gallons (7.6 liters) of fuel per hour.

A four-stroke gasoline engine, incidentally, consumes about a gallon (3.8 liters) per hour for every 10 hp (7.5 kW) it puts out.

Raw Water Filters

Even if your engine is directly cooled by fresh water, it will be indirectly cooled by raw seawater that needs to be strained of sand, seaweed, and other debris.

Special bronze through-hull fittings are made for engine water intakes that have built-in scoop strainers to keep out the large stuff.

To deal with the smaller stuff, you need a sediment-trapping raw-water strainer with a glass bowl, mounted between the intake seacock and your engine's impeller pump. The more expensive ones have a drain plug in the bottom so you can easily remove sediment and drain the trap for a winter lay-up.

Runaway Diesels

Anyone who goes to sea should know how to deal with a runaway diesel, which can be a very frightening and dangerous experience. It's fortunately an extremely rare occurrence, but it can happen when a diesel starts to burn its own lubricating oil because of leaky seals, an overfilled sump, or badly worn piston rings.

It will continue to run out of control until it overheats and seizes, or starts to disintegrate. Either way, it's a very traumatic experience; and

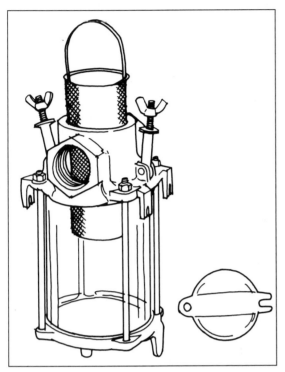

This Perko raw-water strainer has a stainless steel strainer basket that lifts out for easy cleaning, and a drain plug in the bottom casing to remove sediment.

no amount of fiddling with the throttle will make any difference, since the injectors are not providing the fuel.

One answer is to cut off its air supply. Locate the air intake in your diesel and figure out how you would stop air entering there by holding a piece of plywood or aluminum sheet against it or even some substantial kind of cloth. Remember that the suction will be terrific. A few diesels have a sliding plate that can be dropped over the air inlet for this purpose, but most sailboat auxiliaries lack this feature.

Another, safer way to stop it is to aim a carbon-dioxide fire extinguisher at the air intake. It's not a bad idea to have one stationed near the engine in any case. Just remember that the extin-

guisher must be big enough to operate continuously until the engine has come to a dead stop.

Apparently, it is not a good idea to try to stop the engine by operating a valve lifter: A lot of damage can be caused at the speed at which it will be running by the time you think of it.

Spare Parts

If you read through the workshop manual and the owner's manual, common sense will tell you what spares and tools to carry for your particular engine.

It's impossible to generalize, but cruisers with diesels normally carry spare water impellers, filters, sacrificial zincs, and an injector or two. Owners of gasoline engines also carry impellers and filters, plus spare spark plugs, a spare coil and distributor, points, and condensers.

Anyone with an engine should carry spare belts as well as packing for the propeller shaft stuffing box.

Unfortunately, once you get started on a list of possible spare parts, it's difficult to know when to stop. Our advice is to be brave. Take only the absolute essentials. But start your cruise with the engine in tip-top condition, maintain it faithfully, and train yourself never to become overdependent on it.

Stuffing Boxes

Most ocean sailors rely on the old-fashioned type of shaft gland that drips water to lubricate the

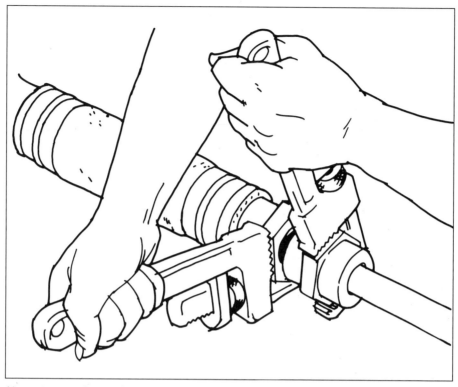

Never try to release the locknut on a propeller shaft stuffing box without a second wrench on the packing nut. Special wrenches are available in boating stores to fit the large-diameter nuts.

packing. It's simple and easy to maintain in primitive cruising areas of the world where you can't find spares for a modern dripless seal—or even find someone who's heard of one.

When the prop shaft is not turning, you should adjust the gland for a flow of about four drops a minute with new flax packing. When this has bedded in after 10 or 15 hours of running, adjust it for a drip rate of one or two drops a minute when it's still. When the shaft is turning, the rate will be somewhat greater and will not only lubricate the gland but also prevent overheating.

Tankage

You're not likely to need a bigger fuel tank than the one you've got. Most coastal cruisers come

equipped with tanks of reasonable size. In any case, it's usually a devil of a job to find space for another fixed tank, and you'd probably need one custom-built for you, which can be an expensive business.

If you're determined to carry extra fuel, it would be better off in a flexible bladder than in rusty jerry jugs lashed to the lifelines. Flexible tanks made of tough nylon with a fuel-resistant coating will fit into all sorts of odd-shaped spaces.

Water Impeller

It's vital to carry a spare impeller for your engine's raw-water cooling system. And it's just as vital that you learn to fit it yourself. Usually, it's a very simple, straightforward job. Consult your engine manual to see if special tools are needed.

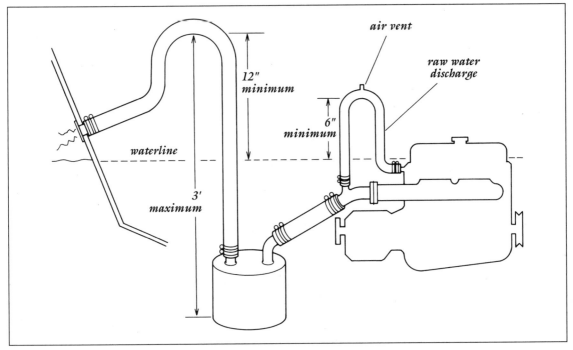

A waterlift exhaust system like this one is quiet and easy to install.

Waterlift Exhaust

Engine exhaust pipes that are jacketed with cooling water are likely to suffer failure of the inner jacket wall sooner or later. If you're planning to take a long cruise in foreign waters, it would be a wise move to replace your jacketed system with a waterlift system before you go.

The waterlift exhaust muffler is a simple canister that collects exhaust water and gases after they've been expelled from the engine but before they reach the exhaust outlet in the hull. The pressure of the exhaust blows the water up and out of the canister every now and then. This results in isolated bursts of water coming from the exhaust pipe, rather than the continuous flow of a jacketed exhaust.

This system is cheaper, simpler, and quieter than a jacketed exhaust system, but it has one little failing you should know about. If your engine turns over but doesn't start straight away, the water will build up in the canister but won't be blown out by exhaust pressure. If you continue cranking too long, raw seawater will flow back into your cylinders via the exhaust valves. For this reason, the best waterlift systems have a drain on the canister.

THINK INVERTED

If your boat turns upside down:

- Will the running engine still get cooling water?
- Can you stop the engine when you're upside down in the dark?
- Can fuel leak out through tank vents?
- Will your engine mounts hold the weight of the engine upside down? (Some have failed to in the past.)

CHAPTER 8

Safety Equipment

Now and then we hear of a truly bad storm at sea that hits a fleet of racing or cruising yachts. All boats carry the specified safety equipment, but some survive and some don't. That leads to the question: What makes the difference? Is it just plain luck?

Similarly, two boats might run ashore in bad weather. One hits rocks and is damaged beyond repair. The other ends up on a patch of soft sand or mud and is refloated undamaged. Is that simply fate, or are there other forces at work here?

Those of us who subscribe to Vigor's Black Box Theory know that there is no such thing as fortuitous luck at sea. The reason why some sailors survive storms or have fewer accidents than others is that they *earn* their luck by constant and diligent acts of preparation and seamanship.

The Black Box Theory is discussed more fully in chapter 19. Meanwhile, think carefully about the following suggestions for safety equipment. Cautious and intelligent preparation for a deep-sea voyage will help you earn the luck you need.

Carbon Monoxide Detector

For the price of a modest restaurant meal for four, you can buy a carbon monoxide (CO) detector. It may be a very good way to ensure that you continue to enjoy eating out in foreign lands.

Carbon monoxide is invisible. It doesn't smell. But it's a killer.

It forms wherever combustion takes place.

There is an old wives' tale that diesel engines don't create carbon monoxide and gasoline engines do, but that's not true. The exhaust from a diesel main engine or generator may contain sufficient carbon monoxide to kill you; so may the fumes from a kerosene or propane burner in the galley, or an unvented stove or heater. Glowing charcoal in a barbecue grill is a rich source of the fatal gas.

Human blood has a great affinity for carbon monoxide—so much so that the gas prevents oxygen from being carried to your body cells. This results in dizziness, nausea, unconsciousness, and eventually death.

All this can happen in a few minutes, if the concentration of carbon monoxide is heavy enough. Normally, the process is slow and dangerously insidious: Most victims don't notice what's happening until it's too late. Hence, the need for a sniffer.

One of the gas's meanest tricks is its ability to travel upstream, against a flow of fresh air, at a mighty rate of knots. So if exhaust gases are being drawn in through the companionway, there's likely to be carbon monoxide throughout the boat, no matter how good the ventilation down below.

The American Boat and Yacht Council recommends that you install a carbon monoxide detector in every sleeping area on board. It's a wise precaution.

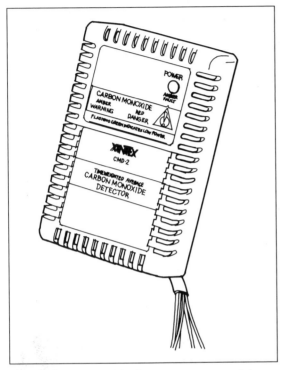

This carbon monoxide detector measures 4 by 2½ by 1¾ inches (102 by 64 by 45 mm), and it sounds an alarm if potentially dangerous fumes are present. It costs the equivalent of 29 fiscal beers.

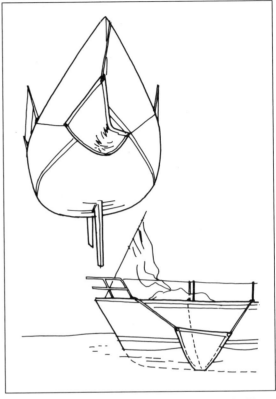

A triangular collision mat in place on a hull. The mat slows down the inflow of water sufficiently for you to make repairs from the inside.

Collision Mat

Everyone agrees that a collision mat is a good idea, but few boats actually carry them. The need for one is illustrated by the fact that a hole in the hull that you can put three fingers through will, if it's near the waterline, let in about 80 gallons (360 liters) of seawater a minute. If the hole is about 4 feet (1.2 m) below the waterline, it will let in about 130 gallons (590 liters) a minute, which is more than any manual bilge pump can keep up with.

A hole near the waterline that you can put your fist through will admit 160 gallons (730 liters) a minute; placed 4 feet (1.2 m) below the

waterline, the same hole will admit more than 300 gallons (1,365 liters) a minute.

These are the kinds of holes that might result from a collision one dark night with a balk of timber or a submerged cargo container. The only way to control a leak like that is to block the hole from the outside.

You can make your own collision mat. A tarpaulin about 4 feet (1.2 m) square, with reinforced grommets at the corners, will do the trick. Slide it on over the bow or stern and work it into position. Be sure to keep the lines taut when it gets near the hole or it may be sucked right inside. That tarp is also useful for catching rainwater, providing shade in the cockpit, and keeping rain out of open hatches.

Alternatively (and this is what most sailors fall back on), you could use a small jib or stormsail, but a dedicated tarpaulin is better, especially if you've practiced with it.

You'll find that working a collision mat into place is not as easy as it sounds, especially if you're alone. And it won't *cure* a leak, but it will slow the leak down sufficiently so you can make temporary repairs.

It will work better if it's on the leeward side while you're drifting, so the pressure of the water helps hold the mat down. And it's more likely to stay in place if you can stop the boat moving forward or aft.

Emergency Steering

If you have wheel steering, it's essential that you carry an emergency tiller and know how to rig it in a hurry. Before you disappear over the horizon, you must fit it to the rudderhead to be sure everything works. You also need to be sure that you can disconnect the primary steering system, whether it's cable or hydraulic.

If your boat has a tiller, you should carry a complete spare tiller assembly from the rudderstock upward.

And if you have an outboard rudder, drill a hole through it near the waterline at its aft edge (or make a slot there). Failing all else, you can pass a line through the hole or into the slot, knot it on each side, and take the line's ends up to the cockpit winches.

EPIRBs

The availability of emergency position-indicating radio beacons (EPIRBs) has inspired much discussion on the morality of their use.

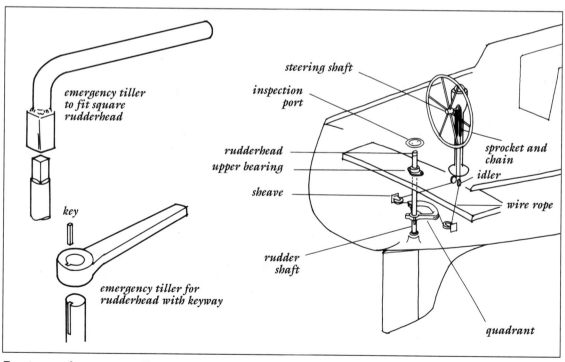

Two types of emergency tillers and the elements of a cable-quadrant steering system

Amateur sailors who take up ocean cruising as a sport often decline to carry EPIRBs. Their thinking is that anyone who goes to sea for sport, rather than for a living, should bear personal responsibility for his or her own safety. They feel it wrong to put potential rescuers' lives at risk, and to be responsible for the spending of tens of thousands of dollars of taxpayers' money.

But people who take up cruising and living on board as a way of life often feel differently. Most of them carry EPIRBs because they feel entitled to the services of rescue personnel, having paid their taxes like good citizens all their lives.

The big question is: Are you entitled to be rescued by New Zealanders when you paid your taxes in the United States? And, since you asked to be rescued (by setting off the EPIRB), are you prepared to pay the bill for your rescue if it's presented to you?

While you ponder the answers to these weighty issues, let's consider how an EPIRB works.

Class A and B EPIRBs transmit on 243 MHz. But they are effective only when a receiving satellite is also in sight of a ground reception station, most of which are in the Northern Hemisphere. This means that if you're in trouble in the Southern Hemisphere, emergency signals may not be passed on immediately—or even before the batteries run down.

The type you need for ocean cruising is the Category I or Category II EPIRB that transmits on 406 MHz. The former automatically turns itself on after floating free from its mount. The latter must be turned on manually. Both cost about three times as much as a 243-MHz beacon but their SOS messages are recorded by satellites and then retransmitted when the satellites pass over a ground station, thus ensuring worldwide coverage around the clock.

A signal from a 406-MHz EPIRB also is coded to identify your boat and provide details helpful to rescuers. For this purpose, you must register Category I and II EPIRBs in the United States. Manufacturers include registration forms with the beacons, and the National Oceanic and Atmospheric Administration (NOAA) issues a decal to indicate that the EPIRB has been registered.

Most EPIRBs will transmit for at least 48 hours and most have batteries good for 10 to 12 years, but you'd be wise to replace them every five years.

Escape Hatches for Multihulls

If you have a multihull, think carefully about how you would get outside after a 180-degree capsize.

Diving down through the companionway and then surfacing through a tangle of lines could be a very hazardous undertaking. If you have no better means of access, you might want to cut an escape hatch in the bottom of the boat if it doesn't already have one.

Now is the time to figure out where, and perhaps even mark its location. Make sure everyone aboard knows where you keep the tools needed to cut out the hatch.

Extinguishers

Fire at sea is a fearsome thing, and extinguishers are essential safety equipment. But most extinguishers found aboard small boats have a surprisingly short discharge time—usually between 8 and 20 seconds.

So use them effectively from the very start. That means three things: Don't delay, get close, and aim low.

You have a choice among dry chemical extinguishers, which can make a terrible mess of everything, carbon dioxide extinguishers, and those using the gases designated FE-241 or FM-200 (which are the successors to Halon 1211 and 1301).

FE-241 is toxic and only used for engine compartments and other unoccupied areas. FM-200 is suitable for occupied areas, but it is less effective than Halon. It doesn't eat up the ozone layer, though, as Halon did.

The rule of thumb about locating extinguishers is to avoid placing them right where a fire is likely to break out—not counting automatic extinguishers in the engine compartment, of course.

Place them nearby, along your escape routes. Usually there should be one handy to the galley and another near the engine. At least one should be at hand in the forward half of the boat, and it's a particularly good idea to be able to reach one from the cockpit.

Firearms on Board

Do you need firearms to protect yourself from those desperadoes lurking over the horizon? Should you take a gun to frighten off pirates and drug runners?

The answer depends partly on where you go, and partly on your own philosophy about owning firearms. Remember, though, that most foreign countries have gun-control laws far stricter than those in the United States. Don't expect customs officials to look kindly upon tourists who enter their countries bearing arms.

Apart from the insult to their hospitality, they regard it as an act of overt hostility. You have to remember, too, that Americans have a trigger-happy reputation abroad. Firearms kill more U.S. residents every year than those killed by guns in the rest of the world's 25 most industrialized nations put together.

Many cruising sailors get along fine without firearms, using common sense about the areas in which they sail and the company with which they mix—just as any careful tourist would.

But if you fear you would be vulnerable abroad without your personal arsenal, here are some points to consider.

- A handgun is not likely to be of much use for anything at sea except shooting sharks—and a dead shark only attracts other sharks.

- A rifle might give a long-range warning to another vessel not to approach; but if they're bent on mischief, you'll probably be outgunned anyway.

- A shotgun is probably your best form of short-range protection, and it will injure rather than kill if you use suitable ammunition.

- You must declare all your firearms to foreign customs officials. They will often confiscate them for the period of your stay, and if they return them full of rust and pitting you have no recourse. If they catch you with undisclosed firearms, they can confiscate your boat.

- If you do decide to take firearms, keep them safely locked up. Make sure you know how to use them and look after them properly.

- Be aware that a flare-launching pistol that uses 12-gauge or 25-mm cartridges might be considered a firearm in some countries. Some sailors advocate their use for personal protection in place of a handgun; but they're more likely to set your boat on fire and make things worse.

Flares

Red flares and white flares are essential safety equipment. You should carry both hand-held versions and rocket-propelled (or pistol-launched) meteor flares.

Red is the accepted color for distress signals. White flares are used to make an approaching vessel aware of your presence.

Federal safety regulations require all boats over 16 feet (4.8 m) in length that are used after dark to carry three Coast-Guard approved nighttime signals, such as red distress flares or SOS distress lights.

The flares must be in good condition, must be ready at hand, and must be no older than 42 months from the date of manufacture. They're usually good for at least 6 years, so don't throw your old ones away.

You'd be wise to carry flares that meet the stringent specifications of the Safety of Life at Sea (SOLAS) Convention of 1983. They're waterproof, easy to fire, and very bright. And you'd be well advised to increase your stock of distress flares beyond the Coast Guard's minimal requirements.

Round-the-world racing boats, for example, are required to carry 12 red parachute flares, 4 red hand flares, 4 white hand flares, and 2 orange smoke flares—which, you'll find, is not a vast inventory when you're desperately trying to attract attention.

By the way, if you pack a leather gauntlet with your flares, you won't be sorry.

Freshwater Still

A reverse-osmosis watermaker is a wonderful thing to have if your freshwater supply runs

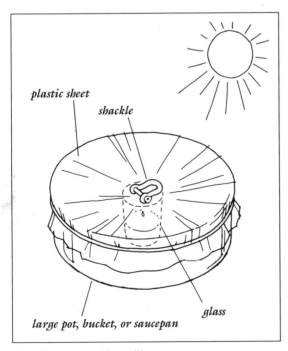

An emergency solar still

out. But they're fairly expensive, so few small yachts carry one (see the section on watermakers, page 94).

You should know how to make a solar still for emergencies.

You need a wide-mouthed saucepan or bucket, some old T-shirts or rags, a tall glass or cup, and a sheet of thin plastic (black if possible).

Put the glass in the middle of the bucket and snug the rags around it. Pour seawater into the bucket until it's about a quarter full; but don't let any spill into the glass.

Tie the plastic sheet over the bucket and make it into an inverted cone by placing a weight in the middle. Then leave the bucket in the sunshine.

Fresh water will condense on the underneath of the plastic, drip off the point of the cone, and fall into the glass. If you're rolling around at sea, some of the drips will miss the glass, so the wider it is, the better. The deeper you can make the cone, the closer you can bring its point to the mouth of the glass, and the more effective the still will be.

The deluxe version of this still incorporates a plastic tube led from inside the glass, under the plastic sheet, and over the edge of the bucket; that way you can sip the water from outside without dismantling the still.

Grab Bag

An abandon-ship bag, or grab bag, is vital to your survival. Most liferafts simply don't have all the essentials for long-term survival at sea, so you'll have to keep them in a container that you can grab as you abandon ship.

You might be astonished to learn how little fresh water is stowed in your liferaft, or how few emergency flares there are. Arrange to be present at a routine servicing and check what's there. Don't rely on a manufacturer's checklist. That could be a fatal mistake.

Here's what you might need to keep in your grab bag to supplement the basics in your liferaft.

In the illustration labels: plastic sheet, shackle, large pot, bucket, or saucepan, glass

406-MHz EPIRB

Manual watermaker (see page 94 on watermakers)

Extra red hand flares and parachute flares

Prescription medicines and spare eyeglasses

Old long-sleeved shirts, floppy hats, and long pants

Flashlight and spare batteries

Fishing kit

Handheld VHF radio and spare alkaline batteries

Signaling mirror (heliograph)

Medicine for seasickness

Pencils and notebooks

If there's room, you should add:

Vitamin tablets

Hand-held compass

Plastic sextant, and a current nautical almanac

Cheap, waterproof quartz watch set on Greenwich Mean Time

Small-scale chart of your cruising area

You can buy conveniently sized abandon-ship bags from boating stores. The best have built-in flotation and a transparent window in an exterior pocket where you can keep a list of the contents.

Abandoning Ship

The old advice is that you shouldn't abandon ship until you have to step *up* to your liferaft.

The reasoning behind this trite and silly-sounding advice is well documented. The great majority of yachts abandoned in gales are found still floating months or even years later, whereas it often happens that the sailors who abandoned these boats in liferafts are never seen again.

It's advice that is easy to offer but difficult to act on when the time comes. In an emergency at sea, there are often great psychological pressures on you to escape from your overwhelming responsibilities: to be done with the physical labor, the stress, the decision making, and the sense of failure that accompany major accidents.

All this is usually happening at a time of great mental and physical exhaustion, of course, and the lure of the liferaft becomes almost irresistible. It's soft and clean and warm in there. You can curl up like a fetus and hand everything over to fate.

The truth is that in heavy weather, it's not easy to launch a liferaft and board it successfully. Rafts get snatched away when large waves break their painters, and they capsize, spilling people into the sea. If no drogue is deployed, they drift to leeward far faster than a person can swim.

Unless your boat is quite clearly about to sink within minutes, it's almost always safer to stay with her, no matter what sort of depressing shambles the interior is in and no matter what damage has occurred to the mast and rigging.

Some experienced cruisers don't carry liferafts because they never want to be faced with the temptation to abandon ship in a crisis. They regard their vessels as their lifeboats and plan accordingly, even to the extent of adding foam flotation and carrying special air bags which, when inflated down below, will float a flooded boat.

Marcel Bardiaux, who made a remarkable singlehanded rounding of Cape Horn from east to west in 1952 in his homemade cutter *Les Quatre Vents*, fitted her with emergency buoyancy—24 5-gallon (19-liter) cans—in the cabin beneath the side decks. It reportedly saved the boat after she was later badly holed on a reef and floated off fully flooded.

Watertight bulkheads fore and aft are safety features that bring great peace of mind, but you must be quite certain the spaces they enclose can't be filled with water from leaks in deck hatches or other openings. If your boat doesn't have such bulkheads, you might be able to add them without too much trouble.

But an old kitbag filled with the right gear is just as valuable in an emergency—as long as you don't drop it overboard.

Ham Radio and HF Transceivers

International regulations forbid the use of amateur radio frequencies by any persons other than licensed ham operators. On the other hand, the international collision regulations allow you to send a distress signal by any means available to you.

Thus, many sailors who aren't hams carry ham radios and use them—and not only for distress signals. Ham operators, who aren't supposed to talk to non-hams, will always do so in an emergency (and frequently on other occasions). Hams may also patch you through to friends and relatives at home, via the local telephone system.

Hams run regular worldwide schedules for yachts at sea, passing on valuable information about the weather and other safety issues. They also track the progress of yachts crossing oceans, alerting rescue authorities if necessary.

There's nothing to prevent anyone from *listening* to ham broadcasts, and thereby gleaning useful information, but to *transmit* legally on the special ham frequencies, you need to be a licensed amateur radio operator. That involves a certain amount of study, discipline, and passing examinations about the theory and practice of radio-wave propagation.

If you've always wanted to be a ham, now would be a good time to get your license—before you disappear over the horizon. When you're at sea, you'll find no shortage of fellow hams on land who are anxious to make contact with you, especially if you're operating a low-powered rig. They're prepared to tweak and fiddle with their receivers and expend the utmost patience so you can pass on a message that a commercial station would reject as unreadable. But one of the drawbacks with ham radio is that you're not allowed to pass a commercial message: You can't order spare parts for your engine or more gin for the grog locker.

If you're not inclined to become a ham, you can buy a standard high-frequency (HF) single-sideband (SSB) marine transceiver, covering more than 1,000 channels and every conceivable marine frequency, that will bring you into contact with yachts, ships, and professional shore-bound radio operators all over the world. With this rig, you can pass commercial messages and order all the spare parts and grog your heart desires. Together with an automatic antenna tuner, an SSB will cost you about the same as a first-class, 10-foot inflatable dinghy. You'll need a fair amount of battery power to run a rig like this: about 30 amps at 12 volts while you're transmitting, and about 2.5 amps while receiving. A custom-built ham rig could get away with far less power.

While marine SSBs have traditionally lacked ham-radio transmit frequencies, some manufacturers are now producing more expensive marine SSBs open to all bands between 1.6 MHz and 27.7 MHz. This range includes the amateur radio bands, thus greatly increasing the temptation for the great unwashed and unlicensed to invade the hallowed domain of clannish hams.

If you're wondering, you don't have to carry a radio at all if you don't want to. There are no international regulations that force you to carry even a VHF. Plenty of people have sailed around the world without transmitters and there's no reason you shouldn't as well. Nevertheless, a VHF is a wise addition to your safety equipment.

Jacklines

When you're working on deck in your safety harness, you have a range of operation limited by the length of your tether. If you want to move forward or aft, you have to unclip and then clip on again. This is not only tedious: It could be dangerous.

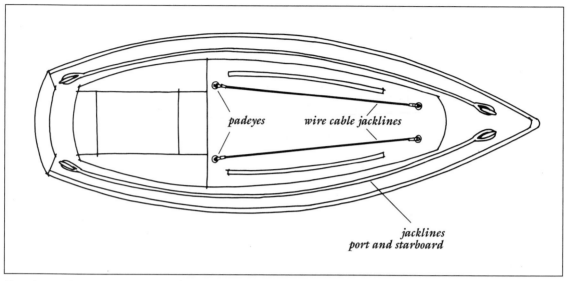

Popular positions for jacklines. The lines on the side decks may be snugged closer into the cabin sides, and they may be made of stainless steel wire, Dacron line, webbing, or tubing.

A jackline gives you the same sort of freedom of movement on deck that an overhead running leash permits your dog in the backyard. Your tether will run fore and aft the length of the jackline without your having to unclip at all.

If you do happen to fall overboard, the tether will slide aft until it reaches the end of the jackline, where it will give you a mighty jerk. At the same time, it will exert a very heavy strain on the jackline and its attachment points.

In theory, the best jacklines run across the cabintop fore and aft on either side of the mast. They are then far enough inboard that you can't fall overboard at all, if your tether is short. In reality, though, you won't be able to move forward or aft along the side decks if you have inboard mast shrouds to get in the way.

If your boat has a raised, flush cabintop and foredeck, that might not be a problem; but the more usual sites for jacklines are along the side decks themselves, close in against the cabin sides. This gives you the whole dog run—from the foredeck to the transom, one side at a time—

without having to remove your clip from the line; but it does mean that you can fall overboard. You can lessen this possibility by having two hooks on your tether, with one only 2 feet (60 cm) or so away from your chest. Clip the closer hook on to some strong point nearer the middle of the boat while you work, without removing the original hook from the jackline.

Stainless steel wire is good material for jacklines that are going to nestle comfortably in the corner formed by the side deck and the sides of the cabin trunk. Placed here, they won't roll underfoot and upend you.

For jacklines that run across a flat deck or cabintop where you also want to walk, 1-inch-wide (25-mm-wide), ultraviolet-ray-resistant nylon webbing is the answer (see also the section in chapter 6 on harness clip-on points, page 61).

Knife

If you've ever trapped a finger or a hand between a winch and a tensioned foresail sheet, you'll understand the need to carry a sharp knife.

It doesn't have to be fancy, just very sharp. Wear it in a sheath on your belt, or in your pocket attached to a lanyard. Anyone whose life depends on rope ought to carry the means to cut it quickly.

Many sailors prefer the faster cutting action of a serrated edge. Some knives feature a slot for opening shackles and a marlinspike for splicing rope. You can pay a lot of money for a good knife, so check your choices carefully and remember that it's the cutting blade that's important. You can always use pliers for opening shackles and borrow grandma's crochet hook for splicing.

Incidentally, if you attach a knife to your belt with a lanyard, make sure the lanyard is sufficiently long to let you reach over your head with the knife. That should be obvious—but some of us had to learn it the hard way.

Life Jackets

You could argue forever about the kind of personal flotation devices you should take over the horizon with you. So to short-circuit all the boring debate, here's a helpful diktat:

- Get a Coast Guard–approved Type I offshore life jacket for everybody on board, or the number of crew likely to be on board at any time. Keep them in a handy place: These are for When the Boat Sinks.
- Also get comfortable float coats or inflatable vests with built-in harnesses for everybody to wear when the weather turns nasty.

Each Type I life jacket will cost you the equivalent of about 14 beers. They are bulky and uncomfortable to wear on the boat, but you'd be very thankful to have one if you were in the water. They provide at least 22 pounds (10 kg) of buoyancy, and they're designed so they will turn most people face up if they are unconscious. This is definitely the life jacket you'll want to wear when you abandon ship in bad weather.

Float coats (64 beers) are not as buoyant as Type I life jackets, and they don't have the same ability to turn you face up in the water. But because they look and feel like sailing jackets, not bulky life jackets, you're more likely to be wearing one when you need it. They will keep you warm in cold weather and help stave off hypothermia in cold water. You're also more likely to be wearing a smart float coat when you go ashore in the dinghy, which is the setting for many drowning deaths.

Some float coats have built-in buoyancy bladders inflated by carbon dioxide cartridges, plus oral inflation. Others have puncture-proof foam sections for buoyancy.

Inflatable vests with built-in harnesses (62 beers) have a purposeful, deep-sea racer look about them. As long as the carbon dioxide cylinder works when needed, and as long as you don't puncture the bladders on anything, they'll provide at least 35 pounds (16 kg) of buoyancy. This is sufficient to keep your head well above water in the roughest conditions.

Coast Guard–approved inflatable vests now come in manually operated versions and automatic versions that inflate when you hit the water. Before you buy the automatic version, make sure it won't be activated by a hefty dollop of spray.

Lifelines and Stanchions

As already noted, you don't need lifelines to sail around the world. You should not place too much faith in your lifelines to keep you on board in any case. But if they catch you only once—if they stop you from falling overboard when you stumble and lose your balance or get swept off your feet by a wave—they've more than paid for their keep.

The Offshore Racing Council calls for double lifelines supported by stanchions. The top line must be at least 24 inches (610 mm) off the deck, but 30 inches (760 mm) is probably better.

Stanchions spaced a maximum of 7 feet (2 m) apart must be bolted through the deck (never screwed) and backed up by a large plate to spread the stress loads.

Lifelines should be made of stainless steel wire and left uncovered so you can see any weakening corrosion.

Incidentally, it's not a good idea to clip your safety harness tether to the lifelines. They're not designed to withstand the immense shock load your body imposes on them when you fall overboard and suddenly come to the end of the tether while the boat is speeding. Use separate jacklines or special eyebolt attachment points for your tether.

Liferafts

As we've seen already, small-boat inflatable liferafts come with no guarantees that they'll work properly when you need them, or that they'll stay afloat long enough for you to be rescued.

The Robertson family's liferaft lasted just 17 days after their yacht went down west of the Galapagos Islands in 1972. Simone and Bill Butler's liferaft was holed when their boat sank in the same general area; but it luckily had special inner sleeves to keep it from sinking.

Some well-documented yachting disasters have raised serious questions about the value of liferafts in really bad sea conditions. When the "Queen's Birthday" storm devastated a fleet of cruising yachts off New Zealand in 1994, the *only* lives lost were those of the crew who abandoned their boat and boarded a liferaft. The liferaft was later found empty.

When a weather bomb hit more than 70 sailboats participating in the Fastnet Race between England and Ireland in 1979, 15 lives were lost, seven of them in "incidents directly attributed to the failure of the liferaft," according to the official board of inquiry. In a sobering footnote, the inquiry board added: "The yachts these seven people abandoned were subsequently found afloat and towed to harbor."

Twelve liferafts were washed overboard and

lost before anyone could board them: eight from their stowage places in the cockpit and four from deck tiedowns. The inquiry board noted that "liferafts clearly failed to provide the safe refuge which many crews expected."

For reasons such as these, and also for the expenses associated with liferafts (from the initial expense through the regular servicings to the need for extra survival gear), some deep-sea sailors choose to do without them.

There are alternatives: You can stow a partially pumped up inflatable dinghy on the cabin top. Some people put their faith in hard dinghies and prefer them for their ability to sail to safety. But can you launch a hard dinghy successfully in a storm bad enough to sink your yacht? Can you launch an inflatable liferaft, for that matter? There are no simple answers to the liferaft problem.

The basic choice is between a coastal liferaft, which has just one buoyancy tube, and an offshore liferaft, which has two tubes, one stacked on top of the other. The coastal raft generally has a canopy that has to be set up manually, while the offshore raft has a self-erecting canopy.

Manufacturers of liferafts are influenced by the fact that about 60 percent of calls for assistance come from vessels within 3 miles of the shore. Steve Callahan, who spent 76 days adrift in a raft in 1982, says that 96 percent of calls for assistance come from boats within 20 miles of shore. Only 10 percent come from boats more than 50 miles out.

This means that few liferafts are built with a 119-day drift in mind, such as the one Maurice and Maralyn Bailey experienced in the Pacific in 1973. Nevertheless, offshore liferafts carry more safety gear and larger ballast pockets than coastal rafts do. If you have them serviced regularly, which is a fairly expensive business, they will last about 10 to 15 years.

You will find that all liferafts are impossibly cramped. A four-person raft is uncomfortable for two, and a six-person raft is uncomfortable for four. Comfort is not a great issue, however, when the alternative is drowning.

The experts say that nothing does more to prevent a liferaft from being flipped over by high winds and seas than a drogue streamed out to windward. If your liferaft doesn't come with a drogue, make sure there's one in your abandonship kit (see the earlier section on grab bags, page 80).

Where to stow the thing on a small boat? On the cabintop just forward of the spray dodger is a favorite place, if you don't have a dinghy there. You'll also need a fiberglass canister for the raft if you keep it out in the sun and open air.

Some boats have a special locker for the liferaft at the aft end of the cockpit, in which case you need only a soft valise to protect the raft.

If you're forced to keep your liferaft down below, think about how you would get it on deck and ready it for launching in the shortest possible time. You might have to dig it out from under a pile of debris in a 180-degree capsize, for example, and you might have to fight a tangle of downed rigging in the companionway. Could you do it? Maybe it would be better just to leave a canister model in the cockpit well for the duration of an ocean crossing and to put up with the loss of foot room.

The decision about whether or not to carry a liferaft is a difficult one that must be left for individual skippers to wrestle with. But despite all the drawbacks, one thing is certain: liferafts do save lives. Although seven lives were lost in liferaft accidents during the Fastnet storm, another 14 lives were saved when crews took to liferafts after their yachts sank.

The Fastnet inquiry board summed it up succinctly: "It is asking a great deal of any small craft to expect it to provide safe refuge in conditions which overwhelm large yachts," they noted, "but this is what liferafts are expected to do." And if you don't have a liferaft, it can't do it.

Emergency Hand Tools

This is a basic list that would serve you well in an emergency. You should add any special tools your boat or engine may need.

Ax, small
Bolt cutters or wire cutters, large
Brace, with bits sized up to 1 inch (25 mm)
C-clamps, several
Drill, hand; 3/8-inch (9.5-mm), and bits
Duct tape, plenty
Electrician's tape
Epoxy glue, sanding and bonding fillers, and fiberglass cloth
Files, triangular, flat, and round
Hammer, ballpeen
Metal snips
Plane, small
Pliers, needlenose, ordinary, and Vise-Grips
Rasp, shoemaker's (flat and half-round; coarse and medium)
Saw, ordinary crosscut and hacksaw with standard and carbide blades
Screwdrivers, slot and Phillips head
Stainless steel seizing wire
Wire clamps to fit rigging
Wood chisels, 1/2-inch (12-mm) and 1-inch (25-mm)
Wrenches, open end, plumber's, and set of socket wrenches

Personal Strobe Lights

It's a good idea to invest in a couple of personal rescue strobe lights, the kind you can attach to your arm over your foul-weather gear with a Velcro strap. Their brilliant strobes run continuously for 28 hours on one size-C battery.

They cost the equivalent of about 10 beers—a good deal. Some singlehanders lash them to a burgee stock and send them up the mast or to the spreaders at night while they sleep. It's probably illegal, because a white strobe can be construed as a distress signal, which will divert ships from their courses and cause great confusion. But if you can take the heat, it's better than being run down.

Rubber Dinghies

Most long-term cruisers use hard dinghies of wood or fiberglass, rather than inflatable dinghies. The hard dinghy is a better sea boat, and it's easier to row and sail. It tows with less resistance and doesn't go "phhht" when you drag it over barnacle-covered rocks or sit down in it with a forgotten screwdriver in your back pocket.

The inflatable is more compact when you let the air out, and it travels fast with a small outboard. It has a great load-carrying capacity, it doesn't knock chips out of your topside gelcoat, and it's wonderfully easy for swimmers to get in and out of.

If you take an inflatable on an extended cruise and subject it to the unusually rough life of a liveaboard tender in the tropics, it will probably last you only three or four years.

Inflatables aren't made of rubber, of course. The two main kinds are made of DuPont's Hypalon, which is good for the tropics and usually guaranteed for 10 years, and polyvinyl chloride (PVC) material, which is excellent in temperate climates and usually guaranteed for five years.

On a small boat, there often isn't much choice about whether to carry a hard dinghy or a soft one. A hard dinghy should be your first choice, but if you can't fit one on deck (even a nesting dinghy), then it's an inflatable for you. But you'd better have a spare bunk to stow it in.

Incidentally, a hard dinghy with a simple sailing rig is an absolute joy in many of those anchorages over the horizon and worth all sorts of sacrifices to carry it over the ocean.

Sails

The sails supplied with mass-production boats are not usually of the best quality. This is one area in which you might consider throwing away your old ones, or converting them to various uses, and getting at least a basic suit of dedicated cruising sails.

The seams should be triple-stitched, and batten pockets should have a layer of cloth between the batten and the sail.

You might even consider a battenless mainsail, cut with a slightly hollow leech, just as a foresail is. Without battens, you can drop the main on any course, even on a run, without having the sail hang up on the spreaders. This is a valuable safety feature. Furthermore, as the majority of sail repairs involve batten pockets, you'll certainly cut down on your sailmakers' bills.

Battens exist only to hold out that floppy outer portion of the sail known as the roach. If you're wondering what effect the loss of a roach has on the mainsail, the answer is: not a great deal. When you're going to windward, the area of the sail that does the most work lies just abaft the mast; and that area is untouched in a hollow-cut sail. Your speed while reaching or running in light winds might suffer slightly from the smaller sail area (due to the loss of the roach). But you probably won't notice much difference in any decent kind of wind. Some boats even balance better with a hollow-cut main: It takes some of the sting out of weather helm. In fact, some of us with cynical minds suspect that roaches and batten pockets were invented by sailmakers seeking to move up to larger homes and bigger cars. We wouldn't trade our hollow-cut mains for anything.

Cruising sailcloth is a compromise between stability (that is, a lack of stretch) and ease of handling. Soft cloth is easier to handle and bag, but it becomes less efficient as it stretches, although on a true cruising boat that doesn't matter so much. A reasonable compromise is polyester cloth (Dacron or Terylene) lightly filled with a stabilizing resin.

It's worth getting a special storm jib for those occasions when you need to beat off a lee shore with maximum efficiency in heavy weather or for when you need to run before a gale. Few modern yachts carry a special storm trysail because a triple-reefed polyester mainsail will do the same work—or almost the same work—without the bother of setting up a separate sail on a heaving deck. A dedicated trysail does, in fact, move the center of effort farther aft, and while this helps most boats to heave to, yours might not need that help.

Have your foresail cut higher than normal and specify a luff length that allows you to fit a tack pendant, so you can see forward under the foot and obviate a lot of chafe on the pulpit and lifelines.

Do you need a roller-furling foresail to cross an ocean? Definitely not. In fact, some experienced cruisers wouldn't touch roller furlers with a 10-foot barge pole. Their creed is: Hanked sails always come down when you want them to. They have a point. No sailor relishes the thought of having to go up the forestay in a gale to cut away a wildly flapping genoa that refused to furl properly. And that sort of thing still happens, despite all the modern improvements in furling gears.

And despite the claims of manufacturers, furling gears don't reef sails very well. There isn't a 150-percent genoa in the world that will reef down to the size of a storm jib and work as well as a hanked-on jib. Ever wondered why racing yachts don't carry reefing furler jibs?

Perhaps the best arrangement is a combination of a roller-furling genoa and a hanked-on inner foresail flown from a removable stay when the weather becomes threatening—a sort of cutter rig, but with only one headsail flown at a time, except perhaps in very light airs. The genoa will be furled completely as soon as a reef is needed, so it's not subjected to the stress of being reefed. You will also find it safer and easier to hank a sail to a stay fastened farther back on the foredeck, and that sail will fill beautifully flat and pull quietly and powerfully.

Safety Harnesses and Tethers

There are some gung-ho cruising types who grab the end of the nearest sheet and tie a bowline under their armpits when the wind pipes up. That's their idea of a safety harness.

But anyone who has fallen overboard and been towed at 6 knots or more knows how easy it would be to drown without a properly designed harness that has a clip at the right position to keep your face above water.

Harnesses need to be really strong. Offshore racing rules stipulate that they must have a breaking strength of at least 3,300 pounds (1,500 kg), which means webbing at least 1½ inches (40 mm) wide. They must be soft too, and easy to put on; otherwise you won't bother to wear them. The chest strap should lie just an inch or two (25 mm to 50 mm) under your armpits. Women, however, shouldn't wear the strap tightened below the bust because when a harness suddenly comes under tension, the pull is savagely upward. There are special Y-shaped harnesses that are said to alleviate this problem, and there are also harnesses built into vests. But the best combination, for men as well as women, is probably the inflatable life vest with a built-in harness. It makes sense to roll both safety devices into one.

Tethers, or lanyards, usually have webbing that's even stronger than the harness webbing (a breaking strength of 4,576 pounds or 2,076 kg is what the Offshore Racing Council calls for), and they should have quick-release snap hooks or snap shackles at each end. The inboard end, the one next to your chest, should be fitted with a snap shackle because it is easier to release under a load than is a snap hook. You don't want to be tied down underneath a capsized boat.

Sea Anchors and Drogues

There is much confusion about the terms sea anchor and drogue. For our purposes, let's say a sea anchor that can't be moved much through the water will stop a boat dead, or nearly so, whereas a drogue (which can be dragged) will merely slow her down.

Sea anchors are supposed to hold boats head-on to the wind in bad weather, which is the best position to avoid capsize. But few modern sailors use sea anchors of the large parachute type because few deep-keel yachts will lie bow-to an anchor streamed from the stemhead when the wind is blowing hard.

Those boats with cutaway forefeet, especially, tend to lie broadside on to the wind and waves, with or without a sea anchor. But shallow-draft boats, centerboarders, and those with canoe underbodies all lie more obediently to a sea anchor, as do most powerboats.

On the other hand, there are a few experienced cruisers who are quite adamant that sea anchors work well in combination with a double- or triple-reefed mainsail. Lin and Larry Pardey, for example, stream a large sea anchor from an adjustable bridle attached to the bow and the stern. Their deeply reefed mainsail holds the bow up toward the wind, and the sea anchor prevents forereaching. They drift to leeward directly in the path of the swirling "slick" caused by their keel, which causes waves to break and expend their energy harmlessly before reaching the boat.

So much depends on individual boats' handling characteristics that it would be folly to dismiss a sea anchor as useless. You have to find out through experience what is best for your boat. Many sailboats, for example, would lie stern-on to a sea anchor with ease. But you'd need a small, watertight cockpit, a very strong rudder, a high bridge deck, and strong storm slides for the companionway.

One thing is certain: You'd need to practice handling a parachute sea anchor before deploying it in a storm for the first time. It's not easy to stream it or retrieve it without getting all those lines tangled.

Drogues are intended to slow a running boat to a safe speed in heavy weather. Too much speed often results in lack of rudder control and the possibility of a disastrous broach. A heavy displacement boat moving at or near hull speed pulls a great quarter wave along with her, which invites an unstable plunging crest to break right there and sweep over the stern. Speed—at least at the beginning of a strong storm system, when the waves are relatively small and steep—is usually dangerous for a nonplaning hull. But as the swells lengthen and flatten with age, speed might become more desirable.

There are many things you can drag through the water to slow you down, from a long bight of thick rope to an old auto tire weighed down with an anchor. The principle is simply to create a resistance that will hold the boat back, and this usually requires a fairly substantial sunken object at the end of at least 200 feet (60 m) of fairly elastic nylon line. It's necessary to sink the drogue somewhat because a breaking wave can hurl a surface-level drogue forward, during which time your boat will lurch forward, too, gathering speed until it fetches up against the drogue again with frightening force.

Some drogues are shaped like elongated cones, others like huge half-watermelons made of webbing. Some are planks of wood bolted to metal frames, and others—including the so-called series drogues—comprise an array of small, cone-shaped sea anchors strung along an anchor line. The Jordan series drogue has been extensively tested by the U.S. Coast Guard, and it allows you to add or subtract droguelets to match your boat's needs. Even if they don't keep them in stock, good marine stores should be able to order one for you. You can buy one, ready-made or in kit form, from Ace Sailmakers (128 Howard Street, New London, Connecticut 06320, telephone 860-443-5556). There is more on the Jordan series drogue in chapter 16 (see page 197).

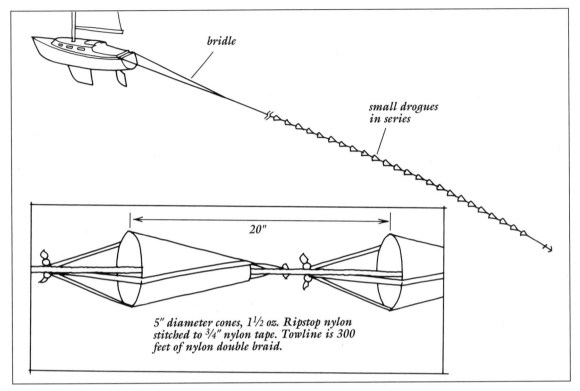

bridle

small drogues in series

20"

5" diameter cones, 1½ oz. Ripstop nylon stitched to ¾" nylon tape. Towline is 300 feet of nylon double braid.

The Jordan series drogue

Self-Steering Disconnect

If you have a wind-controlled self-steering system, you need to be able to disconnect the vane gear if you fall overboard, so your boat will round up, shake the wind out of her sails, and wait for you to catch up.

Most vane-gear tripping systems consist of a long floating line towed astern, with a rescue quoit or a buoyed loop at the end. The line is attached to a snap shackle (see the illustration, page 91). This system depends on the boat's having slight weather helm (a natural condition for most), but sometimes a trade wind running rig of twin foresails is deliberately designed to cause lee helm, and you'd need to take extra care not to fall overboard under that rig.

Signal Mirrors

If you've ever been alerted by the chance flashing of a distant powerboat windshield at sea, you'll know that a signal mirror, or heliograph, makes a very effective distress signal on a sunny day. So get one, or make one from a piece of stainless steel or the lid of can, and put it in your grab bag.

The ones you can buy from your local marine store for the equivalent of about three beers come with instructions about how to aim them. If you make your own, be sure to find out how this works.

Basically, the idea is to punch a hole in the middle of the metal, or to scrape away a tiny piece of a glass mirror's silvering. Hold the mirror a few inches from your face and sight your target through the hole.

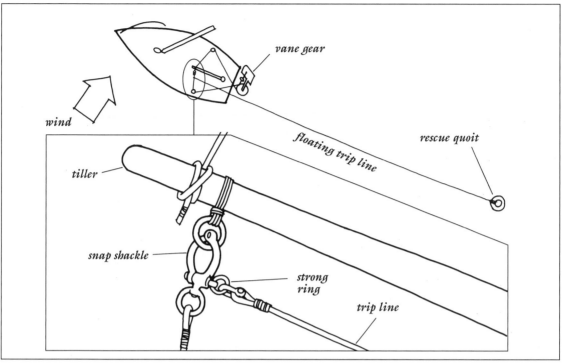

A simple method of deactivating the self-steering if you fall overboard. Pulling on the floating line will open the snap shackle connecting the vane gear to the tiller.

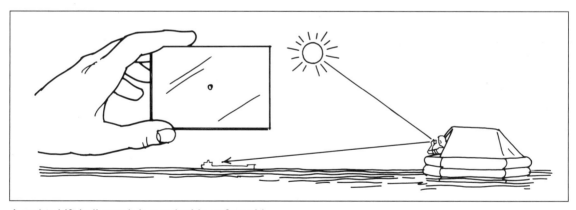

A makeshift heliograph is a valuable safety aid.

If you now hold the mirror still and take your eye away from the hole, the sun will make a little spot on your face or shirt. Tilt the mirror until that little spot disappears through the hole and you'll be on target.

Those are the usual instructions, and they may work fine on land. But you can imagine (quite rightly) that it's nonsense to suppose you can be this accurate on a moving boat at sea. The object of the game is merely to divert the reflection into the right general area. You'll be creating plenty of flashes quite inadvertently.

There is an easier way to do it. Hold two fingers out in a V at arm's length; frame your target in the V, put your eye to the hole in the mirror, and twist the mirror so it reflects light onto your fingers.

Sleep

It may seem odd to list sleep as an item of safety equipment, but lack of sleep causes fatigue, which can be very dangerous at sea, especially for a singlehander. Fatigue causes lapses in concentration and errors in simple calculations. It adversely affects your judgment and can lead to alarming hallucinations.

Anything you can do to make sure you get seven or eight hours of sleep a day is a valuable safety aid, though that doesn't count sleep-inducing drugs, which can have an adverse effect in the long term.

Watches should not last longer than four hours. In heavy weather, if the boat has to be hand-steered, two-hour watches are better if you have at least three capable crew. The watch down below needs at least two hours of uninterrupted sleep at a time to perform adequately on deck.

Singlehanders mostly find it safer to sleep during the day when their boats are more likely to be spotted by approaching freighters. Most of them also take naps, the timing and number of which depend on circumstances, but usually lasting about 45 minutes to an hour. That's really too long for an efficient lookout, because a fast ship can be upon you in less than 20 minutes from first sighting; but it's a reasonable compromise. It is, of course, illegal under the International Regulations for the Prevention of Collisions at Sea to sail a boat without maintaining a constant lookout, but as the singlehander is likely to come off the worse in any encounter with a freighter, the law is not actively applied. So far, singlehanders have notched up a sur-

prisingly good record of not running into one another.

Incidentally, any boat that you intend to keep at sea overnight should have sufficient bunks for the off-watch crew *in or near the center of the boat*—that is, not near the ends of the boat.

The V-berth might look inviting, but most people find the excessively jerky motion up there more conducive to seasickness than to sleep, particularly when the boat is beating. Berths situated far aft are not quite as badly affected, but their motion on the run is still quicker and wider-ranging than that of berths placed amidships.

Smoke Detectors

You may question the need for smoke detectors in a space as small as a boat, but it's possible for a fire to gain a good hold undetected if all the crew is on deck in rough weather at night.

An engine fire can be particularly hard to detect early when the engine is running, and by the time you can smell smoke or feel heat, you've lost precious moments that can make a difference in whether your boat will be saved or not.

Pick up a couple of household smoke detectors at your local hardware store. Fit them where you can get at them easily, because they'll almost certainly go off when you make french fries in the galley.

Through-Hull Fittings

In all likelihood, your boat has several holes through the hull to let in water and to let out water and waste. Take a good look at the special fittings that line every such hole.

Each consists of a threaded pipe with two flanges: one flange pressing tightly against the outside of the hull and another flange in the form of a large hexagonal nut screwed up tightly against the inside of the hull.

You'll notice that there's also a seacock or gate valve attached to the tailpiece of each through-hull fitting. Some seacocks have flanges of their own that are bolted through the hull into the outside flange and sometimes the tailpiece screws right into them.

Examine the material your through-hulls are made of. If they're made of cheap plastic, throw them away. They will eventually become brittle and crack, which could be unpleasant if it happens in the middle of the ocean. Be careful, though: What you think is cheap plastic might in fact be Marelon, a tough, long-lasting nylon reinforced with glass. Marelon is all right to use.

But the through-hulls with the best reputations are still the bronze ones. If you're going to change, you might as well use bronze. A $1\frac{1}{2}$-inch (40-mm) bronze through-hull will cost you about the same as 10 beers in a restaurant. Bronze is recognized by the Coast Guard, the American Boat and Yacht Council, and insurance companies. Bronze makes everybody very happy.

Now take a look at the shut-off valve that stops water from coming into your boat when you remove the hose from the through-hull fitting. If it's a gate valve, throw it away. Gate valves are not seagoing valves, although many manufacturers still fit them to seagoing boats because they're cheap. You can't tell when a gate is properly closed, for a start, and the spindles inevitably fail after a few years, so you can't open them or shut them. No, you need a proper seacock on every through-hull.

Proper, in seacock terms, translates to bronze, of course. Bronze, with a hefty flange, is the marine engineer's dream seacock, though the dream comes at a price. What you'd pay for 28 beers will buy you one $1\frac{1}{2}$-inch (40-mm) seacock.

Tapered plug seacocks and T-bar seacocks are the old standbys, but they freeze easily and require an inordinate amount of fiddling and maintenance to keep them working properly.

The ball-valve seacock is a more modern design that is almost maintenance-free, apart from a smear of petroleum jelly once a year, and it never seems to freeze up. It consists of a bronze body with a hole running through the middle of a chromed-plated bronze or stainless steel ball turning in Teflon seals.

Ball-valve seacocks made of Marelon have gained wide acceptance. They are completely corrosion-free and although they still don't inspire the degree of confidence that bronze does, the worst thing their detractors can find to say about them is that they will melt in a fire. So, of course, will the hose attached to them—not to mention the fiberglass hull.

And in case you're wondering, no, brass is not an acceptable substitute for bronze or Marelon. Seawater loves to eat the zinc away, leaving a weak porous mass of debilitated copper you can poke a finger through. No brass under water, please: never, ever.

All hoses connected to seacocks should be retained by all-stainless steel hose clamps screwed up firmly, but not so tightly that it cuts or distorts the rubber. You need two clamps on each seacock, and another two at the inboard end of the hose, making four in all for each hose. And watch those clamps when you buy them. Some say they're stainless steel, but in fact they have a mild steel screw. Test them with a magnet to be safe. (If it's magnetic, it's *not* stainless steel.)

Just in case the worst happens, and the whole seacock cracks or falls off when you step on it accidentally, keep handy a tapered plug of softwood that you can hammer into the through-hull fitting to seal it off. If the plug is to be of any use in an emergency, you should wire it to the seacock.

Vangs and Preventers

A boom vang, or kicking strap, keeps the mainsail leech taut and stops the boom from lifting on a reach or run. That makes the mainsail more efficient on a reach and safer on a run when it might otherwise tend to jibe unexpectedly.

A boom without a vang also allows the top half of the mainsail to sag off to leeward, forward of the mast, on a dead run. This promotes very exciting gunwale-to-gunwale rolling. If you're planning to go over the horizon, you need a vang.

The usual arrangement is a three- or four-part purchase led from the boom to the base of the mast. The important thing is that the boom should be able to swing fully from side to side without the vang tightening or loosening. That is achieved by placing the mast end of the vang tackle directly below the pivoting point of the boom (the gooseneck).

You can also get fancy rigid vangs with springs or hydraulic mechanisms that hold the boom up as well as down, but they aren't necessary. It's just more stuff to go wrong. It's true that a rigid vang does away with the need for a boom topping lift, but you may regret the lack of a topping lift when the end of your main halyard disappears up the mast at sea and you have no alternative halyard to fall back on.

Preventers are useful on long runs dead before the wind, to stop the boom swinging over in an unexpected jibe. If you can unshackle your boom vang from its attachment point at the foot of the mast, and then lead it forward and outboard to a strong fitting on the gunwale, it will make a fine preventer. Simply make it fast, and then haul the mainsail sheet tight against it to keep the boom rigidly fixed in place. Alternatively, a line may be led from the end of the boom to a fitting on the foredeck. Some sailors even lead the line through a block on the foredeck and then back to the cockpit, so they can cast the line off without having to go to the foredeck when a jibe becomes necessary.

Always keep a sharp knife handy when the boom is held out by a preventer. If your pilot is grossly inattentive, the boat will jibe despite the preventer. Those of us who have suddenly found ourselves sailing backward in the middle of the night after such a jibe—with the mainsail awkwardly held out to weather under great tension, and large seas pouring in over the transom—can tell you that cutting the preventer is the only quick way out of a bad mess. But be sure—double sure—that no one is standing to leeward of the boom when you slash the preventer.

VHF Radio

It's not necessary to carry a very high frequency (VHF) radio when you sail over the horizon, so if your boat doesn't have one, that's all right. But it does seem a bit short-sighted not to carry such a valuable safety aid and information source when a brand new one costs as little as 68 fiscal beers.

The best kind for your purposes is the fixed-mount VHF that operates off your ship's battery and feeds a 3-dB gain antenna at the masthead. Its appetite for electricity is surprisingly modest.

If you don't have the space or the battery power for a fixed-mount VHF radio, get yourself a hand-held version that accepts alkaline batteries. To increase its effective range of reception and transmission, you can connect it to a masthead antenna.

Remember that the VHF works on the line-of-sight principle: The sending and receiving stations must be able to "see" each other without the bulge of the earth or a big mountain coming in between. So, the higher the antenna, the greater the range. For example, two yachts, each with a 20-foot-high (6-m-high) antenna, can expect good VHF communication with each other at a 10-mile range. If one of them were transmitting to a coast station with an antenna 1,000 feet (305 m) high, the range would increase fourfold to 41 miles.

Don't forget to pack a cheap VHF radio in your abandon-ship bag if you can afford it. It's often the best (sometimes the only) way to get a passing freighter to notice you in your little liferaft.

Watermakers

A watermaker is another piece of equipment you don't need to sail around the world. But if you can afford one—and you don't mind giving it a lot of tender loving care—a reverse-osmosis watermaker will reward you with about a gallon (3.8 liters) of sweet, pure, fresh water for every 30 watt-hours of battery power it consumes.

A compact, electrically powered watermaker weighs about 25 pounds (11 kg), makes about 1½ gallons (5.7 liters) an hour, and can be converted to manual use if you run the battery flat. But they're expensive—about the same as a good 10-foot (3 m) inflatable dinghy.

A good alternative is a small, manual, reverse-osmosis watermaker that will keep you alive as long as you can squeeze the handles. An hour of squeezing produces about 2 pints (1 liter) of fresh water, which is worth its weight in gold in a liferaft. The nice thing is that it costs only as much as 200 beers, or less than a quarter of an inflatable dinghy, so you may be able to afford to keep one in your abandon-ship bag.

Waterproof Clothing

Treat yourself to a good suit of foul-weather gear, even if you're never planning to leave the tropics. Some of us have been amazed at how cold and miserable it can get on deck at night in a tropical rainstorm.

Most deep-sea cruisers prefer the kind of suit that has a jacket with a hood and separate pants with suspenders and a high-cut bib.

For warmth beneath, you should wear loose-fitting layers, starting with a T-shirt and a long-sleeved shirt and topped with a woolen or poly-ester-fleece sweater, if necessary.

For those calm, blazing-hot days in the trop-ics, take some loose-fitting, lightweight, long-sleeved shirts. And remember: You don't need designer-label clothing for all this. Thrift-store chic is quite à la mode at sea.

Weather Information

A few modern mariners use radios, fax machines, computers, and satellite communication to find out what the weather is doing around them and to interpret what it is likely to do in the near future.

The rest of us simply shrug and ask ourselves what chance we have, plugging along at 5 or 6 knots, of getting out of the way of a weather system 1,000 miles (1,609 km) in diameter that's approaching at 20 knots.

We all know that lows spin counterclockwise in the Northern Hemisphere. If we're situated right in the middle of the storm track, and we have sufficient time, we might be able to scoot over to the "right" side of the system—the one where the wind speeds are lessened by the speed of the system's forward travel. But apart from that, what use to us are undeciphered weather charts and satellite images? If expert professional meteorologists make mistakes half the time or more, with all the computers and resources at their disposal, what are we amateurs to make of the raw data?

It seems far more practical to take advantage of the short- and long-range weather forecasts available on the single-sideband radio, from shore stations and ham nets, or by satellite phone link to shore.

The problem is always that a high-seas fore-cast covers such a large area: The weather you experience locally might not be anything like that forecast for the region in general. But then, that often happens on land, too. Forecasting is an inexact science.

Your best defense against unexpected bad weather is to be in the right parts of the world at the right times. Ocean cruising guides and pilot charts tell you where and when to expect severe storms.

There are two other ways to defend yourself. The first is to study a book about marine meteo-rology written specially for sailors. Learn what to watch for in the sky. The second is to keep your eye on the barometer. Record its movement in the log every four hours or less. It's the most reli-able long-range warning available.

THINK INVERTED

If your boat turns upside down:

- Can you find your flashlight, first-aid kit, and grab bag in the dark?
- Can you release your tether if it's pinning you under the boat?
- Will your liferaft inflate itself and disappear before you can secure it?

- Will your EPIRB set itself off whether you want it to or not?
- Do you have a spare in case you lose your masthead antenna?
- What if a heater or stove is burning when you capsize? Can you turn it off and find an extinguisher?

Navigation Gear

Navigation is an intensely satisfying pastime. There is profound pleasure in raising an ocean landfall and gratifying fulfillment in bringing a small boat safely to anchor in a foreign harbor.

This happy feeling of accomplishment is heightened by the awe and respect a celestial navigator generates among lesser members of the crew.

And yet there is truly nothing arcane about navigation, especially navigation on a small sailboat that takes place at little more than walking speed. If there is a wall of mystique around the navigator's art, it was built by the professional few to keep out the amateur herd. But some of us who have never had a moment's formal tuition in navigation have managed to guide our boats along coastlines and across oceans with reasonable success—that is to say, without crashing into things too often and hardly ever ending up in the wrong place. There is nothing about small-boat navigation that you can't teach yourself from books. And if mathematics is not your strong point, don't worry: Modern methods require nothing more than simple addition and subtraction, even for celestial navigation.

Many of us cut our celestial teeth on Mary Blewitt's famous little bestseller *Celestial Navigation for Yachtsmen*. In its early editions, this was just a 59-page book that was half theory and half practice. "This a book written for beginners by a beginner," Mary stated modestly. She went on to say that she had written it partly because of "the annoying tendency of navigators in yachts to give the impression that celestial navigation is very difficult—a kind of black magic."

She freely admitted to her mathematical shortcomings. "I do not understand trigonometry . . . my knowledge of geometry is very limited . . . I can add and subtract and that is about all!"

If you are heading over the horizon, and you're wise enough to want to navigate by the sun and the stars, let Mary be your guide. Meanwhile, here is a list of some of the other navigational equipment you might require.

Barometer

This may be a puzzling item to be included among navigational equipment. But two very experienced South African round-the-world sailors, Barry and Patrick Cullen, introduced many skippers to the concept of barometer navigation during the first Cape-to-Rio Race in 1971.

The fleet racing from Cape Town to Rio de Janeiro had to skirt the South Atlantic High, a disk-shaped area of high pressure with wind strengths gradually increasing from zero in the middle to Force 4 at the outer edges. The dilemma facing each navigator was whether to sail close to the center (thereby lessening the distance to be traveled) or to go the long way around the edge (thereby getting more wind).

The Cullens, aboard a famous 47-foot Colin Archer ketch called *Sandefjord,* solved the problem by finding the wind they wanted and carefully noting the barometer pressure. If it dropped, they headed closer in to the center. If it rose, they headed out toward the edge. And so they automatically stayed almost equidistant from the moving center of the high-pressure area, carving a huge but efficient semicircle across the South Atlantic.

There are highs in all the big oceans that can be navigated like that. The only thing you have to make allowance for is the diurnal variation of the barometer, which naturally rises between 4 A.M. and 10 A.M., and also between 4 P.M. and 10 P.M. It falls between 10 A.M. and 4 P.M., and again between 10 P.M. and 4 A.M.

The range of the diurnal variation varies according to latitude, but it's about 0.15 inch (5 millibars) at the equator and about zero at the poles. And it occurs with great regularity regardless of local weather patterns, although they may of course mask its presence.

A mercury barometer has no place on a small boat because of the "pumping" caused by the boat's motion. The brass-cased aneroid model is the one to choose. Even better, if you can afford it, is a recording barograph that shows past fluctuations in pressure on a week-long chart.

More interesting still is the latest development, the digital electronic barometer. It has a liquid crystal display (LCD) screen that gives you a history of pressure changes, plus a current reading. Bulkhead-mounted digital barometers display changes for the past 24 hours. Pocket-sized digital barometers cost about the same as the cheapest handheld GPS, and they keep a record of barometric pressures over the past 12 hours. They're available from retailers of nautical instruments and outdoor recreation stores.

One word of advice—an aneroid barometer is very simple, extremely reliable, and doesn't need batteries. On the other hand, the digital barometer's ability to tell you how quickly pressure is rising or falling, without your having to chart it on graph paper every hour or so, is an impressive safety feature.

Books

For celestial navigation you'll need a current nautical almanac (and next year's, if next year is getting close) and a set of sight reduction tables, which are permanent.

You'll also need Pilots, or sailing directions for the oceans and countries you intend to visit; a guide to the world's sailing ship routes; and books that list navigational lights and radio weather report frequencies.

Incidentally, you might want to hang on to your old nautical almanacs because the sun and star data (only) repeat fairly closely every fourth year. Keep your four-year-old almanacs in your grab bag for emergency navigation.

Chart Table

Small-boat navigators can imagine no greater reward in life than having a special chart table used solely for charts. Too bad that it so often remains nothing but a dream.

Books to Read

The following is a reading list of recommended navigation titles.

The Sextant Handbook, by Bruce Bauer

Celestial Navigation for Yachtsmen, by Mary Blewitt

Emergency Navigation, by David Burch

Boat Navigation for the Rest of Us, by Bill Brogdon

Practical Pilot, by Leonard Eyges

These books are available from International Marine (800-262-4729).

Many of us have noticed that the clear expanse of a chart table is an irresistible lure for cooks and mechanics, who will expropriate it at the drop of a hat for their own messy undertakings and callously ignore the navigator's cries of protest.

Although it may have to be shared with others, you need a good chart table, and even in the smallest of vessels it should measure no less than 21 × 28 inches (530 × 710 mm). A table that measures 22 × 36 inches will accept most charts folded once, which is about as good as it gets on a small boat. But—just so you can drool over it—the ideal measurement for a chart table is 28 × 42 inches (530 × 1,100 mm).

Chart Storage

The only way to store a chart is flat. You will see advertisements for chart stowage in the form of tubes, which seems like a very good idea until you place a chart on the table, and despite your every effort, it curls up as tight as a watch spring. Trying to persuade a curled chart to lie flat so that you can use it is very bad for your blood pressure. And, like Sisyphus, you could work at it forever.

A modest drawer, under the chart table if possible, is the answer. A drawer 2 inches (50 mm) deep will take about 100 charts folded once. The rest can go under the berth mattresses.

If you must stow your charts in tubes, but only if you really must, be sure to take along plenty of masking tape with which to hold them in place on the chart table.

Charts

You'll need charts of different scales for planning, coastal pilotage, near-shore cruising, and long-distance voyaging. The rule about scales is: small scale, small detail.

Try to get the largest-scale chart of your intended port of arrival overseas, at a scale of 1:10,000 to 1:50,000. It brings great comfort.

Once you have been in a foreign country for a few days you begin to pick up local knowledge about other nearby ports you're likely to visit, so you don't need large-scale charts for all ports. But for that first landfall, you're on your own.

Pilot Charts show average wind speeds and directions on the open ocean for every month of the year, as well as the average set and drift of currents. In conjunction with the official Sailing Directions (pilot books), they are essential for planning ocean passages.

The accompanying table has some examples of chart types and scales (see also Plotting Charts, page 110).

Chronometer

A chronometer needn't be one of those exquisitely machined gimbaled clocks in a box that cost half the national debt. A chronometer is simply a timepiece that gains or loses time at a constant rate.

Your cheap quartz watch makes a good chronometer. Most of them lose or gain an average of about 15 seconds a month. You can verify the rate by checking it daily against radio time signals.

If you take two cheap quartz watches with you, you can keep one on Greenwich Mean Time (GMT, or Universal Coordinated Time, UCT, as it is known officially). GMT is the time the navigator always needs, no matter what the ship's time may be.

Compasses

If you know how to check the deviation of your main steering compass, do it just before you disappear over the horizon. It should be one of the last things you do, after having stowed everything in its right place. If you don't know how, call in a compass adjuster. You need to know which way you're going, and a compass is your only guide.

Through-bulkhead magnetic compasses are

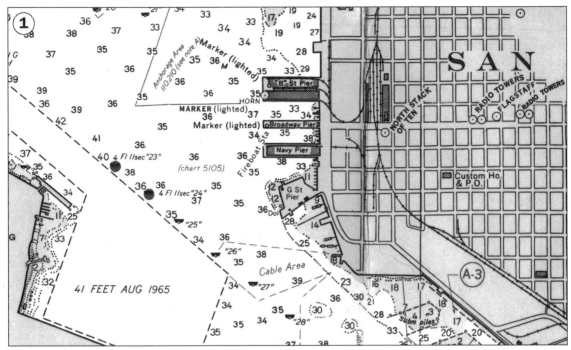

Note the differences in detail in these three charts of different scales. (1) A harbor *chart of San Diego Bay, scale 1:20,000.* (2) A coastal *chart of Puget Sound, scale 1:150,000.* (3) A general *chart of the area between San Diego and San Francisco, scale 1:868,000.*

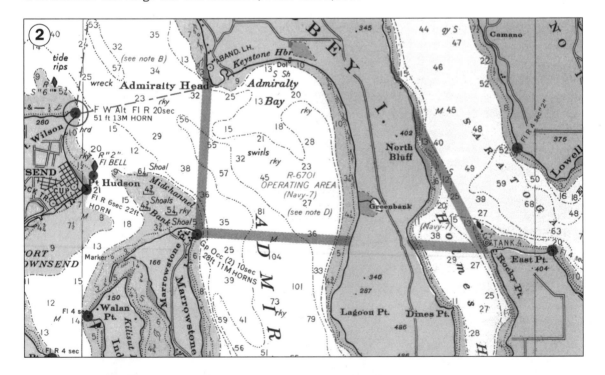

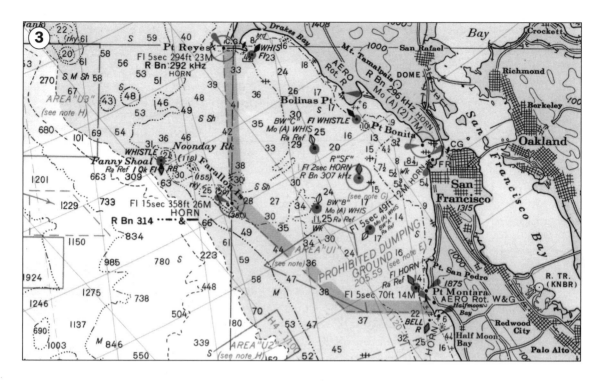

very popular on cruising sailboats because they can be read from inside and outside the cabin. But grid compasses are the easiest to use. They have an azimuth ring that you set to the course you want. After that you merely have to keep the compass needle centered between two parallel lines. Unfortunately, they're very hard to find in small-boat sizes these days.

Besides a steering compass, you'll need a handheld compass for taking bearings of land-

Chart Types and Scales		
Chart Type	**Usual Scale**	**Uses**
Harbor	1:10,000 to 1:50,000	Navigating in harbor; magnified detail of channels, wharves, buoys, lights, and anchorages
Coastal	1:50,000 to 1:150,000	Coastal pilotage; good detail of harbor entrances, sea bottom, buoys, lights, and offshore hazards
General	1:150,000 to 1:600,000	Offshore coastal cruising; shows major navigational marks only, but covers large area
Sailing	1:1,200,000 to 1:8,000,000	Long-distance voyaging; route planning for ocean crossings; scant navigational detail
Pilot	1:15,000,000	Ocean route planning; monthly charts show average ocean wind and weather conditions

marks and quick sightings on approaching ships. If you're canny about it, you can also use your handheld bearing compass to deduce the deviation of your steering compass by standing centrally aft and sighting over the bow. In this position, your hand bearing compass should be well clear of any large metal masses that will affect it. Compare the reading with the course shown on the steering compass. Be aware, though, that if you have steel in the frames of your glasses, or metal fittings on your hat, you may experience some deviation.

Be sure your hand bearing compass is rated for use in the right hemisphere. If you go far south over the equator with a compass rated for the Northern Hemisphere, the edge of the card will dip, drag, and eventually cease to work altogether. Most main steering compasses of the floating, internally gimbaled type do not suffer the same fate. They can tilt without getting hung up, although they may not be very efficient in really high latitudes.

Digital fluxgate compasses work equally well in both hemispheres and can be very convenient, but because they depend on electricity and honeycombs of miniaturized circuits, you should take a magnetic compass as backup in any case. There is no simpler or more reliable navigation instrument on your boat than a magnetic compass.

Some skippers like to install a special telltale compass over their bunks, one that works upside down, so you can see what course the fool crew is steering up there, but a small hand bearing compass of the kind you wear around your neck on a lanyard, is just as good, and a third of the price, though you may actually have to sit up in bed to get a reading.

Dead Reckoning

You'll need to know dead reckoning if you're planning to cross an ocean. If you've done any coastal navigation, you should know how to do this already. But dead reckoning is one of those esoteric pursuits that people talk about a lot—and practice very little. If you have shied away from it in the past, take heart. There are few things simpler.

Imagine your boat is at a spot marked A on the chart. Now imagine that you sail northeast at 4 knots for 2 hours to position B. If you can plot position B on the chart, 8 miles from position A in a northeasterly direction, you can do dead reckoning. All it involves is speed and time, distance and direction.

Most celestial navigators get a position fix once a day at sea, taking one sight in mid-morning and another to cross it at noon. If they need to know their positions in between, they use dead reckoning. Dead reckoning, in other words, represents your best guess at your position: an unconfirmed fix.

Even if you are a non-celestial navigator who

Fixing Your Position

If you're planning to head over the horizon for the first time, you may be wondering how frequently you need to fix your boat's position.

Let common sense be your guide. When you're in mid-ocean, it's rarely necessary to fix your position more than once a day. If you take a sextant sight in mid-morning, and another at noon, you'll have a handy noon position fix from which to calculate your day's run. But when you approach land, you will need more frequent updates, depending on the proximity of hazards.

It's your responsibility as a skipper or navigator to know the vessel's approximate position at all times, in case you need to call for help. But a good sailor has a tendency to secure a positive fix at every opportunity, whether it's needed or not: This earns valuable points for the Black Box.

relies entirely on GPS, dead reckoning is still a vital skill. Brush up on it before you leave.

Distance Logs

The distance a boat travels in any given time is vital information for a dead-reckoning plot. In theory, it's simple to calculate the distance run. It's simply speed multiplied by time. For example, going at 4 knots for 2 hours gives you a distance of 8 miles (12.9 km). In practice, a sailboat's speed varies with changes in wind speed, so it's more convenient to rely on an instrument that measures the distance run through the water.

Most logs have propellers that spin through the water and turn a dial, just like a car's odometer. Some propellers protrude through the hull and turn the innards of the odometer via a cable. Some propellers, those on taffrail logs, are dragged behind the boat on a long line that turns the log dials directly. Sharks love to swallow that kind of propeller. Other propellers are more like paddle wheels, with the bottom half sticking through the hull. All these different types suffer from fouling from time to time, usually by floating weed. Paddle wheels can be withdrawn into the hull for cleaning, and taffrail logs can be handed and streamed again, but when you're in areas of floating weed all mechanical logs become wearisome to attend to.

Once again, though, a distance log is something you can do without if you have to. With practice, you'll learn to estimate an average speed for every 4-hour watch with surprising accuracy—certainly good enough to derive a daily estimated position (which you need for your celestial sights) from your dead reckoning.

Furthermore, if you carry GPS or Loran-C, it will tell you your exact distance run at the press of a button or two. You will earn points in the Black Box, however, by carrying a backup system. And a distance log is particularly useful when you arrive at a strange coastline and have to run one

course for, say, 2.5 miles (4 km), then another for 1.75 miles (2.8 km), and so on.

Electronic Charts

The ability of loran and GPS to provide continual position updates day and night has brought the magic of space-age navigation to the humble sailing vessel. Electronic chart displays connected to a GPS or Loran-C give you a bird's-eye view of your boat's position superimposed on a nautical chart. You can check the course you laid from a previous port or waypoint, you can see the progress you're making along a new route, and you can judge how far away you are from dangers.

An electronic chart saves you the bother of plotting your position on a chart, and it will give you early warning if your track over the land is different from the course you're steering.

Charts for the whole world come in the form of electronic memory cards or cartridges that are plugged into one of three devices:

- A dedicated chart display
- A shared display, or
- A desktop or laptop computer

Most people prefer the dedicated displays with screens measuring about $3\frac{1}{2} \times 4\frac{1}{2}$ inches (90 × 115 mm), or the portable chart plotters that look like ordinary handheld GPS sets but have screens about 3 inches (75 mm) tall and $2\frac{1}{4}$ inches (60 mm) wide. The portable plotters use cartridges not much bigger than a postage stamp—each one holding between six and 80 nautical charts—and they will run for about 12 hours on one set of alkaline batteries, according to the manufacturer. Most astonishing is the price—about the equivalent of 280 beers, or a little more than a top-grade handheld GPS without any ability to screen charts.

Shared displays let you use one screen to switch between two or more instruments, such as radar and a GPS chart plotter, or a fishfinder and a plotter. Sharing a display screen saves on space

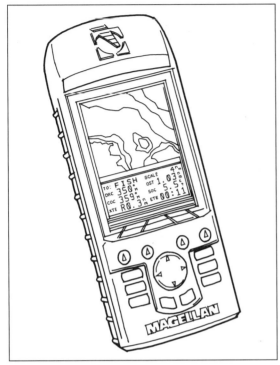

The Magellan Nav 6000 portable GPS displays your position on electronic charts stored on plug-in cartridges little bigger than a postage stamp.

and sometimes money, but it means that at least one of the instruments must be controlled from a keyboard mounted somewhere else, which can make for difficult or awkward operation.

Desktop or laptop computers can run very powerful plotting programs using position inputs from a GPS. They give you a large display and, as usual, offer far more features than you're ever likely to need, including rotating the chart image, zooming, changing scales, and many other helpful tricks. If you have room on your boat for a laptop or a waterproof desktop computer, this is a very tempting choice.

All this is still a good deal more expensive than buying paper charts and parallel rules. But as the prices of electronic gear inevitably come

down when their popularity soars, the chart plotter is likely to be an affordable option for most boats in the near future.

There are drawbacks, however, the most serious of which is that electronics are seriously allergic to salt water, and there's often plenty of that around on a small sailboat, even inside the cabin, when crew shed their foul-weather gear.

So until absolutely waterproof and foolproof chart plotters come onto the market, you'd be foolhardy, if not negligent, to rely solely on GPS and electronic charts.

In addition, some electronic charts are missing small details and some are displayed in black and white. You don't pick up lights shown with magenta blobs on paper charts as easily, or note depths shown in different shades of blue.

At the risk of being dismissed as Luddites, those of us who find it difficult to place our complete faith in the newest and cleverest navigational systems scientists have ever devised would advise you to stock up on paper charts first. If there's any cruising money left over, go electronic by all means.

Emergency Navigation

The ability to go somewhere in a liferaft or dinghy after abandoning ship is an important morale builder. It has been observed that castaways who have some control over their fate have a better chance of survival than those who feel totally helpless.

Even if your liferaft is incapable of being sailed to safety, merely knowing its rate and direction of drift and its proximity to land provides you with important information and enables you to make decisions based upon facts.

Unfortunately, your raft is not likely to contain any navigational equipment, so you'll need to stow some emergency equipment in your abandon-ship bag—a collection that could include
Pencils and writing paper or notebook
Handheld compass

Plastic sextant (see information on sextants, page 111)

Current nautical almanac

Cheap, waterproof, quartz watch set on Greenwich Mean Time

Small-scale chart of your cruising area

This would be a wonderful hoard of navigation gear for a castaway. But you could get by without any of it—except perhaps the pencils and writing paper—if you had a copy of a good book, such as David Burch's *Emergency Navigation*. For the price of six beers you can buy a paperback copy of *Emergency Navigation*. It's difficult to think of a better investment in safety.

If you can afford to buy a spare GPS and tuck it away in your grab bag, you can do without the sextant, the almanac, and the watch—as long as you have a large supply of batteries. Most portable GPS sets will flatten their batteries in about 12 hours of continuous use. But you wouldn't be making continuous use of it, of course, just switching it on for a minute or two once a day for a position check.

Some of us frequently wonder why manufacturers don't make clockwork GPS receivers for emergency work. The technology is reasonably cheap and widely available. In many underdeveloped countries you can buy clockwork AM/FM radios. A few minutes of winding provides about an hour of playing, with a clockwork motor driving a tiny generator. A clockwork GPS could be a lifesaver.

GPS and Differential GPS (DGPS)

Countless sailboats have circumnavigated the world without the help of the Global Positioning System (GPS), so we know it can be done. But if you can afford the comparatively modest price of a GPS receiver you should definitely take one over the horizon with you.

The Essentials

This equipment list reflects our opinion of the very least you should carry for navigation during an ocean passage.

Barometer
Charts and plotting charts
Lead line
Nautical almanac and sight reduction tables
Pair of compasses
Pair of dividers
Paperback copy of *Emergency Navigation*, by David Burch
Parallel or roller rules
Pencils
Plastic sextant
Portable GPS
Protractor
Quartz watch
Shortwave radio receiver
Steering compass and hand bearing compass

To complete this list, add some necessary skills: a good grounding in dead reckoning and a basic knowledge of celestial navigation.

A GPS is a prime safety feature because of its ability to give you a position fix at any time—in fog or in a blizzard, day or night, anywhere on earth.

A standard GPS is accurate to within about 300 feet (91 m), half the length of some ships. If you add a differential receiver to upgrade the signal, which the U.S. Department of Defense deliberately degrades to confuse its enemies, you can obtain accuracy to within 50 feet (15 m). But you have to be reasonably close to land to pick up the special VHF or FM differential correction (DGPS) transmission.

For the price of 60 beers you can buy a simple, handheld GPS that the manufacturer says is waterproof. In fact, some of them may not be totally waterproof; sometimes it's a marketing ploy, as *Practical Sailor* magazine demonstrated in its tests on handheld VHF radios. The manufacturer will honor the warranty and promptly replace any unit that quits working because water has seeped in—but that's not a whole lot of help when you're lost in mid-ocean. So do some homework before you make your choice, or keep your GPS in a waterproof bag.

Fixed-mount GPS receivers usually live down below in the navigation area, where it's drier and safer. Their screens are larger and more readable. They are increasingly being equipped with chart plotters, which makes them a bit more expensive than ordinary GPS sets.

GPS has become the primary means of navigation for cruising sailboats, so you need to decide what sort of backup to carry. The choice is between a second GPS and a sextant.

If, like many of us, you're concerned because the Department of Defense has the ability to switch off its GPS system entirely; and if, in addition, you believe that it would have the temerity to do so in the face of worldwide protest from professional navigators, you don't have to do any thinking about your choice of navigation aids. You will obviously want to carry a GPS and a sextant, even if the sextant is a cheap plastic one. There is more discussion along these lines in the section on sextants (page 111).

Hardware for Navigation

Apart from a GPS and a sextant, what does a small-boat navigator need in the way of hardware? For a start, get a pair of those lovely, shiny brass dividers—the kind you can work with one hand. You can just as easily prick your miles off the chart with a tawdry pair from a cheap school geometry set; but those somehow don't give you the same feeling of confidence. And, in any case, a navigator needs to keep up his or her professional appearance—if only to intimidate lesser members of the crew.

Apart from dividers, you'll need:
Parallel rules, or a roller rule
Pencils of the correct hardness
A pair of compasses
A 12-inch (30-cm) rule
A 180-degree or 360-degree protractor

The right pencil is an individual choice that you have to work out for yourself. A soft pencil leaves very legible black marks and doesn't gouge the chart, but it makes a smudgy mess when you try to erase it. A hard pencil leaves less legible marks and will abrade the surface of the chart if you press too hard, but it is easier to erase afterwards.

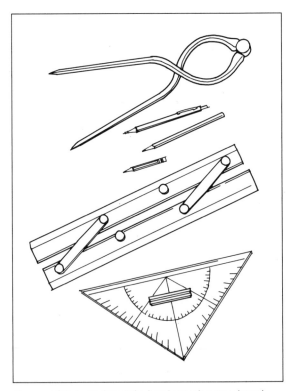

Some of the navigator's basic tools: one-hand dividers, pencils, parallel rules, and a triangular protractor

HF Radio Time Signals

If you're not carrying a ham radio or an SSB communications receiver, you'll need an ordinary shortwave radio receiver so you can check the accuracy of your chronometer at sea.

Continuous time signals from U.S. stations WWV and WWVH can be received almost anywhere in the world on frequencies of 2.5, 5, 10, 15, 20, and 25 MHz. These broadcasts are operated by the National Bureau of Standards in cooperation with the Naval Observatory.

You can also listen to time signals from the British Broadcasting Corporation (BBC) and get the world news as well. Before the news, the BBC's World Service broadcasts six "pips" to count down the last five seconds to the hour.

Idiot Sheets

There is a certain order in which you have to perform the steps when you're working a celestial sight. Each step is simple, but if you miss a step, or perform them in the wrong order, you're in trouble.

All too often, the navigator is short of sleep; and if the weather is rough, he or she might be fatigued as well, and very liable to make silly little mistakes.

That's where an idiot sheet can be of such great help.

Simply note all the steps you take in working out a sight and write them down on one page with spaces for all your observations and reckonings. Don't forget places for the date and a log reading.

Make worksheets like this for sun sights, moon sights, planet sights, and star sights. Then photocopy a good number of each and keep them in your chart drawer. You'll find that you can use each one several times if you use a pencil and an eraser.

No matter how much it feels like cheating, using these prepared work sheets is a good, safe practice.

```
              MOON SIGHT FORM

Date ...............           DR: Lat ..........Long ...........
Log ...............
Time:                                OBS. ALT: ..............
Hours  Min  Secs                     IE ..............
.............. (Chrono)              Dip ..............
.............. (Correctn)        APP. ALT:
.............. GMT              Main correctn+ ..............
                             -30' for upper limb: ..............
                             H.P. (L U correction)+ ..............

       G H A                        TRUE ALT:

Hours: ..............
M/secs .............. ②
v corr.
for mins............. ②          DECLINATION ..........
G H A _____                       +/-d corr: ..........
                                  (for mins of GMT)
Ass. Long........... Ass. Lat ..........  Declination ........N/S
(W-)
(E+)                        ④ From      Hc      d      Z
L H A _____                  tables  ....................
                            d corr. (+ or -)
                           ③for mins of dec. .........
                            CALC. ALT.

INTERCEPT:    .............. towards/away (True alt. greater, towards


From almanac:    GHA    v    DEC    d(+ or -)    H.P.


Ⓔ Enter Moon correction tables at back of almanac with:
   (1) Apparent altitude; (2) H.P. from daily tables (for hour, GMT)
① From back of almanac - Altitude Correction Tables, Moon.
② From  "    "    "   - Increments and Corrections.
③ From loose card in tables - Corrctn to tab. alt. for mins of dec.
④ Enter tables with (a) Assumed lat. (b) Declination (c) LHA.
```

Sample work sheets for a moon sight (above) and an ordinary sun sight (following page). If you pencil in the figures, you can use these photocopied work sheets again and again.

Loran

While European manufacturers are combining GPS sets with loran for unprecedented navigational accuracy inshore, United States authorities regard loran as outdated and are constantly agitating to close the system down in order to concentrate on the Differential Global Positioning System (DGPS).

Loran works by triangulating signals from land-based radio stations and is remarkably accurate in guiding you back to a spot you have visited before—so much so, that commercial fishermen use loran to locate their most productive fishing spots.

Because GPS has duplicated their functions, loran receivers are becoming harder to find. Furthermore, their range is limited, although it's sometimes possible to receive various signals all the way across the Atlantic when propagation conditions are good.

If your boat already has a loran, well and good. But don't go out now and buy one specially.

Navigation Calculators

A navigation calculator seems like the answer in so many ways. It stores all the data from the nautical almanac and it does all the work of the sight reduction tables.

All you have to do is enter a few details, such as the observed angular height of a celestial body and the time you observed it, and it works out a position line for you.

Then you drop it, or lose it overboard, and suddenly you can't navigate. You are defrocked. The crew will jeer at you.

You don't need a navigation calculator to sail over the horizon. Take one, by all means, because they're such fun to play with. But use it as backup only.

Noon Sun Sights

Although this discussion more properly belongs in a book devoted to navigation, a brief description of a noon sun sight is included here for two reasons. First, it is a very important tool for the amateur navigator. Second, once you discover how simple and useful it is, you will take noon sights even during coastal navigation.

The noon sight is important because with a cheap sextant and a current nautical almanac you can find your way to almost any destination in the world by placing yourself well to the east or west of it, and then running along a line of latitude.

How do you ascertain your latitude? The sun tells you at noon.

```
                    SUN SIGHT FORM
Date ...............            CHECK INDEX ERROR!

Log reading .........          Dead Reckoning Position

Time: Hrs  min.  sec.          Lat:         Long:

....................  (Deck watch)   Observed altitude:

....................  (watch correction)  Index error:  ±

       _____               Dip:

       _____  (G M T)      Refraction:

                                Semi-diameter:   _____
                                TRUE ALTITUDE:   _____


GHA for hours:

Increment for mins and secs:   _____

GHA:.........................

Assumed longitude (W- E+).....

LHA..........................._____

                                _____


From the tables:               Declination ............ (N or S)

Altitude .................

Correction d ............      Azimuth ................ (Sign)
                     _____

Calculated altitude: _____  _____  Assumed latitude .........(N or S)


        Intercept = ....... towards/away

        (True altitude greater towards)

                --ooOoo--
```

Noon sun sights have three advantages over other sextant sights.

- No accurate time is needed.
- There's nothing to plot on a chart.
- The working is simple arithmetic.

What you need to know is the sun's maximum altitude when it passes over your meridian—that is, at noon. You start measuring it with your sextant five minutes or so before noon by your watch, and you turn the micrometer screw to keep up with it. If you check every half minute or so, you'll find the change in the sun's height slowing down at the top of its orbit and actually staying in one place—at its highest point—for a minute or more. Just leave the micrometer screw there. Don't start following the sun down again. It's easy to make that mistake, and then you'll never know what the maximum was unless you made a note of each sight.

Now that you have the maximum altitude of the sun's meridian passage, you can work out your latitude as follows.

1. Correct the maximum altitude observed on your sextant by allowing for the following:

a. Index error. This is a usually small, variable sextant error applied to all sights. It's easy to identify and allow for (see the sidebar on index error, page 110).

b. Dip (of the sea horizon). Tables in the nautical almanac give the dip correction for the height of your eye above water.

c. Refraction. This corrects for the "bending" of light rays in the atmosphere. Once again, the nautical almanac gives corrections for different sun angles—though there won't be much, if anything, if the sun is high overhead.

d. Sun's semidiameter. Depending on whether you shot the upper or lower limb of the sun, you must add or subtract half the sun's angular diameter to get the correct angle. As the sun is about 32 minutes wide, you will usually add 16 minutes to a lower-limb shot, and subtract 16 minutes from an upper-limb shot.

More accurate semidiameters are given in the almanac, but they are rarely necessary.

The sum of all these errors is added to your observed altitude (or subtracted from it) to find what's called the true altitude. In practice, after the first day you can simply use one figure for the combined error, and it's really quick and easy to convert the observed altitude to the true altitude.

2. Subtract the true altitude from 90 degrees to find the zenith distance.

3. Now modify the zenith distance with the sun's declination given in the almanac, for the nearest hour of Greenwich Mean Time.

If the sun is in the *same hemisphere* as you are (north and north, or south and south), you *add* the declination to the zenith distance.

If you and the sun are in *different hemispheres,* you *subtract* the declination from the zenith distance.

And that's it. The result is your latitude in degrees and minutes.

Here's an example:

By dead reckoning, you're at latitude 38°34′ N

1.

43°20′	Observed (sextant) altitude
−2′	IE (index error)
−3′	Dip (for an eye 8 feet or 2.4 m above water level)
−4′	Refraction
+16′	SD (sun's semidiameter)
43°27′	True altitude

2.

90°00′	
−43°27′	
46°33′	Zenith distance

3.

46°33′	
−8°31′	Sun's southerly declination. Subtract when "name" (N or S) is different from your latitude. Add when it's the same.
32°02′ N	This is your latitude to the nearest mile.

Off-Course Alarm

If you're planning to singlehand your boat across an ocean, you'll find that life suddenly becomes very interesting as you approach land. So many famous singlehanders have run aground while they've been sleeping down below that a very good case can be made for equipping your boat with an alarm that will warn you when your boat veers off course because of a wind switch.

This is not an item you can buy across the counter every day; speak to a store specializing in marine electronics and they'll help you find what you need.

Plotting Charts

For obvious reasons, ocean charts are drawn with very small scales—far too small to enable you to plot a celestial sight with any accuracy.

> ### Sextant Index Error
>
> You need to check your sextant's index error frequently because it can vary with changes in temperature and for other reasons. Here's a quick way to perform a check:
>
> 1. Set it to approximately 0° and look at the sun through appropriate shades.
> 2. Two suns will be visible. Move the index arm so that the suns' edges just touch, then read the sextant.
> 3. Reverse the suns, edge-to-edge again, and read the sextant.
> 4. One reading will be on the ordinary degree scale. The other will be on the minus side.
> 5. Subtract the smaller reading from the larger one. Now halve the result. This is the index error.
> 6. Note the error to the nearest minute. Always add it to the observed altitude if the error is minus (that is, off the ordinary scale) and always subtract it if the error is positive (that is, on the ordinary scale).
> 7. If the index error exceeds 3 minutes, the sextant should be corrected.

The answer is the large-scale plotting chart, available from any nautical chart agent. It's basically a blank Mercator chart on which you notate your latitude and longitude. Some plotting charts, like the Baker's Position Line Chart (published in England by Imray, Laurie, Norie & Wilson), incorporate a compass rose for your convenience.

Radar

Radar is useful but not essential for ocean cruising. It's comparatively expensive and consumes more electricity than a small sailboat can afford to spare for long periods. But when you're approaching land and the fog closes in, radar comes into its own. It's also a great help when you're crossing shipping lanes in bad weather.

Like most electronic equipment, radar sets are becoming more compact, more economical in their use of electricity, and cheaper all the time. No doubt the day will come when all coastal and deep-sea sailboats will carry radar, especially radar combined with a GPS input that shows your boat's position on the radar screen. But for the present, let's just say that while it would be an advantage to have this safety feature, it's not strictly necessary.

Radio Direction Finders

Radio direction finders (RDF) seem to going the way of sextants. They're hard to find now because their function has been usurped by loran and GPS.

An RDF set has a revolving, directional antenna that picks up low-frequency transmissions from charted coastal stations. You turn the ferrite rod antenna until the transmission fades away, or nearly so, and then you know that the antenna is pointing directly at the station.

You can read, from a built-in magnetic compass, the direction in which the antenna is pointing, *et voilà!* You have a position line you can plot on the chart. Now you can either follow your nose directly to the transmitter or, if you take a bearing of another RDF station, you can cross the two position lines and obtain a position fix.

In practice, it's not quite that easy (nothing ever is on a yacht). RDF radio waves make sharp deviations from course as they pass over the boundary between land and water, and there are other factors that affect the accuracy of the system. Nevertheless, it works in fog, rain, snow, and hail. It works by day or night, and it works from a long way away—up to 100 miles or so. So if you have a working RDF, don't throw it away. It could still be useful.

If you don't have an RDF, you can use a cheap AM radio in an emergency. Most portable radios with ferrite rod antennas are directionally sensitive and will give a fairly sharp null (little or no broadcast reception) when the antenna is pointed end-on to the transmitter.

Some charts note the position of AM/FM broadcast stations, but if your favorite station isn't marked you must be quite sure you know where its signal is coming from.

If you're approaching a small ocean island, such as Barbados, you will have no trouble finding it this way, nor will you want for lively music.

And here's a tip: The cheaper the radio, the better it works as a direction finder. Expensive radios have better antennas and extra circuits to improve reception, and they disguise the null zone, which is precisely what you *don't* need.

Sextants

Now we come to the big question. Do you need a sextant?

Based on one fact, the simple answer would have to be no: Boats have sailed right around the world without sextants, and more are doing so all the time. But the better answer is yes. The sextant is still an important item of safety equipment, and you should know how to use it to plot a position line on a chart.

It is becoming increasingly difficult to sup-

port the latter stance, however, because the alternative to the sextant, a portable GPS set, now costs less than 60 beers, or about one quarter of the price of a good new sextant. You can take along four GPS sets for the price of one sextant.

But what if the Department of Defense cancels the GPS system, or somebody at the Pentagon presses the wrong button and accidentally sends the constellation of satellites flying into space while you're halfway across the Pacific?

Could such a thing happen? We just don't know. But put it this way: Which of the following two systems do you regard as the more stable platform for navigation?

The first is a fleet of 21 man-made satellites orbiting in a very hostile environment, subject to collision with all sorts of space debris, vulnerable to being shot down by enemy rockets, and filled with electronic equipment with an unknown propensity for malfunction over the long term.

The second is a much vaster constellation of stars and planets, placed in space by someone or something unknown to us, that has been in existence since the dawn of time and is likely to be there for at least the next million years. And yet it is a system over which we have no control whatsoever. Furthermore, although it looks mighty permanent, we have no actual guarantee that it will still be there tomorrow.

Tough choice? Not really. Become a latter-day wimp. Take a sextant, even if it's just to earn points in the Black Box. It should be the best one you can afford. There is great satisfaction to be derived from handling a beautifully crafted metal sextant, but a plastic one with a micrometer screw will suffice.

Use your GPS for everyday navigation, but practice with your sextant, your almanac, and your tables. You might even find, as many of us do, that it's a very gratifying pastime.

There's no doubt that despite everything, many cruisers regard sextants as old-fashioned and unnecessary. They, too, have a point. If the person at the Pentagon in charge of the GPS system runs off to South America with the cash, and the satellites come crashing down about our ears, all those cruisers stuck out in the middle of the ocean who depend solely on GPS can simply go back to the oldest navigation system of all—dead reckoning. Thousands of ancient seafarers used it to find their way around the world, including Columbus; and they didn't even have decent charts. We can surely do as well as they did.

But while we're on the subject, there are other aspects of GPS navigation worthy of some consideration. As we know from the experience of Russia's space station, *Mir*, computers do sometimes go wrong; and there aren't always astronauts on hand to fix them. Thus it would seem likely that the computers aboard the orbiting GPS satellites could go wrong too. Would they all go wrong once? If they were hit by a meteor shower, perhaps they would.

And here's something else to ponder. You may have heard that the GPS system is due to crash because of the millennium bug, when its computers will mistake the date digits 00 for 1900 instead of 2000. In fact, one of the rumors at the time of this writing was that the GPS system would die *before* the year 2000 because it follows its own time system, not Greenwich Mean Time or Universal Coordinated Time (UCT).

And then there's the question of computer hackers. They have already broken into Pentagon files. What if they reach the software that controls the GPS system? The Pentagon already uses its software to make the system less accurate for anyone other than the U.S. military. What if the hackers shut it down completely?

Clearly, it's impossible for most of us to evaluate the real threats to the GPS system, and there is no real reason to be alarmist. But any cautious navigator will see the sense of carrying a sextant and double-checking the GPS positions whenever possible.

Ship's Log

In chapter 15 we will discuss the importance of the ship's log as a way of proving your competence to a court or maritime authority (page 180). But a well-kept log is also a great aid to navigation and safety in general.

You should make a point of noting barometer pressures at the change of every watch, and the amounts of fuel and water remaining. It's a good idea to keep a column for formal remarks, such as what kind of jib allowed you to heave to best in a gale-force wind or what kind of anchor best buried itself in a sandy bottom covered with grass.

Some sailors like to combine the formal and informal logs, and include details about what brand of ice cream tasted best and the last time they changed their underwear. But some of us feel the informal chatter is out of place in a document that might be quoted in open court one day, or at least scrutinized by an admiralty lawyer or an insurance agent. It's a good idea to keep a personal, informal log, particularly if you want to write about your trip afterward or give a slide show, but it's better kept separate from the ship's log.

Sounding

Often, when you arrive safely on the other side of the ocean, there will no convenient marinas for you to tie up in. You will have no choice but to lie to your anchor.

That being the case, the first thing you'll want to know is the depth of the water, which you ascertain by sounding.

An electronic depth sounder does this for you in the most convenient way. It measures the time a sound signal takes to travel from its transducer to the bottom of the sea and back again.

The signal has a frequency of between 50 and 200 kHz, which is too high for the human ear to pick up. The rule is that the higher the frequency, the greater the detail the depth sounder produces, but at the cost of penetration. The lower the frequency, the greater the depth it will record, but at the price of poorer resolution.

Sportfishers are concerned with detail, but most sailors aren't, so you should choose a 50-kHz transducer if you frequently navigate along bottom contour lines in deep water.

Depth sounders used in combination with large-scale charts will give you useful information about your distance offshore at night, or in fog, and enable you to run along a contour line to stay out of trouble.

The depth sounder is undoubtedly the electronic instrument with the best record of reliability on small boats, but if you don't have one, there is another instrument with an even better record, as long as you can tie a reliable bowline. It's the sounding lead, a 6- or 7-pound (2.5 to 3 kg) lead weight on the end of a 20-fathom (36-m) line.

Its advantage is that it works by gravity, which, unlike electricity, is constantly available and always free. Its disadvantage is that the lead must be tied to the line with a very secure knot lest (as some of us have experienced with con-

sternation) the two come to a parting of the ways. A further advantage of the lead is that its hollow can be armed with grease or soft soap to bring up a sample of the seabed, which helps you choose the type of anchor to deploy.

Plaited Dacron is said to be best for the line, because it doesn't kink as easily as stranded line, but some of us prefer three-strand Dacron nevertheless, because we can thread small pieces of marked canvas between the strands to indicate depths.

THINK INVERTED

If your boat turns upside down:

- Will your charts end up on the cabin roof smothered in ketchup and peanut butter or soaked in seawater?
- Will your sextant and your handheld GPS stay in place?
- Is anyone likely to get a pair of dividers in the eye?

CHAPTER 10

Electricity

You don't need electricity to sail around the world. It's legal to be without electrical power: You can do very well with kerosene lamps, just as many sailors have done in the past. But electricity runs so many safety devices, and is so convenient for lighting and powering motors of various types, that the modern sailor would be almost foolhardy to go to sea without it.

Today's boats have brighter navigation lights, more efficient pumps, electric anchor winches, pressurized water, bow thrusters, and push-button sail reefing. Modern inverters allow 12-volt DC batteries to power 110-volt AC household appliances, such as microwave ovens, television sets, and computers.

But when you cross an ocean, you must be self-sufficient in your electrical needs. You have to be able to generate electricity and store it—and that's when things start to get interesting. If you haven't done so already, you're going to spend a lot of time thinking about electricity.

How Many Batteries?

The first question is: How much electricity do you need? The second is: How many batteries are needed to store that amount?

There is a logical way to calculate your needs. Make a list of all the electrical items you use during an average day, then note beside each one the length of time each item's in use.

Most of these items will be rated in watts, but if the consumption of some is shown in amps, multiply the amps by the battery voltage to get watts. Most small sailboats will have 12-volt batteries.

For example: If your anchor light draws 10 watts and it's in use for 10 hours a day, you will list it as drawing 100 watt-hours. And if your bilge pump draws 48 watts for 0.2 hours a day, then you put its consumption down as 9.6 watt-hours. The reason we're working with watt-hours will become clear in a moment.

Now work out the watt-hours for every single bit of equipment on board that draws current from the ship's batteries. Don't forget the starter motor on the engine. It will probably draw between 1,200 and 3,600 watts (depending on whether it's turning over a gasoline engine or a diesel), but it works for a very small fraction of an hour every day. (For a list of average wattage loads, see Appliances and Their Electrical Appetites, page 117.)

When you have your full list of watt-hours, add them up and divide the total by the voltage of the batteries you want (which is almost always 12 volts). The answer is the number of amp-hours you require every day.

The capacity of batteries is marked in amp-hours, so you're now almost ready to calculate the number of batteries you need to make up the ship's battery bank.

For example, the capacity of a Group 24 deep-cycle battery weighing 47.5 pounds (22 kg) is 95 amp-hours. A Group 27 deep-cycle battery weighing 52.5 pounds (24 kg) will provide 115 amp-hours, and a Group 30 deep-cycle battery weighing 66 pounds (30 kg) will give you 130 amp-hours.

Their sizes vary with their capacities, so choose batteries that fit the space you have for them, and for convenience in lugging them around. Two small batteries may work better for you than one big one.

Now for the bad news. Only 40 percent of your battery capacity is available for normal use. So you need a battery bank with a capacity 2.5 times your average daily draw. Thus, the battery capacity needed to give you a daily draw of 90 amp-hours is 225 amp-hours; you could use two Group 27 batteries.

Only 40 percent of their power is available because it's not good for the battery's life to let it drop below a half-charge before recharging. Also, it's difficult to top up the last 10 percent of a battery's capacity during ordinary recharging.

You can certainly run your batteries flat every time, if you wish. In that case, you will get the full number of advertised amp-hours out of each. But even deep-cycle batteries (which are deliberately designed to be far more resistant to this kind of maltreatment than are ordinary starter batteries) will have their lives shortened drastically by constant deep discharge.

If you're wise, you'll learn to live with the 40-percent rule, and you will install a battery bank with an amp-hour capacity 2.5 times greater than your actual daily draw. Anything less will eventually make your life miserable.

You could, if you wished, reserve one battery for starting the engine, and that one could be a cheaper starter battery, like the ones used in cars. Just remember, though, that you'll have to keep that starter battery charged up at all times, because car batteries react very badly to being deeply discharged. They don't last any time at all if you do that to them regularly. Auto manufacturers assume their batteries will be recharged immediately after use.

In fact, though, you can use a deep-cycle battery for starting your engine, as long as it can deliver current fast enough. You'll know if it can by the number of cold-cranking amps (CCA) marked on the casing. For diesel engines you'll need 2 CCAs per cubic inch (per 16 cc) of piston displacement. For gasoline engines, 1 CCA per cubic inch (per 16 cc) will do. A good, conservative installation will either have identical deep-cycle batteries for starting the engine as well as for all ordinary needs, or one starter battery and one or more deep-cycle batteries.

Although they need maintenance now and then, flooded lead-acid batteries are preferable to gel batteries, in our opinion, because a simple hydrometer will give you information about the health of individual cells. Although gel batteries are sealed and maintenance free, they can be damaged by alternators or battery chargers with high constant voltages. They also cost more than twice as much as deep-cycle, wet-plate batteries.

Six-volt golf-cart batteries are designed to take a lot of abuse, and they give excellent service on small boats. Connect them in series for a 12-volt or 24-volt system.

All batteries should be fully protected by a proper, acid-proof battery case, and they should be held down firmly in case of a capsize.

Keeping Batteries Charged

How do you keep your batteries charged when you're cruising and unable to plug into shore power? If you're like most people, you run your engine or a separate generator. But there are other ways. We'll look at them one at a time.

ENGINE-DRIVEN ALTERNATORS

You may want to upgrade your alternator because a modern, multistage regulator (which we'll come to in a minute) allows faster charging from a larger alternator.

If you're using one of these "smart" (and expensive) regulators, your alternator's rating in amps should equal between 25 percent and 40 percent of your battery bank's capacity in amp-hours.

For example, if you have a 200-amp-hour battery bank, your alternator output should be between 25 percent and 40 percent of 200, or 50 to 80 amps.

If you're still plugging along with the regulator the engine manufacturer supplied, and you haven't entered the "smart" age yet, you should be sure the regulator limits the charging rate in amps to 10 percent of the battery's capacity in amp-hours. A higher rate of charging than this, without proper regulation, will greatly shorten battery life.

Thus, your regulator for your 200-amp-hour battery bank shouldn't constantly put out more than 20 amps. Many do, of course, for the simple reason that it takes forever to recharge a 200-amp-hour battery bank from an input trickle of 20 amps. Some people are prepared to accept the damage from a faster charge rate and buy new batteries more frequently.

By the way, only the electrically naive believe that charging a 200-amp-hour battery at 20 amps for 10 hours will restore it to a full charge. The truth is that charging a battery is like paying taxes: You have to put in a lot more than you'll ever get out. It can be as much as 10 or 20 percent more, depending on the smartness of your regulator, among other things.

All these remarks about engine-driven alternators also apply to alternators driven by dedicated generating plants, although the latter are more likely to possess sophisticated regulation.

OTHER GENERATORS
Cruising yachts often top up their amp-hours from alternators driven by small propellers dragged through the water or large propellers turned by the wind. In addition, solar panels can make a substantial contribution to the day's electrical requirements.

Here are some rough comparisons of their outputs, taken from manufacturers' brochures.

Water-driven generator: 5.25 amps at 5 knots

Wind-driven generator: 7 amps at 15 mph (6.7 m/s)

Solar panels: two 35-watt rigid panels will put out about 1.5 amps, or about 18 amp-hours over a daylight period of 12 hours, on average. The rule of thumb with solar panels is that a rigid panel will generate amp-hours equal to about 25 percent of its rated wattage each day.

Water generators can make a substantial contribution to your store of electricity while you're at sea, but they will do nothing for you while you're in a marina or swinging to your anchor.

Wind generators work well when you're at anchor, but many cruisers are surprised at how little wind there is in anchorages much of the time; an anchorage is, by definition, sheltered, and the wind frequently dies down at night. Most wind generators need a fairly good breeze to produce anything worthwhile. On a very small boat, the whirling blades of a large wind generator (about 4 feet or 1.2 m in diameter) may constitute a hazard in strong breezes.

Solar panels are a kinder, gentler solution—especially if you are headed toward the tropics and abundant sunshine. They are very popular on cruising boats. The brighter the sun, and the more squarely it strikes the panel, the more electricity a solar panel will generate. The three main types of panels are monocrystalline, polycrystalline, and thin-film panels. Monocrystalline panels, the most efficient, are naturally the most expensive. These panels and the polycrystalline panels are almost rigid. While thin-film panels are flexible and often more convenient for a small boat, they are less efficient than the two other types.

Air Marine's sleek wind turbine produces 72 watts in 15 knots of wind and will start generating power in a 5-knot wind. The carbon-matrix blades span 45 inches (1.14 m).

Lightweight, portable *gasoline generators,* such as those made by Honda, are carried by many cruisers to work 110-volt and 220-volt AC appliances, such as power tools and microwaves. They will also recharge 12-volt batteries in an emergency. But be aware that their DC output is very small, so they will take a long time about it.

Appliances and Their Electrical Appetites

Here is a list of most of the electrical appliances found on small cruising boats and an approximate indication of the number of watts they draw from your battery bank. Not all these appliances are found on every boat, of course, and you'll have to decide for yourself exactly what your needs are.

The items marked with an asterisk are essential in most cases and highly desirable in others.

Autopilot	40
Bilge pump*	24 to 180
Blender	30
Blower fan for gasoline engine*	36 to 72
Cabin lights, incandescent or fluorescent*	
	10 to 20 each
Cabin heater	100
Cabin fan	12
Depthfinder*	3 to 6
Galley fan	40
GPS*	3 to 6
Loran	5 to 9
Microwave oven	1,000
Navigation lights*	12 to 25
Pressure pump	84
Radar	20 to 50
RDF	12
Refrigerator	84
Shortwave radio receiver*	
	1 to 2 (or alkaline batteries)
Soldering iron	80
Speed and wind instruments	1 to 2
Spreader lights	24 to 30
SSB radio	
	12 (receiving) to 240 (transmitting)
Strobe light	9
Tape deck	12 to 24
Toilet, electric	200
Vacuum cleaner	120
VHF radio*	
	6 (on standby) to 60 (transmitting)
Washing machine	60
Weatherfax	120
Windlass	400 to 900
Windshield wiper	40

Inverters

You don't need an inverter for safety or seaworthiness, but you might want to consider one if it's your intention to use household appliances such as computers, TV sets, blenders, and power drills.

Inverters convert the 12-volt direct current (12V DC) from your ship's batteries into 110-volt alternating current (110V AC) with little loss of efficiency and none of the noise and fumes associated with generating 110V AC with a gas- or diesel-powered generator set.

Inverter output ranges from 50 watts to about 2,500 watts. The right wattage for your boat depends on the size of your battery bank. The rule of thumb is that you need an inverter with an output in watts equal to five times your battery bank's total amp-hours.

For example, if you have a 200-amp-hour battery bank, you can comfortably support a 1,000-watt (1 kW) inverter without the need to recharge your batteries constantly.

"Smart" Alternator Regulators

Most cruising sailors regard their engines' alternators as the most convenient way to recharge their batteries. But no real sailor wants to run an engine longer than necessary, so the need is to return large amounts of energy in the shortest time.

The best way to do this is with a high-output alternator working through a smart regulator. But even if you decide to stick with your factory-supplied alternator, a smart regulator will still get your batteries charged more quickly and do them the least harm.

Standard auxiliary engines come with alternators producing anything between 25 and 55 amps, but a smart regulator can handle an amperage roughly 25 percent to 40 percent as large as your battery capacity in amp-hours.

Thus, a 200-amp-hour battery bank can be recharged much more quickly than normal, and without damage, by an alternator with a maximum output of 80 amps.

Sophisticated regulators sense the state of charge of your batteries and supply them with the maximum current only while they can absorb it. They usually work through three stages of charging—the bulk, absorption, and float stages—staying with each one as long as it is beneficial.

A smart regulator will cost you about 60 beers, and a 75-amp alternator will cost about twice as much. A 1,000-amp inverter costs about 240 beers, and the ultimate tool for power management—a smart box that controls your inverter, monitors your battery, and regulates your alternator—goes for about 270 beers.

A modern sophisticated power system adds up to a lot of money. Its entire purpose is to shorten battery recharging time and to give the batteries a longer life. Weigh the costs. You must decide for yourself whether it would be cheaper and simpler to continue to charge in the old, unsophisticated manner (perhaps with help from a wind generator, a water generator, or solar panels) and replace your batteries every two or three years.

Wiring

If you're upgrading your boat's electrical system, don't forget the wiring. Increased loads mean heftier wire. The majority of boat systems work on low voltage, which requires thicker wire than do household voltages. Furthermore, boat wiring, besides calling for a substantial thickness of top-quality copper wire, also needs multistranded wire for resistance to vibration.

Wire that is too thin causes a voltage drop at the end of its run. That's not just inefficient: It's dangerous. Thin wire gets hot and can start fires.

A voltage drop of 10 percent is acceptable for cabin lights and other circuits where voltage isn't critical, but electronic gear and navigation lights should not be subjected to a drop of more than 3 percent. Because voltage loss is proportional to wire length, long runs need thicker wire. How thick? Here are two tables to guide you.

American Wire Gauge (AWG) Sizes for a 10-Percent Voltage Drop at 12V DC											
Total Current on Circuit in Amps	Distance Run										
	Feet: 20	30	40	50	60	70	80	90	100	110	120
	Meters: 6	9	12	15	18	21	24	27	30	33	37
5	16	16	16	16	14	14	14	14	12	12	12
10	16	14	14	12	12	12	10	10	10	10	8
15	14	14	12	10	10	10	8	8	8	8	8
20	12	12	10	10	8	8	8	6	6	6	6
25	10	10	10	8	8	8	6	6	6	6	4

Note: *Distance Run* is the total length of the wire from the source, to the appliance, and back to the source.

American Wire Gauge (AWG) Sizes for a 3-Percent Voltage Drop at 12V DC											
Total Current on Circuit in Amps	Distance Run										
	Feet: 20	30	40	50	60	70	80	90	100	110	120
	Meters: 6	9	12	15	18	21	24	27	30	33	37
5	14	12	12	10	10	8	8	8	8	8	6
10	12	10	8	8	6	6	6	5	5	5	4
15	10	8	6	6	5	5	4	4	3	3	2
20	8	6	6	5	4	3	2	2	2	2	1
25	8	6	5	4	3	3	2	1	1	1	0

Note: *Distance Run* is the total length of the wire from the source, to the appliance, and back to the source.

Wiring Color Code

Many production sailboats, but by no means all, conform to recommendations of the American Boat and Yacht Councils for the colors used to identify wires in DC systems under 50 volts. If yours is one of those that does comply, the tables on the following page will help you determine which wire goes where and what each wire is for.

The Essentials

Here's a helpful list of requirements for a cruising boat's electrical department in regard to the generation and storage of power. But you don't need it all. Start at number 1, and stop anywhere you like after number 3.

1. Deep-cycle, wet-plate batteries, possibly with one ordinary battery reserved for starting the engine

2. An engine-driven alternator and/or:
3. Alternative charging source(s). One or more of these: solar cells, wind generator, water generator
4. Smart regulator
5. Portable gasoline generator
6. Inverter
7. Combined inverter controller and alternator regulator

Color Code for Marine Wiring: American Boat and Yacht Council's Recommendations for DC Systems Under 50V	
Color	**Use**
Brown	Generator armature to regulator; generator terminal/alternator auxiliary terminal to light to regulator; fuse or switch to pumps
Dark Blue	Fuse or switch to cabin and instrument lights
Dark Gray	Fuse or switch to navigation lights; tachometer sender to gauge
Green	Ground or bonding wire
Light Blue	Oil-pressure sender to gauge
Orange	Ammeter to alternator or generator output and accessory fuses or switches; distribution panel to accessory switch
Pink	Fuel-gauge sender to gauge
Purple	Ignition switch to coil and instruments; distribution panel to instruments
Red	Positive main
Tan	Water-temperature sender to gauge
White or Black	Return, negative main. Either color is acceptable, but not a mixture of both.
Yellow	Generator or alternator field to regulator field terminal; bilge blowers; fuse or switch to bilge blowers
Yellow/red stripe	Starting switch to solenoid

Standard Color Codes for 120V AC Wiring	
Color	**Use**
Black	Identifies the "hot," current-carrying line
White	Neutral ground return
Green	Noncurrent-carrying line grounding a metal cabinet or chassis

THINK INVERTED

If your boat turns upside down:

- Will your batteries stay in place?
- Will they leak acid?
- Can salt water short-circuit any wires and cause a fire?

CHAPTER 11

The Galley

ooks on small sailboats usually work under conditions that range from woefully inadequate to atrocious. There is rarely sufficient counter space, for a start, or any place at all to put down a hot pan. Much of the food the cook needs at hand is actually located in spots that a contortionist would have trouble reaching. Even the readily accessible staples are commonly buried in a cupboard directly behind the stove, so the cook risks third-degree burns simply to get at the salt and pepper.

All of the cook's woes are multiplied vastly at sea, and when the weather turns foul—the very time when hot, nourishing food is most needed—it often becomes impossible to produce a meal in a small galley. Considering the number of meals a cook is expected to produce and the frequency of their production, it is a mystery to many of us that yacht designers believe the space and facilities allotted to the average galley to be adequate.

But it's not only the space and the layout that are less than desirable: There's also the hardware.

Stoves that use propane or butane gas are dangerous (much more so than natural gas stoves on shore). Propane from a small leak will sink to the bilges, where it mixes with air and is retained like a bomb—just waiting for someone to light the fuse.

Stoves that use kerosene or diesel fuel must be preheated with raw alcohol. This is a never-ending source of excitement that can develop into a major hazard if the burner is opened too soon and hot spurting kerosene flares up like Vesuvius erupting.

Many production sailboats have stoves that use alcohol alone. They were once greatly favored because rumor had it that an alcohol fire could quickly be extinguished by water. In fact, burning alcohol can float on top of water, and throwing water at an alcohol fire may just spread it farther abroad. But besides that, alcohol is very expensive and doesn't put out as much heat as propane, kerosene, or diesel.

The kind of fuel you cook on is one of two galley subjects that cruisers never tire of discussing. The other is refrigeration.

For some reason, Americans—more than any other nation on earth—love ice. We use it in big chunks in iceboxes, and small chunks under our oysters, and in our drinks. The phlegmatic British will drink their beer warm, if necessary—indeed, some actually prefer it that way: They claim that chilling inhibits the volatile vapors that give beer its best flavor. The French don't need ice for their wine, and Canadians are prepared to suffer quietly for the sheer joy of sailing. But Americans need ice. That means refrigeration, and refrigeration on a small boat means two things:

1. You'd better be able to fix it yourself if you plan to cruise to less-developed countries.

2. You'll never have to wonder what to do with your spare time.

These things, and others mentioned in the alphabetical list below, should be considered very carefully if you're thinking of fitting out your production cruiser for ocean work. (And for a look at the *practical* side of cooking in a small boat on the open ocean, see chapter 18, Gastro-Navigation.)

Bowls and Mugs

If you, like many coastal cruisers, have never cooked or served a meal at sea, you will scarcely appreciate how handy bowls and mugs can be in place of plates and cups or glasses. Few meals at sea are eaten at the table; most are eaten from the lap.

A deep bowl retains its contents even if the boat is rolling her gunwales under. A deep mug,

---

Rum Punch, Traditional

The rule of thumb for Caribbean planter's punch was: "One of sour, two of sweet, three of strong, four of weak." It's not for the fainthearted or the lily-livered.

Take the juice of one lime or lemon. Add two heaped teaspoons of sugar, three ounces of best Jamaica rum, and four ounces of dry gin.

Then sip: Don't gulp.

---

half-filled, serves the same function for soup or drinks. Keep your household dinnerware for meals in port, but invest in some mugs and bowls for meals at sea.

Rubber adhesive sprayed on the bottom of a bowl or mug, and allowed to dry thoroughly, will prevent it from slipping on a canted surface.

Cooker Placement

Most cooking stoves are gimbaled on a fore-and-aft axis so that they remain level as the boat heels to port or starboard, but occasionally you'll see a stove that is gimbaled athwartships. Presumably, this is to keep the stove level when the boat is pitching. But pitching is the lesser of the two evils. Heeling is the main villain. If your stove is presently gimbaled on a side-to-side axis, you should think about relocating it for sea work, if it's at all possible.

Alternatively, you can confine all cooking at sea to a single-burner, bulkhead-mounted stove. This, in any case, is what you'll probably be reduced to in rough weather. Force 10 makes a fully gimbaled, single-pot, seagoing model with a 16-ounce (473.6-ml) bottle of propane that will last about $3\frac{1}{2}$ hours at full flame. Using gas this way is not the most economical way to cook; but it's justifiable if you use it only during storms.

The last word in seagoing mugs. This gleaming stainless steel mug has a low center of gravity to deter it from tipping over and a neoprene pad on its base to stop it from slipping on a canted surface. The walls are double, to keep things hot or cool longer, and it has a snap-in lid. But a mug of such magnificence is not cheap: about 11 beers, from West Marine.

Check Your Gimbals

Have a careful look at the pivoting point of your stove gimbals. The pivots should be level with the hot plate so the motion of a pan on the hot plate resembles that of a seesaw.

If the pivot point is higher than the hot plate—as you will sometimes see—your stove will swing like a pendulum. Although you can restrain the pots with special gates, or fiddles, their contents may be hurled out by centrifugal force in a seaway.

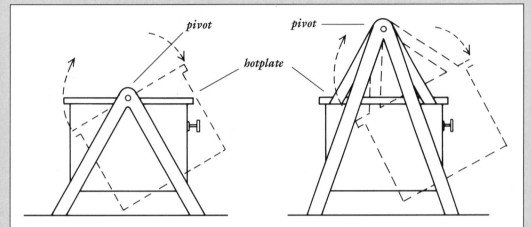

A cooker must be gimbaled so that its top surface, upon which the pots and pans will rest, is in the same horizontal plane as the pivot point (left). If it pivots from a point higher than the hotplate (right), it will swing wildly and spill the contents of the pots.

Cooking Fuels
ALCOHOL

Most production boats are fitted with alcohol stoves because they're less likely to explode or experience a runaway meltdown than gas, kerosene, or diesel stoves. The fact that they're not particularly efficient, or that the fuel costs an arm and a leg, is of no concern to a manufacturer anxious to cut down on liability claims.

So if you have an alcohol stove, do your best to get rid of it before you disappear over the horizon to places where denatured alcohol is rare, expensive, and laced with poison because people tend to drink it. In much of the world, it's dyed a bluish purple and called methylated spirits, but addicts still drink it after straining it through a loaf of bread, even if it does—and it eventually does—make them blind. This is surely not the kind of behavior you want to support by keeping the manufacturers in business.

KEROSENE (PARAFFIN) AND DIESEL

Kerosene is available all over the world and was king of the cooking fuels when the Primus stove was at the height of its popularity. But the world's wilderness spots are now being converted to gas cookers—even though liquid petroleum gas costs more—because gas is undoubtedly the simplest fuel to use and provides the best temperature control.

Kerosene fuel is regarded as safe: At normal temperatures it will not mix with air and form an explosive mixture, as gas or gasoline will do. The principle of a kerosene stove is that the fuel is heated in a vaporizer until it turns into a gas, at which stage it burns easily.

But to get the cycle going, you need to heat the burner first with denatured alcohol. Some kerosene stoves specially fitted with preheaters will emit a fine, high-pressure cloud of kerosene that will actually burn, but in our experience, these preheaters are not as efficient or as reliable as alcohol. The burner is usually surrounded at its base by a small circular bowl, which is meant to be filled with alcohol. Seagoing boats should fill the bowl with a piece of fiberglass gasket material to soak up the alcohol and prevent the burning fuel from spilling because of the boat's motion. Hardware stores sell that kind of gasket for the doors of household wood stoves.

One of the advantages of kerosene is that, at the rate of a gallon (3.8 liters) or so a week for lighting and cooking, you can easily carry a six-month supply.

Another is that you can use kerosene for lighting—even for running lights and anchor lights, if you wish—and a cabin heater. It will thin oil-bound paints and clean paint and varnish brushes. It will displace water from shorted electrical circuits, just like its close relative WD-40, and it will dissolve grease. You can even run a gasoline engine on it for a short while in an emergency, if the engine is hot enough to vaporize it.

You can run a diesel engine on it too, because diesel is another close relative of kerosene, only a little rougher around the edges—it's not so highly refined. Kerosene won't give the pistons as much lubrication as diesel fuel, but it will get you home in an emergency, if you take it easy. And finally, if your compass develops a bubble, you can top it up with kerosene.

Diesel fuel will also run stoves and heaters, but it won't run wick lamps because it makes too

Weight of Food

How much food can your boat carry? For cruise-planning purposes, you should figure that galley stores will weigh 5 to 6 pounds (2.3 to 2.7 kg) per person per day. That includes the weight of packaging.

To calculate how much of a load will put your boat an inch down on her marks, use this formula:

Pounds per inch immersion = waterplane area in square feet × 5.34

(Or, in metric, kilograms per centimeter immersion = waterplane area in square meters × 10.25)

A close approximation of your boat's waterplane area is given by this formula:

Waterplane area in square feet (meters) = waterline length in feet (meters) × waterline beam in feet (meters) × 0.76

much smoke and soot. It is the hottest-burning liquid fuel: Some cruisers who cook on it say they have trouble keeping the heat low enough for simmering (although you can buy a metal heat diffuser from a hardware store). Nevertheless, if you have a diesel auxiliary anyway, there is an advantage to carrying just one type of fuel for the engine, the cabin heater, and the galley.

Both diesel and kerosene burners tend to become blocked by soot or coke every so often, but most have self-pricking devices that work at a flick of the wrist.

If you're watching pennies, kerosene and diesel are the cooking and heating fuels that give you the best value for your money, but be careful where you buy kerosene. A one-gallon (3.8-liter) container of deodorized kerosene listed in the catalog of a nationwide U.S. chain of boating stores sells for the equivalent of 3.6 beers. The same stuff from our local household fuel merchant sells for 1.08 beers a gallon (3.8 liters) if you provide your own container.

BUTANE AND PROPANE

Cooks love it and nervous skippers hate it, but most cruisers use liquid petroleum gas (LPG) in their galley stoves because it's so easy to work with. LPG is mostly propane, sometimes butane, and sometimes a mixture of both.

It's heavier than air, so you have to be very careful not to let any unburned gas escape and collect in the bilges. That can't be said enough times. Many small boats have been blown to smithereens when a mixture of gas and air was accidentally ignited by a tiny spark.

Safety regulations call for the gas canister to be housed in a vapor-tight compartment separated from the main cabin and vented directly overboard. And although the gas bottle has a manu-al shut-off valve, you should install a separate solenoid shut-off, an electrically operated switch that allows you to turn the gas supply on and off from inside the boat. Many solenoid controls incorporate a sniffer that detects LPG gas and sets off alarms before it reaches explosive quantities in the cabin. If you don't have this double arrangement, be sure to install a separate LPG detection system. If there's ever a leak, you need to know about it quickly—even before you can smell it.

Propane tanks hold from 6 to 20 pounds (3 to 9 kg) of gas, and a 10-pound (4.5-kg) tank will supply cooking fuel for a cruising couple for about six weeks.

Refilling those tanks when you're out in the

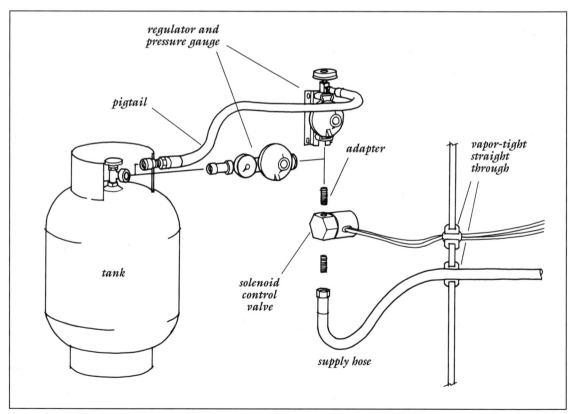

The basic set-up for delivering liquid petroleum gas (LPG) to the galley cooker. You can mount the regulator directly on the tank, if you wish, or you can place it on the wall of your LPG locker.

wilderness can be a problem, although, as mentioned earlier, the world's wild spots are fast being converted from kerosene to LPG. Be sure, before you leave civilization, to buy any international cylinder adapters you need, and be prepared to lug your cylinders for long distances to refill centers.

Compressed natural gas (CNG) is a wonderful cooking fuel, probably the best of all: It is lighter than air, and thus far less likely to lie around in explosive pools. The problem is availability. Suppliers are few and far between in the United States and totally absent from much of the rest of the world.

Cooking Fuels Compared			
Fuel	Btu per gallon (3.8 liters)	Comparative cost per hour	Hours per gallon (3.8 liters)
Alcohol	64,600	$0.21	32
Kerosene (Paraffin)	129,350	$0.07	32
LPG (Butane or Propane)	91,000	$0.10	17

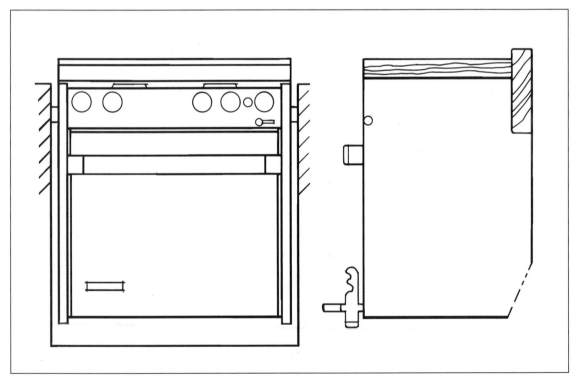

Force 10's popular propane galley range has two or three burners, an infrared flame broiler, and an oven. It's made of stainless steel and set in gimbals. It's not cheap: the two-burner model retails for about 396 beers.

Cupboards

Ideally, your galley cupboards, nooks, niches, and crannies should be sufficiently commodious to store at least a week's worth of food. Transferring cans, packages, eggs, and vegetables from bulk lockers under the bunks or up forward is not something you want to do too often at sea.

But on a very small boat, you may not have cupboard space in the galley to last a week and you will have to go foraging and rummaging more frequently. At least you will have the compensation that almost all the stores you need are only a couple of paces away from the galley.

Cupboard doors, like all locker doors, should have louvers or holes cut in them for ventilation, as well as positive catches that will not open accidentally if a can is flung against an inside release during a heavy bout of rolling.

Rum Punch, Tafia

Tafia is the West Indian Creole name for rough rum, often applied to any drink by crews of old sailing ships. Here's a recipe for tafia from the French sailor and cook Florence Herbulot, author of *Cooking Afloat*.

"The first essential is a bottle of good white rum. Next you need an empty bottle, an attractive looking bottle, with a really good stopper. Each time that you open a tin of fruit in syrup, pour any surplus syrup into the bottle. Do not waste a drop! When the bottle is half full of syrup, add the juice of a lemon (or two if they are small) and fill the bottle with rum.

"Do not worry that it will take too long to half-fill the bottle with fruit syrup; it is surprising how much you get out of one tin. The variety of flavors that go to make up a tafia is one of its great merits; it never turns out the same twice, but is always excellent. You will be proud of it, believe me!"

Dining Table

Dining is rather too elegant a word to describe the process of eating food at sea, unless you are sailing on a very large yacht. On a small boat, a dining table is used only in port. At sea, people mostly eat from bowls in their laps. Although there are some highly organized crews who set higher standards and eat regular meals at set times in dinettes, furnished with folding-leaf tables that have deep fiddles at their edges to stop the plates and cutlery sliding off. Such grace and refinement is not the norm, however, at least, not at sea.

The old rule of thumb was that a yacht's saloon table should be fitted with fiddles at least 1½ inches (40 mm) high, which is fine for plates; but a 2-inch (50-mm) fiddle has a better chance of preventing a mug of hot coffee from sliding into your lap. Fiddles can be fitted with pegs or hinges so that they can be removed or folded down to allow the table to be used flat for other work, especially for navigation on a small boat lacking a chart desk. If you're lucky enough to have a gimbaled saloon table, you'll find it a great place to set things down while you're cooking.

Fire Extinguishers

For obvious reasons, the galley is a potential source of fires, so you should keep an extinguisher handy. Use a Type B gas or powder extinguisher that will deal with oil and fat fires—not one filled with water.

Tempting as it may be, don't place the extinguisher in the galley itself: You might find yourself cut off from it by the very fire you want to fight, or you might get burned trying to reach through the flames for it. Locate the extinguisher on a bulkhead nearby, on an escape route from the flaming galley.

Remember that there are other ways to fight a galley fire, too. A fire will go out if you

• Cool the burning material
• Starve it of oxygen

• Remove the combustible material

You can place a close-fitting lid on a pan of flaming oil to starve it of oxygen. And you can quickly smother a small galley fire with baking soda, salt, flour, sand, or a wet blanket.

Freshwater and Saltwater Faucets

It is very handy to have two faucets for the galley sink: one for fresh water and one for salt water. Fresh water is such a precious commodity in the middle of the ocean that few small boats risk washing dishes in it.

If you have a watermaker and tanks full of drinking water, then it is more convenient to do all the washing up in fresh water. But the normal practice is to wash in salt and rinse off in a mere mist of fresh water.

Onion Soup

This is the classic recipe for British naval Commander E. G. Martin's onion soup, the object of frequent praise aboard his famous cutter *Jolie Brise*, which won the first Fastnet Race in 1925. It's delicious and easy to prepare, even in rough weather on a single-burner stove.

"Place four medium-large onions, peeled and cut into quarters, into a covered saucepan with 3 to 4 cups cold water," said Commander Martin. "Add 2 tablespoons Bovril (or other strong beef stock), 4 ounces butter, a dessert spoonful of Lea and Perrins's Worcestershire sauce, a little black pepper, and (when the cooking is nearly done) a small glass of sherry or rather more white wine. Boil gently for 30 minutes or until the onions have fallen to pieces and are soft, stirring occasionally."

If you find that recipe too glutinous for your modern arteries, you can reduce the butter to 2 ounces and substitute 5 beef stock cubes for the Bovril without doing grievous harm.

Saltwater supplies to the galley faucet are often provided from a tee-connection to the engine's cooling water line; but some of us have been aboard boats where the engine sucked in air through the faucet instead of water from the sea, unless the faucet was plugged shut with a glob of plastic putty. This was inconvenient, because the faucet could not be used while the engine was running. It was also dangerous: If someone forgot to plug the faucet, the engine would soon be cooking along with supper.

If you arrange a saltwater connection from the engine supply in this manner to avoid having yet another hole through the hull, add a stopcock in the line to the faucet. You'll have to open it and shut it when you want to use the faucet; but it beats searching for the glob of putty and wondering whether it has been sucked back into the line to clog the innards of the engine.

Fridges and Freezers

You don't need a fridge or a freezer to cross an ocean, or even to sail around the world. If you can train yourself to do without ice for your sojourn on board, you will be a much happier and more relaxed person. The bliss when you finally step ashore and down that first freezing drink will rank as one of the great experiences of your life.

While the majority of sailboats cruising around the world do not carry refrigeration, the majority of American boats do. But refrigerators and freezers that work so well on shore have two disadvantages on small boats. They use a lot of power, and they break down more frequently because they work in such atrocious conditions. These faults make the cost and bother of refrigeration unacceptable to many sailors from Europe and countries in the Southern Hemisphere, whose cultures do not center on ice cream and cool drinks to the extent that America's does. If they can't have ice, they don't miss it. Lucky them.

But North Americans have an ongoing affair with ice: Like most affairs, it's costly. Whether or not you should invest in refrigeration depends (a) on your ongoing ability to pay for it and keep the machinery maintained, and (b) on the reason for your voyaging.

If you are sailing with a fixed-term plan, say to circumnavigate the world in three years, and you don't want any delays in godforsaken places while refrigerator parts are rushed to you by ostrich or camel, you may well opt to play the Spartan and go without ice. On the other hand, if your plan is to live aboard and simply "go cruising," that is, to wander the high seas like a gypsy caravan, wandering from fleshpot to fleshpot, time without end, then you probably need ice, and you probably have the time and money to spend on it.

For the price of about 760 nicely chilled beers you can buy a 12-volt refrigeration system with a freezer plate to fit an 8-cubic-foot (226-liter) ice-box. It will draw nearly 6 amps at full load, which means you can run it flat out for about 7 hours on a 100-amp-hour battery before you need to recharge the battery. (Remember the 40 percent rule?) In practice (because it's not running the compressor all the time), you'd get refrigeration for about 20 hours. Maybe. And then the battery would need to be recharged.

For the price of about 1,030 beers you can buy what is probably the most popular system of all among American long-distance cruisers: the eutectic-plate, or holding-plate, system. This provides super-cool freezing of a metal plate by means of a compressor coupled to the boat's engine. This system cools a holding plate from room temperature to –20°F (–29°C) in about 45 minutes. In normal use, the compressor needs to be run only for one or two hours each day.

Unless you can install these systems yourself

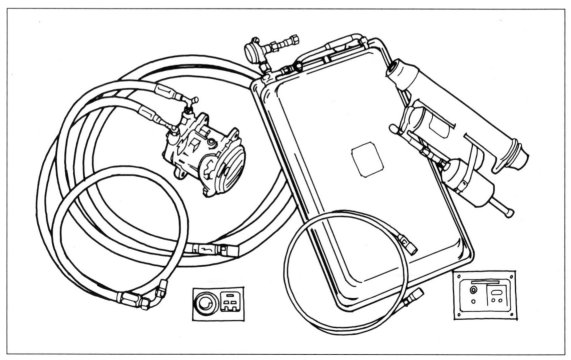

A holding-plate refrigeration kit from Technautics. This Islander model has a compressor driven by the engine that will cool the holding plate from room temperature to –20°F (–29°C) in 45 minutes.

(some are designed for owner installation), you should add quite a few more beers to the cost of your ice cubes. Some manufacturers, anticipating the inevitable, supply what they call "cruising kits" for their cooling systems. They cost the equivalent of another 45 beers and contain the bits and pieces you need for routine maintenance. When something happens that's not routine—and you can be sure that it eventually will—you're on your own.

There are small household-type fridges that run on the heat from a gas or kerosene flame, and you might be tempted to buy one because they are very efficient. Resist the temptation, however, because the dangers associated with a constantly burning open flame on a small boat are too great to live with. Don't try to rationalize this by using the fridge only in port where it's calm: You'll still

be leaving a flame burning when you go ashore. It's just not worth the risk, and your insurance company will confirm that. There is, it seems, no cheap, simple, long-lasting, and reliable way to make ice on a small boat.

It's true that in the relentless heat of the tropics nothing brings greater joy to the heart of a hot and sweaty sailor than the sound of ice tinkling in a tall glass. But it's too bad that it so often has to come from a friendly neighbor whose freezer, by some miracle, is still working.

Galley Straps

You'll see galley safety straps for sale in marine stores. The idea is that the duty cook can lean back against one, or even sit on it, to gain some stability when the boat is lurching at sea.

However, some sailors don't think it's a good idea to have the cook pinned in like that: It's then impossible to free oneself quickly and leap out of the way of a spilled pan of boiling water. Experience is the only thing that will tell you whether you need galley straps on your boat.

Some boats have a restraining bar instead, which the cook leans against. To be any safer than a strap, however, a restraining bar must be carefully designed for each particular galley.

Incidentally, it's standard practice on some boats to make cooks wear a plastic rainsuit top and pants for protection against scalds, no matter how hot and uncomfortable it makes them. Cooks are particularly vulnerable when the boat is well heeled over and the galley stove is higher than they are. In theory, nobody should have to work under those conditions, but in practice, when you're beating through the trade winds and stuck on the same tack for two weeks at a time, you have no choice.

Fish Tahitienne

Your friends won't believe they're eating "raw" fish when they try this delicious appetizer for the first time. It's wonderful with almost any kind of freshly caught fish, and you can easily make it at sea.

Place the fish—either in fillets or cut into small cubes—in a plastic container with a lid. Sprinkle it generously with lemon juice (fresh or bottled) and leave it to marinate for an hour or two with the lid on. Then add some olive oil and pepper, and let it marinate for two more hours.

You'll know when the fish is "cooked." It will appear a solid white, with no trace of transparency. The lemon juice will have cured it right through and firmed it up to a wonderful chewiness. It takes longer than cooking, but the flavor is tangy and delicate. If you have a fridge, it will keep for several days. Otherwise, eat it within 24 hours (see also the recipe for Ceviche, later in this chapter, page 131).

Hot Water

Hot water for the shower is one of those little luxuries that compensate for the hard times on a small boat. If you don't have a shower, you prob-

Ceviche

In a port where you can lay hands on some chili peppers and cilantro (coriander leaves), try this tasty Mexican version of the Fish Tahitienne appetizer, called Ceviche.

Ingredients

1 pound fresh fish, clams, mussels, or scallops
¼ cup lemon juice
1 tablespoon green chili pepper (jalapeño) diced, with seeds removed
1 tablespoon finely chopped cilantro
¼ teaspoon powdered ginger (optional)

Method

Cut meat into small cubes. Then place in a plastic container with a lid and sprinkle on the powdered ginger. Marinate in the lemon juice for three to four hours, with the lid on, and stir occasionally.

If you have a fridge, you can keep it there for several days: It will be improving all the time. Otherwise, as with Fish Tahitienne, eat the Ceviche within 24 hours. You'll find this to be a very popular appetizer in warm climates when you invite friends on board for a drink.

ably don't need a water heater. And even if you do have a shower, you can boil water in a pan on the stove, or you fill a black plastic bag with water, leave it on deck, and let the sun, if any, do the work for you.

But if you're going to run the engine for a couple of hours each day to charge batteries and keep the icebox cold, you might as well run the hot exhaust water through a heat exchanger that will warm up a tank of fresh water for you.

You can buy ready-made tanks with capacities from 6 to 20 gallons (20 to 75 liters) that use shoreside power when you're at the dock and the engine's cooling water when you're under way. They cost from 100 to 190 beers, not including installation charges.

Ovens

An oven is almost essential if you're planning to live aboard your boat for a long time, despite the fact that it takes up a lot of space and despite the fact that it's empty most of its life.

As to the latter criticism, you can use it during an ocean passage to store pots and pans or almost anything else that takes your fancy, though on those rare occasions when you want to use the oven at sea, you'll have to unpack and repack, which might be sufficient nuisance to dissuade you from using the oven in the first place.

The smaller the boat, the less likely it is to have an oven, but a boat of, say, 30 feet or more on deck should have room for an oven. The cook will be very glad to have it aboard: There is only so much you can do with a stove-top range before the crew begins to complain.

Some very attractive propane stoves with ovens are available from marine stores, most of them with thermostatically controlled ovens and piezo-electric ignition. They come in stainless steel, complete with gimbals and safety sea rails to stop things from falling off the stove top. They cost about 330 beers.

An alternative for a small boat is a two-burner propane cooktop with a broiler tucked in underneath; complete with gimbals and pot holders, they cost about 230 beers.

You can still find kerosene and diesel stoves with ovens, if you look hard enough. They have many fans among the deep-sea cruising fraternity, but if you care a jot about keeping the cook happy, nothing beats a propane stove and oven for sheer ease of working.

A large boat with a separate generator can run a 120-volt or 240-volt electric stove, which is also very convenient; but in the absence of a generator, don't be tempted to run an electric stove with an inverter coupled to a couple of house batteries. The draw is from 200 to 300 amps at 12 volts, which will flatten your batteries in a matter of minutes if it doesn't fry them immediately.

Fresh Sprouts

On a long voyage, when you've used up all your fresh salads and are craving something green, fresh, and crisp, sprouts are the answer. They're a wonderful source of vitamins B and C.

Put a heaped teaspoon of dry alfalfa seeds in a wide-mouthed glass quart jar. Cover the seeds with lukewarm water and let them soak overnight.

Place some cheesecloth or an old nylon stocking over the mouth of the jar, secure it with a rubber band, and drain off the water. Rinse the seeds with warm water again, and drain again.

Now prop the jar up at a 45-degree angle in the sink, mouth downward, so the seeds will continue to drain. Cover the jar to keep most of the light out.

Rinse the sprouts two or three times a day to keep them damp, but not flooded. Within three or four days, the seeds will have sprouted and developed two yellow leaves.

Now expose them to as much light as you can give them without leaving them in direct sunshine, which will dry them out and kill them.

When the leaves turn green, the sprouts are ready. By this time, the jar will be crammed full of crisp, moist sprouts at their most nutritious. They'll keep for a day or two in the jar, and three or four days in a fridge, but if you don't hide them from the crew and ration them, they'll disappear in a flash.

Mung beans also sprout very successfully, and you can also try adzuki and wheat, which are sold in bulk as whole-wheat berries. (For more on sprouts, see June Vigor's Sea-Tested Tips in chapter 18, page 212.)

Paper Towels

Paper towels handily placed on a roller where the ship's cook can easily grab them to mop up spills or swab out a frying pan are a great convenience. They are so valuable in the galley that their use must be deliberately restricted on board, especially by nongalley crew who tend to grab them in passing for blowing their noses, wiping their hands, or cleaning their glasses.

They are bulky, so you can't carry an endless store of them. You also have the problem of getting rid of them. It is certainly legal to throw them overboard when you're at least three miles from shore, but anyone who cares about upsetting the earth's ecology, or merely littering a pristine ocean, will have qualms of conscience in doing so. And yet, who wants to cram landfills with bulky paper towels?

Be firm. Let the cook be in charge of the paper towels, and let the cook guard them jealously, for the only reason they are on board at all is to make the cook's unenviable job a little less onerous. As for the rest of the crew, remind them of the existence of handkerchiefs; and remind them—if necessary—that handkerchiefs can be washed when they're soiled, and used again.

Pressure Cookers

The smaller the boat, the greater the need for a pressure cooker. It cooks food quicker and uses less water. For instance, you can roast a chicken in 15 minutes or whip up chili con carne in just five minutes. You're more likely to have chili than chicken on a small boat in mid-ocean. But the point is that quicker cooking times will enable you to use less fuel.

There is another trick that pressure cookers can perform, too, which is especially useful on small boats without ovens: You can bake in them.

Some of us who have crossed more than one ocean in small, ovenless boats have been vastly impressed with the ability of pressure cookers to act as tiny ovens. In fact, the mouth starts watering at the mere recollection of how a new-baked loaf of bread smells and tastes on a calm day in mid-ocean.

You need to remove the weight valve from the lid of the cooker. If you have one of the new cookers with spring-loaded thermo-valves, you

Pressure-Cooker Bread

Ingredients
3 cups (750 ml) flour
1 tablespoon cooking oil
1 tablespoon sugar
1 teaspoon salt

½ teaspoon sugar
½ packet (⅛-ounce or 3.5 grams) active dry yeast
1 cup warm water

Method
Pour warm water (105 to 115°F or 40 to 46°C) in a bowl. A ceramic bowl is best, but plastic will suffice. Add ½ teaspoon sugar and sprinkle yeast on top. Stir, and leave for a minute or two; then see if the yeast is starting to work.

If the yeast is foaming, add 2 cups of flour to the mixture and stir in 1 tablespoon sugar, 1 tablespoon cooking oil, and 1 teaspoon salt.

Add the rest of the flour slowly until you can knead the dough with the palm of your hand. Knead for 10 minutes. Add flour until the dough no longer sticks to your hands and is looking smooth and satiny.

Lift the dough and put 1 teaspoon cooking oil in the bottom of the bowl. Replace the dough, then flop it over, so that all sides of the dough are covered with oil, which will prevent it from drying out on the surface. Cover the bowl with a clean cloth, and set it aside for one hour in a warm place to let the yeast rise.

After 60 minutes (or when the dough has doubled in size) knead it a second time, punching it down for about two minutes. Then replace the cloth and leave the dough to rise again in a warm place for 45 minutes. This rising will be complete when a dent remains in the dough after you have prodded it with a finger.

Now oil the inside of a 4- or 6-quart (4- to 6-liter) pressure cooker and place the dough inside. Keep the cooker covered and in a warm place; then let the dough rise for a further 60 minutes, or until it has doubled in size again.

Now place the pressure cooker on the stove top with its lid on, without the pressure regulator. You do not want pressure to build up: The pot is simply acting as a tiny oven.

In a proper oven, you would cook the dough for about an hour at 400° F. With a pressure cooker for an oven, however, you start off with a medium-low flame. You'll see steam starting to come out of the hole in the lid after 20 or 30 minutes, and that's your signal to reduce the heat to a low simmer for another 30 minutes. The bread can easily burn now, so use a metal heat dissipater over the stove flame if necessary.

After the final 30 minutes, turn the bread out of the pressure cooker and tap the bottom. If it's firm and sounds hollow, the bread is done. If it feels soggy and sounds dull, put it back in the cooker and give it another 10 or 15 minutes.

simply need to ensure that pressure will not build up during baking. And you'll need a heat diffuser of some sort if your galley stove produces a particularly fierce flame, even on the low setting. In the olden days, asbestos pads were used for this purpose, and they proved to be very efficient. Today's stainless steel diffusers, which are available from hardware stores or camping gear stores, don't work quite as well, but probably offer the benefit of longer life for the cook, if that's important to you.

A modern, 4-quart (4 liter), thermo-valve pressure cooker in gleaming surgical stainless steel costs the equivalent of about 64 beers at a marine store. It's not cheap, but by way of consolation you'll find you can also use it as a standard saucepan, which you need to have on board anyway.

Pressurized Water Systems

A pressurized water system is a dangerous thing to have in the galley of a seagoing boat because

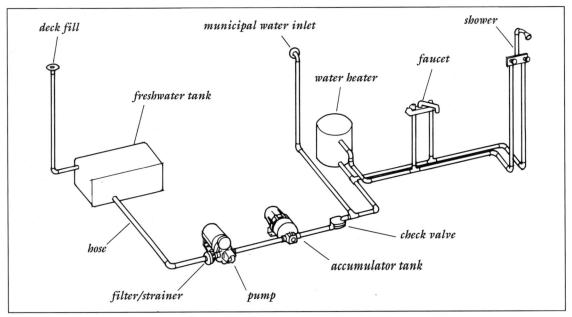

A pressurized freshwater system. The accumulator tank is a small reservoir of air under pressure that absorbs shocks in the water system and reduces the number of times the pump turns itself on and off.

it continually tempts the cook to be a water wastrel.

In theory, it's more convenient to get fresh water by turning a faucet on than by pumping it by hand or foot. But in practice, one tends to leave the faucet on that little bit longer than is really necessary, or to turn on the tap to wash clean a plate that could have been dry-cleaned with a paper towel. These little dribbles add up to a lot of water on an ocean crossing.

The physical act of pumping acts as a psychological barrier to water wastage. Every time you have to use the pump when you are hundreds of miles out at sea, you are reminded just how precious that fresh water is, and how finite the supply. While manual pumps tend to conserve water, pressurized systems waste it—no matter how disciplined you and your crew may be.

Then, too, there is always the risk of a leaking

or broken pipe or fitting, which could lead to the automatic emptying of your entire freshwater supply into the bilges or overboard, unless you have carefully arranged for separate tanks with shut-off valves between them. It's not very likely to happen aboard your well-appointed vessel, naturally, but it has happened before aboard other boats. Without doubt, it will do so again.

Pressurized systems are usually served by electric diaphragm pumps that are activated in one of two ways. There is either a switch attached to the faucet itself, which you must turn on and off. Or there is an automatic switch built into the plumbing system that senses changes in water pressure; it switches itself on when the pressure drops and off when it builds up again. With the latter system, you only need to turn the faucet on—and the pump, sensing the release of pressure, will send more water gushing your way.

There is another form of water delivery that combines a swivelling faucet with a built-in electric pump that you switch on and off as needed. It could not have been better designed to make the purists shudder, because its total function seems to be to replace the simple manual pump with an expensive electric motor and pump and thus save you the muscular fatigue of exercising your forearm for a few seconds. This is not the place for moral judgments, however, so you will have to decide for yourself whether or not you need such a pump when you're fitting out your boat to cross an ocean. But here's a hint: The answer is no.

Sinks

Sinks on small sailboats are never big enough to satisfy the cook, so there is no point in offering any advice other than to fit the biggest stainless steel sink you can, and preferably two, for easier washing up.

But the placement of the sinks can make life interesting for the cook. As the boat heels over, an outboard sink (that is, one near the hull) will often dip below the level of the seawater outside. This not only means that it won't drain. In an extreme case, it may allow water to travel back up into the sink or start a siphon action with the potential to sink the boat if the sink drain plug isn't firmly in place.

The farther inboard (toward the middle of the boat) you can place your sinks, the happier the cook will be and the safer your boat will be.

Vacuum Flasks

You can get a lot of pleasure from a little vacuum flask. Filled right after the evening meal, before the galley has been shut down for the night, it provides hot soup, chocolate, or coffee for the night watch on deck. And it saves the effort and disturbance of firing up the stove down below.

A larger flask will also cook meals. Oatmeal porridge, for example, will cook itself overnight

Beer Bread

Ingredients
3 cups self-raising flour
12 fluid-ounce (355 ml) bottle of light beer
½ teaspoon salt
2 teaspoons sugar

Method
It doesn't get much simpler than this. Mix the flour, salt, and sugar. Add beer and stir thoroughly. You can mix in herbs such as sage, if you like. About a half-teaspoon of crumbled dried sage leaves would be about right.

Without waiting for the mixture to rise, scoop it into an oiled bread pan or an old coffee tin, sprinkle grated cheese on top if you like, and bake at 400°F (200°C) for 1 hour (or until done).

The finished crust resembles that of crunchy scones. But after a few bland and breadless days at sea, the smell and taste is delicious.

Incidentally, be sure to use a light-colored beer for this bread. A dark beer will give it a strong, bitter flavor.

The sugar is included to mask some of the bitterness of the hopped beer. If you'd prefer a flavor more like sourdough, leave out half or all of the sugar.

and keep itself warm for a hearty dawn breakfast. There are no doubt many other meals that a wily cook could prepare in a similar fashion.

Washing Up

A good rule is that the cook should never have to wash up. If you apply this rule, you will unfortunately find that it encourages the cook to have no conscience about dirtying pots. He or she will use every pot and pan, and every knife and fork and spoon you possess, with gay abandon, feeling nothing for the poor dish washer. Nevertheless, it is very important to keep the cook happy. An angry cook is a dangerous animal aboard a small boat.

If you are singlehanding, you will be a lot less profligate with the utensils, and you will quickly learn which meals require the least washing up afterward. And there is always the singlehander's washing machine. Simply shove all the dirty dishes, pots, and pans into an orange bag or a netting sack, throw them overboard, and let them trail and churn in your wake for a few hours. If the sharks don't swallow the sack, you'll save yourself a lot of work.

Water Purification

Even if you have a watermaker on board, there will probably be times when you'll have to top up your freshwater supplies from sources that will make you pause to think.

If you consider that experts now consider *every* source of fresh water in the United States to be contaminated (and that includes all of our wilderness areas), you can judge for yourself the odds that you're going to find uncontaminated water in less developed countries.

City water supplies that have been specially treated ought to be safe enough, but even in the United States, cases of contamination crop up often enough to make you wonder just how effective wholesale treatment actually is.

So the safest attitude to adopt is that all water you bring aboard needs to be purified before you can use it. You might want to consult your family doctor about this before you leave home shores, but make sure he or she understands that the safest method of all—boiling for several minutes—is not practical on a small boat, except for very small amounts.

Outdoor recreation stores sell various kinds of filters and tablets that will kill and/or remove microbial and chemical adulterants, but they are usually packaged in small sizes suitable for backpackers.

Luckily, household bleach does a pretty good job of cleaning up dirty water. The rule of thumb is to add one teaspoon (5 ml) of 5.25-percent liquid chlorine bleach, such as Clorox, to every 15 gallons (55 liters) of water. This is much more than you'll find in any public drinking water, which contains about one part of chlorine to a million parts of water; but it's easier for you to calculate. The chlorine will do its work within about 10 minutes, then break down after being exposed to light and air.

The smell and taste of chlorine disappears with time; if you can leave the filler cap off your tank for 30 minutes or so, most of the chlorine will dissipate. Be cautious when you take your first taste of the chlorinated water. If the chlorine content is still too high, you'll burn your mouth and throat. A good way to test it is to pour a little in the palm of your hand and sniff it. If it smells no stronger of chlorine than does the normal city household supply, it will be ready to drink.

Unfortunately, this is not a permanent treatment. Your newly sterilized water is now once again vulnerable to infestation by algae and contamination by bacteria. But any stored water that is open to the air suffers from the same handicap. The answer is to repeat the chlorine treatment at appropriate intervals, according to your particular circumstances.

When you're cleaning and flushing a water tank, add one cupful of 5.25-percent liquid bleach for every 50 gallons (190 liters) of water. Pump it through all your pipes and faucets within a few minutes—before it loses its potency—and make sure the area is well ventilated to carry off any accumulated fumes, which you should not breathe.

There are a couple of caveats to be aware of. The first is that chlorine corrodes stainless steel. If you have stainless steel water tanks or fittings, don't seal chlorinated water in them. If you allow the chlorine to break down quickly by leaving the filler caps or vents open for 30 minutes, there should be no trouble.

The second caveat is that you should never add bleach to tanks connected to a reverse osmosis watermaker: The chlorine will damage it. Disconnect the watermaker when you're purifying your water supply, and reconnect it only after you're sure the chlorine has dissipated.

Water Needs

You can live very well on half a gallon (1.9 liters) of fresh water a day, even in the tropics, if you don't waste it on such frills as washing yourself, but most authorities advise you to carry a gallon (3.8 liters) per person for every day you plan to be at sea, which automatically provides an emergency reserve.

If you want to earn points for your Black Box, you should divide your water supply among two or more tanks or containers in case of leaks or contamination.

Good water will remain sweet for at least six months in sealed containers, provided they are not filled completely and are stowed out of the sun.

To save water for drinking and the needs of the cook, most sailors in the tropics wash or shower in salt water, then rinse themselves with a mere lick of fresh water. A fine spray from a plastic bottle that used to contain window cleaner will do the job nicely if you wipe off the layer of dew with a washcloth.

You can shower on deck in tropical rainstorms, of course, but the water can sometimes be surprisingly cold. Just be sure the rain won't quit after you are all soaped up.

All ocean voyagers should have some method of catching rainwater. Some cruisers catch water in buckets placed underneath the gooseneck of the main boom, with the boom lofted slightly by the topping lift. The standing instruction here is to throw away the first few bucketfuls until all the salt and grime has washed off the sail, but in practice, most of us take so long to find the bucket that the water is running clean and pure by the time we are organized.

You could fruitfully spend some of those boring hours on night watches thinking up other ways to catch rain. You could line the cockpit with thin spinnaker cloth, for example, and a plastic through-hull fitting at the lowest point could lead fresh water down below. It's possible for a singlehander to catch all the ship's freshwater requirements from rainwater, which is probably the purest supply available anywhere.

Water Tanks

You should have two or more fixed water tanks capable of holding a combined amount equal to a gallon (3.8 liters) per person per day for the

Survival Rations

If you ever have to take to the lifeboat you will need about ⅔ pint (315 ml) of fresh water and 600 calories (2,500 kilojoules) of food per person per day. That is about the minimum needed to sustain life in an emergency. You can get the calories from 5 to 6 ounces (140 to 170 g) of hard candy, sugar, or fatty cookies.

Floating Fresh Water

Fresh water floats on top of salt water for a long time, until wave motion stirs things up. So if you're ever adrift in a lifeboat, you will find the whole surface of the sea is fresh water after a tropical downpour in a calm. Scoop the top inch (25 mm) or so into your dinghy or raft before it mixes with the salt water.

length of time you propose to be at sea, unless you're planning to sail around the world nonstop, in which case you'll have to use a watermaker or catch rainwater. If the tanks are interconnected, be sure to place stopcocks in the lines so that a leak in one won't empty the other as well.

Make certain before you sail that your tanks are full. That important detail has been overlooked more than once in the last-minute flurry of departure.

Try to keep a week's supply of fresh water in jerry jugs or one-liter plastic pop bottles, in addition to your fixed tankage. Leave a small air space at the top of each container: If you have to throw them overboard as you abandon ship, they will float and you can retrieve them.

Most tanks on production boats are made of fiberglass, but tanks of polyethylene, aluminum, or stainless steel are also suitable. Marine or outdoor quality plywood, sheathed with fiberglass, makes good water tanks, too. Galvanized steel tanks are best avoided because they rust easily if they're nicked inside.

If you use flexible water tanks of nylon lined with polyvinyl chloride (PVC), they will fit themselves into all sorts of oddly shaped places, but be very careful that they don't chafe through as the boat moves.

Watermakers

For information on watermakers, see chapter 8 (page 94).

Working Surfaces

If there is any way you can add to the number of working surfaces in the galley, you will gladden the heart of the cook. Few small sailboats have sufficient space in the galley where food can be prepared or hot pans put down—even temporarily. Many of us have stepped down from the cockpit into a bowl of delicious something-or-other injudiciously placed on a companionway step by a harassed cook trying to dish up four suppers simultaneously.

Even a couple of square feet of plywood, hinged and arranged to flap up when needed, or to slide away like a drawer, improves the galley considerably, especially if you furnish it with deep fiddles to prevent things from flying off when the boat lurches.

Good hot food is important to keep the crew fit and morale high, particularly in bad weather. The preparation of meals therefore ranks as a safety feature, and it should be accorded the importance it deserves.

THINK INVERTED

If your boat turns upside down:

- Can your cupboard doors break open?
- Will the stove stay put? What will happen to the boiling water?
- Are there glass food and beverage containers that could break loose, splinter, and slash bare feet?
- Will the gas switch itself off, or will it fill the cabin with an explosive mixture?

CHAPTER 12

Creature Comforts

When applied to small sailing boats at sea, the word comfort is a relative term. On your boat, you may experience more comfort or less comfort than another person on another boat; but you'll never experience comfort as the word is understood on land.

Creature comforts at sea are directly related to the size of the boat and the amount of money available. The more money you're prepared to spend, the more comfortable you're likely to be.

In the first place, a big boat is more comfortable than a small one; no boat smaller than about 45 feet (13.7 m) in overall length is going to have an easy motion in heavy weather. In the second place, a big boat also has the capacity to carry fuel and generators to power the kind of gadgets that make life much more pleasant on land: freezers, fridges, microwave ovens, air conditioning, hot water showers, computers, satellite television, and telephone service to the whole wide world.

But even on small boats, it's possible to improve comfort by degrees. A little shade to keep you out of the broiling tropical sun; a little curtain to give you some privacy in your bunk; an overhead handrail to grab while you're crossing the cabin. All these small comforts add up.

Air-Conditioning

This is one of the greatest comforts of all; but air-conditioning is a mixed blessing. You don't need air-conditioning to sail over the horizon, yet it does allow you to get a good night's sleep when you're anchored in some tropical lagoon. It's wonderful to feel cool and refreshed in steamy weather, but air-conditioning also makes the heat feel much worse when you step outside and into the cockpit—so much so that you could end up lurking in your nice cool cabin and never go ashore at all.

Air-conditioning is the ultimate luxury on a boat of any size, and it demands a lot of power at high voltage—too much for most small boats. Cruisers with planned itineraries usually consider the expense, maintenance, and noise of air-conditioning to be unwarranted, but permanent liveaboards often think differently. Some even go so far as to enclose their cockpits with plastic screens so their "verandas" can be air-conditioned, too.

You can buy an air conditioner for a small boat for about 600 beers, to which you'll have to add the cost of installation, ducting, through-hull fittings, a seawater strainer, hose, and hose clamps. And if you don't already have the generating facilities to keep your air conditioner running when you're not plugged in to 115-volts or 240-volts at a marina, you'll have to add a few hundred beers for those, too.

A more expensive version of the air conditioner has a reverse cycle unit that heats as well as cools, drawing warmth from seawater when air temperatures are low.

It's the opinion of some cruisers that air conditioners on yachts are not only more trouble than they're worth, but that they are contrary to the spirit of adventure that attracts most people to small-boat cruising in the first place. What, after all, is adventure without a little hardship? Hardship sweetens adventure, so that we remember it and savor it when we are safely back home.

So live dangerously. Get hot. Sweat a little. You can boast about it later.

Biminis

Those of us who have suffered heatstroke on a small boat during an ocean crossing are all in favor of Bimini tops that provide shade from the searing trade-wind sun. Not all boats can fit dedicated Biminis, though, because the main boom has to be high enough to clear the Bimini, and the Bimini has to be high enough to clear you when you're standing up. A fold-down Bimini also requires a messy clutter of aluminum tubes and hardware that can be a source of intense irritation to those who believe sailboats ought to combine elegance with simplicity.

A better arrangement for cruising boats is a removable Bimini awning, attached to the companionway dodger with Velcro or a zipper, extending aft to the boom gallows (see the section on Biminis in chapter 6, page 55.) If you've been resisting fitting boom gallows, this is just another reason why you should take the plunge. Noel Coward was right. Only mad dogs and Englishmen go out in the midday sun.

Bunks

No matter how hard you try, or how long you practice, you never seem to be able to get comfortable in a bunk that's too short for you.

The minimum bunk length that designers strive for is 6 feet, 4 inches (1.9 m), but all too often production boats are made with smaller bunks because of customer pressure for the maximum number of berths.

Don't buy a boat if there isn't at least one bunk in the main cabin or aft cabin that fits you. The only exception to this rule is where a saloon berth abuts a locker that you could break into for a foot well. You can stow your bedding in there when you're not using the bunk.

A bunk that is too wide is uncomfortable at sea because it offers no lateral support when the boat is rolling. The maximum width for the average person should be about 21 inches (535 mm), though it can taper from 13 inches (330 mm) at the foot end, out to 21 inches (535 mm) at mid-thigh, and back to 16 inches (405 mm) at the

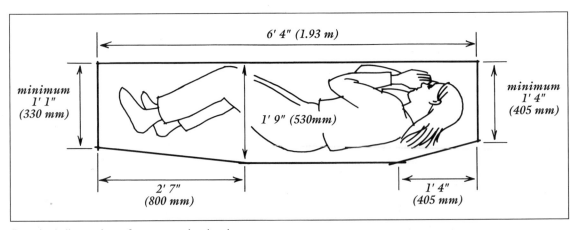

Practical dimensions for a seagoing bunk

head end. You might find this restrictive at first, but you'll soon get used to it.

You need a lee cloth to keep you in your bunk at sea. The few boatbuilders who do supply them often use sailcloth for the purpose; but if solid sailcloth makes you claustrophobic, use net instead. A lee cloth is usually fastened by a lengthwise batten screwed or bolted to the bunk frame beneath the mattress, close to the outer edge of the bunk. It is held in place by three or four lines lashed or clipped to eye straps firmly bolted overhead. When it's not in use, the lee cloth lies flat beneath the mattress.

Mattresses for double berths should be made in two lengths, with a lee cloth brought up through the split between the two. This will save you from rolling steeply downhill across a wide expanse of bed and crashing into the hull at breakneck speed.

Cabin Heating

If you plan to cruise in cold climates, you'll appreciate a cabin heater. It's possible to do without one, but heaters dispense cheer and comfort out of all proportion to their size. When the weather is cold and wet, and everything in the cabin is dripping with condensation, warm dry heat down below is a wonderful blessing.

The size and type of heater you need depends, as usual, on the size and type of your boat. Some of us have cruised in boats so small that a Coleman pressure kerosene lamp was adequate to heat the cabin and dry out our soaked underwear as well. But the majority of cruising boats would be better served by a compact heater permanently mounted on a bulkhead.

Such heaters will burn propane, diesel fuel, kerosene, or solid fuel—charcoal, cardboard packaging, coal, wood pellets, and any kind of driftwood you can scrounge from the shoreline.

If you have a diesel engine, a diesel heater is a good idea. Like a kerosene heater, a diesel heater can be fed by a pressurized fuel tank, usually

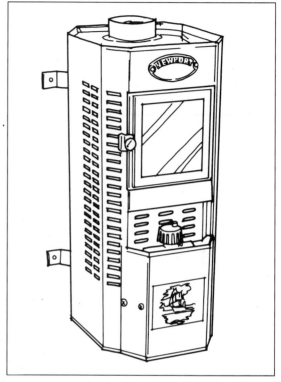

This "shippy" little cabin heater by Dickinson Newport mounts on a bulkhead. It has a glass door and burns diesel or kerosene fuel.

holding about 2 gallons, but many cruisers prefer to raise the fuel tank above the heater and let gravity take care of delivering the fuel.

Some bulkhead heaters come with glass fire doors to create a cozy fireplace atmosphere, and they all have a good "shippy" look about them. They range in price from 120 beers to 240 beers, and you'll need to vent them through the cabin-top with a stainless steel flue and deck-pipe cap, or Charley Noble (which will cost you a few more six-packs).

Don't be tempted to use a household kerosene heater. They are too easily tipped over on a boat. And while alcohol heaters are small and cheap, they put out comparatively little heat and are very expensive to run for long periods.

Heating Needs

You can estimate pretty closely the hourly amount of heating you need for your cabin in British Thermal Units (Btu/hour) by multiplying the volume in cubic feet by a number varying from 10 (warm climates) to 20 (cold climates).

For example, the number for southern California would probably be 12 or 13; Florida would rate 10; Washington state would rate about 15 or 16; and New England would be about 20.

For example, let's say you have a cabin measuring 10 feet by 8 feet by 6 feet, or 480 cubic feet. If you live in San Diego (13), you'll need a heater capable of putting out $480 \times 13 = 6,240$ Btu/hour. If you live in Maine (20), your heater should be capable of producing $480 \times 20 = 9,600$ Btu/hour. (Multiply cubic meters by 35.31 to convert to cubic feet. Multiply Btu by 1.05 to convert to kilojoules.)

A major problem with household kerosene heaters and free-standing alcohol heaters is that they are unvented. Both give off the silent killer gas carbon monoxide, and can only be used in a cabin that is so well ventilated that it draws in a constant stream of freezing cold fresh air from outside—which rather defeats the object of heating the cabin in the first place.

The dangers of carbon monoxide can hardly be overstated. It has been the cause of many deaths on boats as well as a host of close calls. Even such sensible cruisers as Lin and Larry Pardey nearly managed to kill themselves when they left a flame burning in a cabin closed tightly against cold weather.

Any burning flame will produce carbon dioxide. Even if your heater is vented, a small break in the flue will allow the gas to escape into the cabin. You can't see it, and you can't smell it. It will just peacefully put you to sleep, and that will be the end of your cruise. So, as was suggested in chapter 8 on safety, be aware of the danger and invest in a carbon monoxide detector for every separate sleeping area (see page 75 for more on detectors).

Cockpit Cushions

When you're on watch in the cockpit for four hours or more at a time, the seats start to get hard. All-weather cushions ease the discomfort in the nether regions, but they come with their own set of problems.

Yachting author Don Casey describes some of them in his book, *This Old Boat.* "My original experience with cockpit cushions was a typical set constructed of polyurethane foam covered with reinforced vinyl (Naugahyde) and closed with a metal zipper. A more worthless combination I cannot imagine. While the vinyl was ineffective at keeping the water out, it was great at keeping it in; within days the foam was full of water and was never again dry. The soaked cushions were as heavy as lead and only slightly softer. The always-clammy vinyl was uncomfortable to sit on, impossible to sleep on, and a ready source of second-degree burns in summertime."

If you cruise the hot and humid trade wind routes, you will also find that sitting on vinyl-covered cushions promotes the dreaded "botty" rot, or diaper rash. You will probably end up as Casey did, throwing the whole mess overboard.

Luckily, there is a viable alternative. Closed-cell foam, 2 inches (50 mm) thick, covered with a light-colored acrylic canvas such as Sunbrella does not absorb water. The cover will get soaking wet from rain or spray, but it will quickly dry out again.

It's more sensible to make a full-length cockpit cushion in two or three pieces, because a single piece is an unwieldy beast. But you have to make sure the three pieces together fit snugly between the end of the cockpit and the companionway bulkhead; otherwise they'll separate and develop uncomfortable gaps when you lie on them. It's hardly necessary to say, of course, that the zipper should be corrosion-proof: The YKK #10 Delrin zipper is the industry standard.

Closed-cell foam cushions make handy life preservers for someone who has fallen overboard, and you'll find it easier and faster to throw the smaller portions into the water.

Incidentally, closed-cell foam isn't as comfortable as the open-cell polyurethane foam used for bunk mattresses because it's not as "springy." It tends to pack down after a while and get hard, which means you'll have to shift position now and then or swap cushions, while the foam recovers.

Fans for Cooling

Electric fans can make the difference between deep sleep and wakeful misery in a hot, humid, airless bunk in the tropics. It's bliss to feel that cool air streaming all over your sweaty body.

There are many 12-volt fans on the market, but the guiding principle is that you'll be better off with a powerful fan quietly working at half speed than a puny little fan working its guts out and vibrating noisily at full speed. Be cautious about buying any fan that draws less than 1 or 2 amps at 12 volts.

Many cruisers find it's not necessary to have an oscillating fan. A fan blowing in a steady direction sets up its own air currents, and it blows on you all the time instead of merely giving you a tantalizing puff every now and then. Most fans on the market are designed to oscillate, but you can turn the oscillation off and set them in one position.

Food and Drink

The moment you get over that initial feeling of queasiness after leaving port, food and drink suddenly assume an exaggerated importance, and as the voyage wears on, you start to look forward to mealtimes with great anticipation. It's not that the food is more delicious or better prepared at sea than it is on land—usually the exact opposite is true—but simply that you strangely feel more ravenous most of the time.

Meals also serve the important purpose of breaking up the working day, and they are often the only times when most of the crew can get together for a brief period to indulge in a little civilized conversation.

The wise boat cook will therefore prepare larger-than-normal helpings of food and try to provide a wide variety of meals—say 10 main meal recipes, and five or six different breakfasts. A clever cook, or one seeking favors from the crew, will also ensure that the galley provides a steady supply of little surprises in the form of an exotic dessert, a small bar of Swiss chocolate, or a packet of those extra-crunchy potato chips. A word of advice for cooks: One surprise a day is usually sufficient, so ignore the heart-rending pleas for more. It doesn't serve you well to spoil your crew—and if you cave in there will be no end to their demands.

On a long passage, someone often develops an insatiable longing for a certain kind of food or an unusual food combination, such as curry and pineapple. This feeling, well known to pregnant women, is very real. It is often accompanied by tingling in the mouth and a great hollowness in the stomach, even after a large normal meal. Some of us who have lusted after thick, raw, sweet, sticky condensed milk must confess to raiding the galley, night after night, and sucking it straight out of the can. If there is no curry and pineapple on board, and no condensed milk either, there is not much that can be done about these perverse longings (which probably need the attention of a psychiatrist rather than a cook). It has been found, however, that the longing diminishes if the sufferer is given frequent fizzy drinks. Carbonated drinks are usually too heavy and bulky to carry on small boats, and perhaps their lack (in combination with the bland taste of warm, flat water from the ship's tanks) accounts at least in part for the weird longings. Beer is the most popular carbonated drink, but a soda maker that uses carbon dioxide cartridges is a great asset in hot, calm weather. It supplies the tingle that the jaded palate craves.

There are also flavored powders that make fizzy drinks. Have a good supply of those on board, sealed in foil packages. Had there been some fizzy-drink powder aboard our yacht during one particular race across the South Atlantic, some of us might never have become involved in a nasty and long-running skirmish over the effervescent fruit salts in the first-aid kit.

The night watches deserve a little treat or two tucked into a small Tupperware box or canvas bag. Jerky and hard candy are always appreciated, as are an apple or a banana. A vacuum flask of coffee, tea, or drinking chocolate is nice, too, though it verges on spoiling the crew. Incidentally, it's a good idea to have a separate box or bag marked for each night watch; otherwise the first night watch will gobble up everything without a trace of conscience and lie flatly about it afterward.

Lack of fresh salad vegetables can also set off cravings in hot weather, but you can easily grow sprouts that will calm down your frenzied taste buds until you can get to a produce stand ashore. The instructions are given in chapter 11 (page 132).

The Head

A group of visitors from another boat once came aboard our 31-footer while we were anchored in the roadstead at Fernando de Noronha, 200 miles off the coast of Brazil.

One woman disappeared discreetly into the head. When she came out, she whispered something to another woman who then went straight to the head herself. She, in turn, came out and whispered something to her husband. But while

he was in the head, the women could contain themselves no longer.

"How do you keep your loo smelling so nice?" they blurted out.

We were so taken aback we didn't know whether to blush with pride or faint with surprise. It wasn't a subject that normally came up in polite conversation.

The fact is that most small boat toilets smell bad—not just because somebody's aim wasn't too good in rough weather, but also because seawater trapped in a pipe quickly develops the most vile smell, thanks largely to anaerobic bacteria. The problem is that you can clean the toilet as much as you like and it will still smell; only nobody will believe it's the seawater that's making the stink.

One of the reasons why our toilet didn't stink, at least not as much as most, was due to its construction. It was a British-made Lavac that didn't have the usual complicated double-action pump attached to one side that sprays water and drips every time you use it. Instead, the Lavac used a remote, sealed diaphragm pump mounted on a bulkhead. The toilet seat had an airtight seal; when you put it down, the pump created a vacuum as it withdrew the contents of the bowl, and that vacuum drew in more water behind it. In general, our toilet spread less of its contents around the head.

But the main reason why our head smelled so good on that auspicious occasion (a reason we never divulged to our guests) was simply that my wife, June, had just poured a cupful of sweet-smelling disinfectant into the bowl, as it was her habit to do every couple of days. We became the talk of the anchorage, and at one stage, we considered giving guided tours of our head.

Apart from masking the smell with perfumed disinfectants, what else can you do? Vinegar poured into the bowl and pumped through the system will cure the problem for a while, and it will dissolve some of the salts encrusted on the

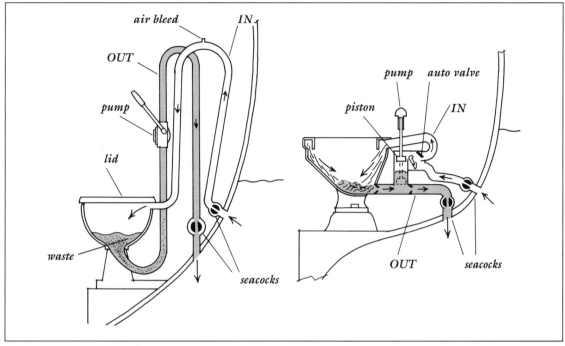

The Lavac toilet (left) makes use of a diaphragm pump mounted remotely on a bulkhead and a lid with an airtight seal. Both inlet and outlet lines loop high above water level to prevent siphoning. Other toilets (right) use a double-action piston pump to empty the bowl and pull in flush water.

hoses, to boot. But few small boats can carry enough vinegar to keep that kind of treatment up for long.

Sometimes the problem lies with the kind of hose used in the toilet plumbing. In that case, you can improve things greatly by installing a special type of hose such as the series 101 No-Odor Super Head Hose, which is designed to give "maximum resistance to odor permeation." It costs twice as much as normal heavy-duty vinyl hose, but it is probably worth it.

Marine retail stores stock many different kinds of treatments for heads and holding tanks, some based on aerobic bacteria, others on enzymes and chemicals.

Long-term cruisers who use any treatment at all prefer the enzymes or aerobic bacteria to the chemicals, which simply kill the bad bacteria and mask the stink.

Good ventilation is vital for the head compartment—a large louver in the door or bulkhead, and an extractor fan or large vent. That way, any lurking smells will be sucked out and dispersed by the wind instead of invading your living quarters.

Headroom

Standing headroom is not a necessity on a small yacht. As the famous English designer Uffa Fox is reputed to have said, If you want to stand up, go on deck.

There are two places where standing headroom contributes greatly to creature comfort, however: the galley and the toilet.

Nobody can produce good meals while crouched over in a galley without headroom, and they shouldn't be required to. And if you've ever tried to pull your pants up while you're bent over, you'll know why headroom in the toilet compartment is desirable.

Heavy-Weather Clothing

There are few things more conducive to misery than sitting in the cockpit of a small boat in rough waters in cold pouring rain. It takes the best kind of foul-weather gear to keep you dry and happy under those circumstances.

A good offshore jacket and pants will now cost you about 120 beers, or twice as much as a little handheld GPS receiver. If this seems to you to be a bad investment, think again. Grit your teeth and pay the man his money. When the time of misery approaches, you will be very thankful you did. In the waterproof clothing market you get what you pay for, and if you pay a miserable amount, misery is what you're going to get.

Most of the best foul-weather gear now incorporates breathable fabrics such as Gore-Tex. They work on the principle that a molecule of water vapor is smaller than a drop of water. Thus, your body sweat, in the form of vapor, can escape through minute holes in the fabric; but the rain and seawater can't penetrate to wet you. That, in any case, is the theory. The practice still has a little catching up to do.

When choosing any type of foul-weather gear, be sure that it fits you well at the neck, wrists, and ankles. Hook-and-loop fabric fasteners such as Velcro are excellent for making exact closures, but you can get awfully wet and cold under your foulies if even small amounts of water find their way in.

If you choose cheaper waterproofs without Gore-Tex, they must have vents in carefully chosen places to let out the water vapor (which will otherwise collect as pools of condensed sweat). While such vents work well on shore, they are very likely to let water in if you're doused by heavy spray or a wave.

Pilot Berths

If you're part of a crew of four or more, heaven is a pilot berth with a curtain. You can snuggle up in your bed any time of the day or night and not be disturbed by what's going on in the cabin. It's extraordinary what a sense of privacy a thin curtain brings—and privacy is a very important issue on a long passage.

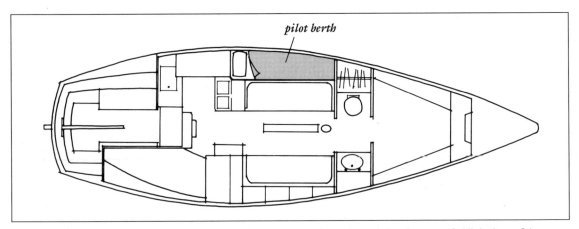

Even small boats can have pilot berths. The accommodation plan of the Camper & Nicholson 31 shows a pilot berth above and outboard of the port settee.

A pilot berth works best on a fairly beamy boat, because it is tucked under the side deck between the outer hull and the back of the settee. If you're singlehanding, though, or cruising with just one other person, a pilot berth may be a waste of space that could better be devoted to lockers or bookshelves.

On a boat with a large crew, even if there are no pilot berths, every person should have a private area that nobody else touches. A bunk is the best place, but bunks often have to be shared or used as settees at times. Instead, a small locker or shelf (or part of one) could be a crewmember's personal space. The skipper should make sure everybody is aware of the need for privacy and understands that they should not touch anything they see or find in somebody's private place. If you have not yet been to sea for a long spell in tight confines with other people, this may sound a trifle melodramatic, but it's not. Some of us who have had to make do with a miserly cubby hole in the forepeak for a private place would have given our back teeth for a whole pilot berth.

One other important aspect about living in close quarters with others is neatness. The golden rule is: Clean up behind yourself. Crew members who leave their personal gear, or tools they've been working with, lying around are a constant source of irritation to others. And it's surprising how easily irritation can flare up into anger after a few incidents, and how easily anger can turn to rage. It's something to be aware of before you sail over the horizon for the first time.

Reading Lights

A reading light over your bunk is a nice touch of home comfort, but in truth, very little reading gets done in bunks at sea. When people go to their bunks, they are tired and they go straight to sleep.

Some cruisers do manage to get a lot of reading done, but it's usually done in the cockpit when they're supposed to be keeping a sharp lookout for ships and other dangers.

Nevertheless, a bunk reading light is really appreciated in port, where more than 90 percent of a cruiser's life is spent. If you have no electricity on board, then a bulkhead-mounted kerosene lamp will have to do—but it will be hot in tropical climates, and not particularly bright. There seems to be no truth to the old rumor that reading in poor light will harm your eyes. Electric light is so much brighter and so much more convenient that it seems worthwhile to make a special effort to provide it, even if the system consists of nothing more than a single battery and a couple of solar panels to charge it.

Spray Dodger

A canvas hood over the main companionway adds greatly to the comfort of a sea passage. It keeps rain and spray out of the cabin but still permits the sliding hatch to be opened for ventilation. A spray dodger also provides a cozy windbreak for the crew in cold weather, and a patch of shade in blazing sunshine.

Most dodgers are made of acrylic canvas supported by stainless steel hoops hinged at their lower ends to enable the dodger to be folded flat in a semicircle on the cabintop. The favorite color for a dodger is blue, to match the mainsail cover and the dinky little winch covers. But blue is hot, and those of us who have had light, sand-colored dodgers will tell you they make a lot more sense in the tropics.

A dodger should have windows of the same durable, flexible plastic used for see-through panels in sails, but it should be thicker. Because the plastic tends to stretch more than the acrylic material, it's best to have two forward-facing windows separated in the middle by an inch or two of cloth that will take most of the strain. Side windows are a good safety feature, but they shouldn't extend too far toward the aft edges of the dodger for fear of weakening the structure.

Stainless steel tube is the correct material for the hoops, which should be held open firmly with the aid of turnbuckles. The whole dodger must be very firmly supported in the raised position because it inevitably becomes a handgrip as you move from the cockpit to the side deck. It's possible to lash a dodger firmly in place with nylon or Dacron cord, but until it's fully stretched, you'll need to be constantly adjusting your lanyard.

There must be provision for lashing the dodger down when you fold it to reduce windage during a storm at sea, or while you are at anchor. If you are tempted by the glowing advertisements for hard-topped dodgers, find out in advance if they will fold down in an emergency and figure out where you would stow them—if you could handle them at all in a gale of wind.

A good dodger should have a leather strip along its after edge where it forms a handgrip, otherwise it will quickly become dirty and wear through the fabric. It should also have a strip of Velcro or a hefty zipper for attaching a Bimini awning that is stretched aft to provide shade in the cockpit.

If your cockpit is very small and your boat has a tiller, the size of the dodger might need to be restricted. You need to be able to stand up in front of the tiller and still be behind the end of the dodger. You also need to be able to see over the dodger when you're standing, so it should be no higher than nose level: There are occasions when peering hopefully through the plastic windows just isn't good enough.

One other very important thing about dodgers is that they should not interfere with the use of cockpit winches. The winch handles must clear the dodger (for more on dodgers, see chapter 6, page 59).

Showers

This may come as a surprise to some Americans, but no great harm befalls you if you don't shower every day. Showers are, after all, a modern invention. Not that long ago, no one in the whole world showered; only the rich enjoyed the luxury of soaking in a bath, and that was only once a week. It's true that the Romans had elaborate public bathhouses, and probably showers too, but the untamed northern tribes from whom many of us are descended regarded them as extremely decadent and one of the major reasons for Rome's subsequent decline and fall. In any case, when the bathhouses disappeared, the world happily forgot all about bathing for centuries. The Dark Ages weren't called that for nothing.

Some modern cruisers have no problem turning the clock back to those times, but others, having fallen into the habit, become very itchy and uneasy if they can't shower every day.

This poses a problem, because it's not easy to install a shower on a small boat. There's not usually much space, for a start, although you can convert the whole head into a sort of plastic shower stall with the throne in the middle. You can then sit on the throne and spray yourself with a handheld shower head—but only if you have an electric pump pressurizing the water. And unless you have some way of heating the water, either a propane flash heater or a heat exchanger in the engine, it will of course be a cold shower.

Few small boats carry sufficient fresh water to allow for showers. Besides that, there's also the question of drainage. Showering on a small boat is like pouring buckets of water over yourself in a corner of your front room at home. There are no drains to carry the wash water away to the public sewers and get rid of it. So you either let this dirty, sticky, hair-laden waste water run underneath the carpet—through the bilges to the sump under the galley floor—where it will fester and bubble until you get around to pumping it overboard, or you fit a small electric pump in a hole in the toilet floor, which will expel the waste through yet another hole in the hull of the boat.

Bigger boats with pressurized hot water systems and machines that make fresh water from seawater often have room for separate shower

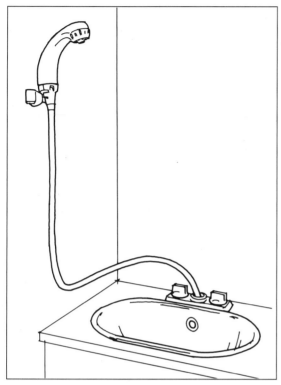

A neat and practical shower arrangement features a multifunction head that doubles as a sink faucet and—when the hose is extracted—a shower spray nozzle.

stalls, and boats with sugar-scoop sterns frequently have a freshwater shower tucked into a small recess in the aft stairway. But the majority of cruisers have weaned themselves off showers and relearned the use of a washcloth, which is very economical with fresh water. A couple of cups of warm water in a wash basin will do it.

In warm waters, many people have a daily swim and then wipe themselves down with a washcloth dipped in fresh water to remove the salt; or they mist themselves with a fine spray from a garden sprayer or a small spray bottle, and then towel off.

In rough weather, with freshwater supplies running low, you can wash all over with the moist-

ened paper towels marketed for wiping babies' bottoms. Or you can wait for calmer weather and a rain shower, and get up on deck with the shampoo.

If you can spare the fresh water, a gallon-sized (4-liter-sized) garden spray with its container painted black and left in the sun to get warm provides a good shower. You can also buy a commercially made black plastic container, complete with a tube and shower head attached, to hang in the rigging.

Even if you have learned to forgo the daily ritual of a shower, it's a real luxury to be able to wash your hair at sea, particularly if it's long. Nothing makes you feel cleaner, fresher, and more presentable than newly washed hair. If you wanted to give someone a wonderful present at sea, you could hardly do better than hand over a gallon or two of fresh water that you'd saved from your own precious ration.

In a nutshell, you could say that showering is not a priority on most cruising yachts; but if you can manage it, it's a great comfort. Most of us shower to get rid of body odors that nature probably intended to be attractive eons ago, but that now seem offensive in a crowded high-rise elevator. When you're all in the same boat, however, and nobody is able to take showers, one smell cancels out another—so no offense is given and none is taken.

Ventilation

Every boat needs ventilators that provide a steady flow of fresh air through the accommodation, not only to carry away heat but also to get rid of the moisture that builds up from condensation.

A boat with poor ventilation is likely to become a riotous playground for mold, mildew, rot spores, and other disagreeable growths that will either discolor or devour the fabrics, furnishings, and wood surrounds. Lockers and enclosed spaces need ventilation holes, too, lest their insides turn slimy black or green.

As we saw in chapter 6, the natural flow of air in most sailboats with forehatches hinged on the forward edge is from aft forward, and this effect is exaggerated by a raised dodger over the aft companionway. Air gets sucked in behind the dodger and travels through the galley and main cabin to the forecabin, where the partial vacuum created by the open hatch sucks it out again.

It hardly seems to matter which way the wind is blowing for this circulation to be in operation, although it is strongest when the boat is lying bow to wind.

So be sure to take advantage of this natural flow when you're arranging fans or additional ventilators. Go with it: Don't try to fight it.

The most effective long-term ventilation is provided by 4-inch (100-mm) cowls feeding into Dorade boxes. When production boatbuilders do deign to provide ventilators, they often have 3-inch (75-mm) cowls, but it's worth remembering that a 4-inch (100-mm) cowl pushes through almost twice as much air as one an inch (25 mm) smaller in diameter.

On a small boat, you might want to remove the cowls and replace them with deck plates when you go to sea, especially if you're expecting bad weather. All Dorade boxes should be provided with a means to seal them off from below.

Incidentally, you can buy low-lying, streamlined ventilators that look very sleek, but they can't possibly do the work of the traditional solid, stand-up ventilator. And while a solar-powered ventilator sounds like a good idea, the traditional cowl ventilator will outperform it in the long run and you'll never have to replace a motor or a battery.

Weather Cloths

Weather cloths of acrylic canvas or sailcloth laced to the lifelines on either side of the cockpit provide shelter from beam winds and flying spray. They can look smart, too, and they provide a place for the boat's name or identification number. Still, they do have a couple of drawbacks.

First, they limit your vision to windward from the cockpit. Second, they create windage well aft of the boat's center of lateral resistance, so that she will tend to gripe in every puff, and become hard-headed. Thirdly, they are likely to be carried away and take the lifelines with them if you are hit broadside-on by a plunging breaker while you're hove-to or lying ahull.

On the whole, a dodger that will provide reasonable shelter for the crew on watch is preferable to weather cloths. Most cruisers don't bother with them.

THINK INVERTED

If your boat turns upside down:

- Will you be able to open the door if you're in the head?
- If it's a sliding door, will it come off its runners and jam closed?
- If it's a hinged door, will it be jammed shut by debris in the gangway outside?
- Can the smallest member of your crew kick the door open?
- Or do you need to keep an ax in the head?

CHAPTER 13

Self-Steering Gear

No one who has experienced the tyranny of the tiller will ever go to sea again without some form of self-steering device—for no more fiendish a punishment could be devised than to force a sailor to sit at the helm hour after hour, day after day, week after week.

Most sailboats can be persuaded to sail themselves to windward at the cost of a little efficiency. But few will maintain a course without occasional correction from the rudder when the wind is abeam or aft of the beam, which it is for most of the time during the majority of ocean crossings.

The shorter your boat's keel, the quicker she wanders off course. And by shorter, I mean the fore-and-aft length, not the depth. Some fin-keeled boats with balanced rudders can't be left alone for more than a few seconds without luffing up into the wind—complete with a great bustle of rattling sails and a great crashing of waves at the bow.

If you are singlehanding, there is no question about it: Your boat must be able to steer herself while you cook, eat, sleep, and navigate. If there are just two of you, the crewmember on deck usually has other jobs on the daily list of sailing chores and can't afford to be tied to the helm for four or six hours at a time. A big boat, with six or more crew, has a better time of it. Each person will be at the helm only for four hours out of every 24. But even then, there is no reason to man the helm continuously if she's a cruising boat.

In short, all sailboats that set out to sea on long voyages need some kind of self-steering device. A good system is as valuable as an extra crewmember—more valuable, in fact, because it is on duty 24 hours a day, nonstop. And it never whines about the rain or steals the last can of condensed milk in the galley.

Understanding the Theory

All boats can be made to steer themselves by one means or another, but you'll do better at it if you understand the principles.

To put it very crudely, your boat pivots left and right around an axis that is called the center of lateral resistance (CLR). The CLR lies roughly in the middle of the underwater area. Pressure exerted by the sails makes the boat pivot around the CLR. The mainsail pushes the stern away from the wind, and thereby turns the bow in the opposite direction. The foresails, ahead of the axis, push the bow away from the wind. The force exerted by the various sails depends on two things: their area and their distance from the pivoting point. The farther they are away from the CLR, the more leverage they gain to push their end of the boat around. One of a bowsprit's major tasks, for example, is to gain leverage.

Secret Forces

Apart from the convenience of self-steering, there is a very satisfying magic about it, especially when a wind-vane gear is doing the work for you. It creates a wonderful feeling that you're harnessing secret forces of nature as you watch that vane sensing the wind direction, like an invisible cat sniffing the breeze, and moving the tiller until equilibrium reigns again.

WEATHER HELM

When a boat is properly balanced, there will be a slight bias in favor of the mainsail. Its superior turning power will make the stern fall off to leeward all the time, and the bow will want to turn into the wind. This slight imbalance is corrected by the wheel or the tiller, which is pulled to the weather side just two or three degrees to keep the boat going straight on course. The boat is then said to have slight weather helm, and everything is in balance.

This desirable state of balance unfortunately doesn't last for long because the exact pivot point, the CLR, is constantly changing for various reasons: The boat's speed, the leeway she's making, the amount she's heeling, the condition of the sea, and other factors are among these reasons.

If your boat has a fin keel, she will react quickly to these small changes, wander off course immediately, and need quick attention at the helm. If she has a full-length keel, she will take much longer to react; and before she can change course, the pivot point will have gone back to its average position, thereby removing the stimulus to turn.

If you take a long plank, place it end-down in deep water to represent a fin keel, and move it forward, you'll see that you can very easily turn it to the left or right. But if you place that same plank lengthwise in the water to represent a full-length "cruising" keel and move it forward, you'll find it very difficult to make it change course. Keels come in many different lengths; but the longer the keel, the better she will *track*, or maintain a steady course.

DIRECTIONAL STABILITY

Many production boats have fin keels because they slavishly follow the fashions of the racers. The fin keels found on racing boats are the most efficient airfoils, or hydrofoils. And as their helms are constantly manned by relays of fresh crewmembers, directional stability is not as important to racers as is the ability to claw to windward quickly.

Cruising boats sacrifice some efficiency (which translates mostly to speed, not necessarily windward ability) for better directional stability, which, together with sail balance, is the basis of self-steering.

Whether you have a fin keel or a full-length keel, your boat should be tuned for balance under sail before you install any form of self-steering. It is expecting too much of any self-steering device to overcome vicious weather helm.

Balance often changes as the boat heels. A boat with a hull shaped like a wedge or a diamond will tend to dig her bow in as she heels, and she will try to head sharply into the wind. Her balance will be much less affected if the submerged areas fore and aft remain about equal as she heels. Even then, the mast leaning out over the water creates a powerful sideways lever that also tries to push the bow into the wind. With both these forces in action, overwhelming weather helm might result.

AVOID LEE HELM

Test your boat by sailing with the apparent wind on the beam in a fresh breeze under all plain sail.

If you can keep the boat on course by hauling the tiller just two or three degrees to windward, she's well balanced. But if you need to turn the rudder much more than that to keep her going straight, you need to reduce weather helm by one of the methods discussed below. And if you have to push the tiller down to leeward to keep going straight, you have lee helm.

Lee helm is dangerous and needs to be corrected, not only because it greatly slows a boat down but also because it encourages uncontrolled jibes. A boat with slight weather helm will round up into the wind and stop with her sails ashake if the tiller is suddenly left unattended because a crewmember has fallen overboard. But a boat with lee helm will fall off the wind and sail away fast, jibing and jibing until she tears the rig out of herself.

Bad weather helm usually can't be completely cured if it's a design fault, but it can be greatly tamed by decreasing sail area aft of the center of lateral resistance, or by increasing the sail area forward of the CLR. You can also increase the leverage of the same sail area—by flying it from the end of a bowsprit, for example, instead of from the stem.

RAKING THE MAST
If your mast is raked well aft, you can reduce the mainsail's turning effect by raking it forward a little; this will help get rid of excess weather helm. Don't rake it farther than plumb upright, however, or it will look awful and a new set of problems will come into play. If raking the mast doesn't make enough of a change, you might be able to increase the area of your foresails if you judge the boat to be undercanvased, or, as we noted above, you could move them father forward to gain leverage. As a last resort on a very small boat, you might be able to move the whole mast forward to lessen weather helm; but this solution is unlikely to be feasible on a bigger boat.

An easier cure would be to remove some sail area from the mainsail where it is doing the most damage—along the leeward edge. If the leech ends in a large roach propped up with battens, have the mainsail recut along the lines of a genoa jib with a hollow, battenless leech. This is, in any case, the mainsail shape recommended for safety, convenience, and economy by many experienced cruisers, including the Pardeys.

On many boats, a good balanced helm can be maintained in winds of 15 knots and over only by reefing the mainsail. Find out by experience when you need to reef, and remember to tuck in that reef even when your self-steering device is in command. Not only will you make its life easier and reduce the stresses on it, but your boat will stay under better control.

FLATTEN THE SAIL
Incidentally, a blown-out mainsail—one that has stretched and ballooned with age—will contribute a considerable amount of weather helm. Flatten it, especially in a blow, by tightening the front and bottom edges: Haul the halyard and the clew outhaul tight. Take up the Cunningham cringle (if you have one) or the flattening reef, and zip closed the pocket in the foot. Free the leech a little and let the sail twist at the head. If that doesn't do the trick, it's probably time to invest in a new hollow-cut mainsail. The difference could amaze you.

You can save yourself a lot of trouble by buying a reasonably balanced hull in the first place. If you haven't yet bought the boat you want to sail over the horizon, do some research into which designs suffer the most from weather helm. *Practical Sailor* publishes books that contain details about most popular production boats, and each copy of *Cruising World* magazine features a list of boats whose owners are prepared to tell you their good points and bad points.

Having balanced your boat under sail as best you can, it's time to take a look at what self-steering systems are available.

Autopilots

An autopilot works off the boat's 12-volt electricity supply. It has a heading sensor and an electronic box of tricks that gives orders to the drive mechanism, which attaches to the tiller or the wheel. You can connect an autopilot to a GPS or Loran-C and it will take you to a waypoint as faithfully as a guide dog would. You can even connect it to a little wind vane, so that it steers the boat according to wind direction rather than along a fixed compass course.

When you want to use it, you simply put your boat on course and press a button marked Auto. Your pilot will lock the course in its memory and faithfully keep you going in that direction until

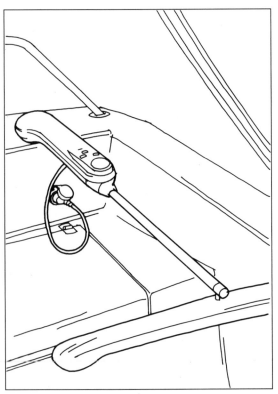

Cockpit autopilots are mounted out in the open, with a push rod extending to the tiller. The Navico TP 100 shown here generates up to 143 pounds (65 kg) of thrust and sells for about 160 beers.

you run ashore or give it new instructions. With the aid of a remote control unit, you can make it dodge around obstacles at the touch of a button or tack through exactly 90 degrees like an Olympic champion.

There are two major kinds of autopilot: the cheap kind that mounts in the cockpit, where it's exposed to the weather; and the expensive kind that is mounted below decks, out of harm's way.

You don't need either kind to cross an ocean, but there are times when an autopilot is an invaluable release from tiller tyranny. If you are tempted to buy one, you might well wonder which type would be better for you.

CANDID ADVICE

Here is some candid advice from the West Marine catalog: "Are you sailing across an ocean? Buy a below-deck pilot. Period."

West Marine is a chain of retail boating stores that sells and repairs a lot of autopilots, most of their repairs being to the cheap cockpit models. The message is plain, and it coincides with the experience of many deep-sea racers and cruisers: Above-deck autopilots do not stand up to continuous, heavy-duty work in all types of weather. Furthermore, they cannot be relied upon to steer for long in conditions where a person would have difficulty steering.

Cockpit autopilots are relatively cheap (they start at about 175 beers) and so tempting that many boat owners succumb to their siren lure. But they simply don't last. And little wonder, considering the conditions they operate under—stuck out there in the bitter cold and the blazing sun, alternately doused with freezing rain and warm salt spray. Only human beings can stand that kind of abuse—and only certain seagoing types of human beings at that.

The expensive, under-deck type of autopilot starts at about 920 beers, which is a sobering financial consideration for a cruiser already committed to investing 800 beers or so on a wind-vane self-steering system. But here an idea presents itself: A wind vane naturally requires wind to work, and it's useless if you're motoring in a calm. But a cheap cockpit autopilot actually prefers steering in a calm, and it will feed right off the electricity your alternator is producing.

WHY NOT BOTH?

So, at the risk of offending the experts at West Marine, why not fit your boat out with a wind vane for times when there is wind and a cheap autopilot for times when there isn't?

If you treat the pilot with kid gloves and shepherd it down below to a nice dry berth at the first sign of wind, rain, or spray, it will reward you with a reasonably long life devoted to steering impossibly boring courses without complaint. And at the first sign of trouble, which will eventually come, you can simply hurl it overboard without remorse.

There is a lot more to be said about autopilots, including the pros and cons of fluxgate compasses, proportional rate correction, and digital feedback, but it all boils down to the same old thing: You get what you pay for. But as far as a cockpit autopilot is concerned, you're not asking for much—so you might as well spend the least money.

Wind-Vane Gears

There are more vane gear systems than you can shake a stick at, but they all work by keeping the boat at a constant angle to the wind, so that if the wind direction changes, the boat's course will change with it. Vane gears need no electricity, but they will only work if there is enough breeze to move a hinged vane and overcome the friction in the system of lines, blocks, and fairleads that transfers power from the vane to the tiller or wheel.

Vane gears are at their best when a boat is going to windward; they react to every minor wind change with great accuracy. As the boat is headed off the wind, the flow of air over the vane decreases and it becomes less effective. When the boat is on a dead run, it may cease working altogether. Many vanes need a flow of at least 5 knots over their surfaces to work properly, so a boat doing 4 knots downwind in an 8-knot breeze will have to be steered by some other method.

Just as a transistor assists in the boosting of a radio signal, the more advanced vane gears develop considerable power from a top-hinged oar drawn through the water at an angle behind the boat. These are called *servo-pendulum gears*.

The simplest form of vane gear, however, resembles the type that used to be found on the old Marblehead model racing boats. Basically, it is a vertically hinged wind vane with a fixed drum that accepts lines from either side of the tiller. As the vane turns with changes in the wind, the tiller also moves until the desired course is regained. Because a small vane has limited power—and because a big vane would be too cumbersome perched on the stern—this kind of self-steering is limited to very small boats, although Sir Francis Chichester's *Gipsy Moth III* had a reefable vane on its own mast that looked like a miniature mizzen.

The next step up in sophistication is represented by the *trim-tab gear*, where a wind vane turns a tab on the trailing edge of the main rudder. The principle is very simple: When the tab turns to starboard, the rudder is forced to port.

Usually, a trim tab needs a reduction linkage to soften its quick responses, which will otherwise lead to oversteering and a lot of yawing around. When a trim tab is in action, the rudder must be free to swing, of course, but sometimes, if the boat is moving at high speed, the trim tab alone will do all the steering required, and the tiller may be lashed amidships. Trim-tab wind vanes are so simple that many cruisers make their own, experimenting and improving as they go.

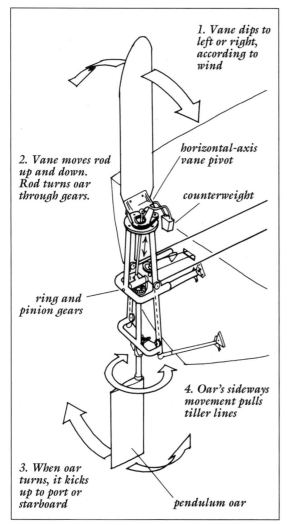

1. Vane dips to left or right, according to wind

2. Vane moves rod up and down. Rod turns oar through gears.

horizontal-axis vane pivot

counterweight

ring and pinion gears

4. Oar's sideways movement pulls tiller lines

3. When oar turns, it kicks up to port or starboard

pendulum oar

A servo-pendulum system like this is used on the Monitor and Aries wind-vane rigs, among others.

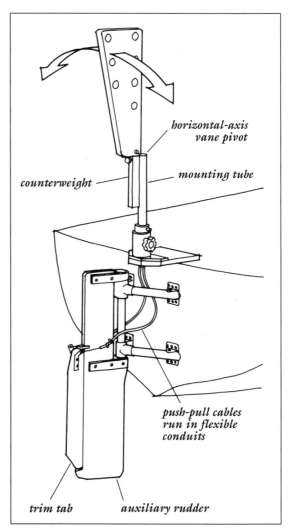

horizontal-axis vane pivot

counterweight

mounting tube

push-pull cables run in flexible conduits

trim tab

auxiliary rudder

In the Auto-Helm system, a wind vane moves cables that act on a small trim tab attached to an auxiliary rudder or a transom-hung rudder. The main rudder can be lashed amidships, or used to trim the boat and take pressure off the vane-steering gear.

Trim tabs work best with outboard rudders, but if you have an inboard rudder you might consider another vane gear system that drives its own auxiliary rudder, such as the Auto-Helm. It's a bit cumbersome and adds to underwater drag, but it has the advantage that it can act as a replacement if your main rudder suffers damage.

A POPULAR CHOICE AMONG CRUISERS

The servo-pendulum type of vane gear, such as the U.S.-made Monitor or the well-known Aries

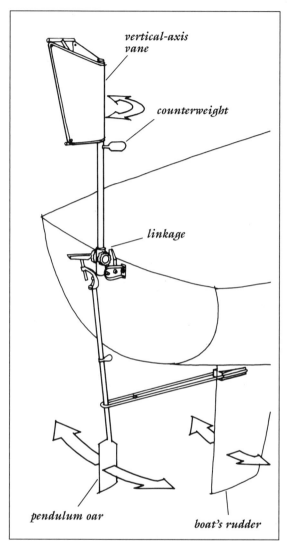

The Saye's Rig uses a vertical-axis vane to control a pendulum oar attached directly to the main rudder by a metal bar. It has proved useful on boats too large for normal servo-pendulum rigs.

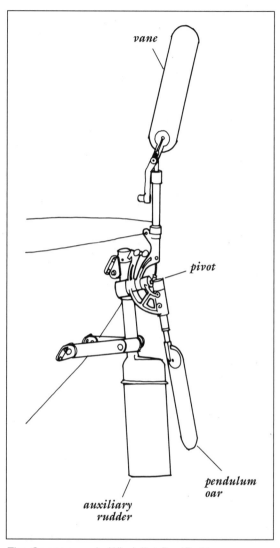

The German-made Windpilot Pacific Plus uses a servo-pendulum to drive an auxiliary rudder. This rudder can be used to steer the boat if the main rudder fails.

(formerly made by Nick Franklin of Cowes, England, and now made in Denmark by Peter Matthiesen of Nordborg), is found on large numbers of cruising boats. It is relatively easy to fit to most kinds of sterns, and it delivers a lot of power with good sensitivity.

A good servo-pendulum gear off the shelf will cost you in the region of 1,200 beers, but second-hand ones are occasionally advertised in the yachting press for 400 to 800 beers.

They are very simple to use and reasonably easy to repair if something goes wrong, even at sea, but they are vulnerable to damage in port, and the pendulum oar should be lifted from the water and securely lashed if you lie ahull or heave-to in heavy weather. Otherwise it is likely to be harmed by wave action.

There seems to be a limit to the speed at which they will operate successfully. After 8 knots or so they may become erratic, especially in following seas. Of course, 8 knots is a more-than-respectable speed for a small boat—so most of us are in no danger of being the victims of erratic vane-gear behavior.

Most servo-pendulums use horizontally hinged wind vanes, which are puzzling in their action at first, continually falling down and staggering to their feet again like sailors at closing time. In use, the vane is pointed edge-on, straight into the wind, and as soon as the wind gets to one side or the other of it, the vane is blown flat, developing considerable thrust as it is forced over.

The Achilles heel of the servo-pendulum, as with all vane gears, is a light following wind, but matters can be improved by bearing off 20 degrees and tacking downwind: The increased air speed will enable the wind vane to steer again. If the wind is so light that you are tempted to resort to the engine, the answer is to put the vane gear to bed and wake up the cockpit-mounted autopilot.

In heavy, following winds there is usually no problem whatsoever. Your servo-pendulum will do a splendid job of running in gale conditions if you are prudent enough to reduce sail—especially if you strike all canvas abaft the mast and run under a small jib.

Steering with Sails

Even if you carry a vane gear and an autopilot, you should still have some knowledge of sheet-to-tiller steering for when things go wrong. Numerous passages have been made by all kinds of boats using nothing but the power of a sail to move the tiller and keep the boat on a steady course.

If you want to earn points for your Black Box, you should practice this kind of self-steering before you disappear over the horizon. If that's not possible, you should at least carry the instructions (in the form of a good book on the subject) and a few yards of surgical tubing.

All the information you need on this subject, and about the setting up of twin running foresails, is contained in *Self-Steering Without a Windvane* by Lee Woas and *Self-Steering for Sailing Craft* by John Letcher. Both books are out of print, but they can be obtained from libraries and out-of-print book dealers.

With some surgical tubing, a few small blocks, and some light Dacron line, you can make a boat sail herself on any course up to a very broad reach using your ordinary, everyday sails. With special twin foresails and booms, you can even run dead downwind in the trades without touching the helm for weeks. On some twin-staysail systems, the sheets are led to the tiller on either side; if the boat goes off course, the sail pulling harder than the other will move the tiller over and put her back on track.

If you can move the center of your sail area far enough forward, you might not even need to attach any lines directly to the tiller. This is the one time you strive for lee helm and accept its dangers. Joshua Slocum made his 37-foot (11.3-m) *Spray* sail herself downwind by dousing his mizzen and setting a flying jib at the end of a very long bamboo extension to his bowsprit, with the sheets hauled flat amidships. A jib sheeted in tightly like that not only pulls a boat's bow downwind, so that she will run with her tiller lashed amidships or even left untended, but it also takes the sting out of the vicious rolling that some sailboats experience when they're running in the trades. Because the jib is sheeted in flat, it develops little forward thrust, so the job of propelling the boat is left to the mainsail.

THE TWISTLE YARD

Another way to curb the rolling is to angle your twin jibs forward in a deep V. One such arrangement, known as the twin-staysail (twistle) yard, was invented by the British sailor and marine engineer Hugh Barkla in the early 1970s. He wrote about it in *Yachting World* magazine. Like many other sailors who longed one day to make a trade wind passage, we cut the article out and filed it away.

The twistle yard places the sail area very far forward, mostly ahead of the forestay, and exerts such a strong, self-steering pull that it will steer some boats with cutaway forefeet directly downwind without the need for lines to the tiller or a self-steering gear.

Sixteen years after reading that article, in 1987, we got our chance to test the twistle yard on an ocean crossing. We were delighted with its performance. It changed the trade wind run from a misery of wild rolling and yawing to a controlled and exhilarating surge of power and stability.

The major problem with the twistle yard lies in describing it to anyone else. Ordinary intelligent sailors just can't seem to grasp the concept of the yard—a pair of aluminum poles joined to each other with a hinge, floating free 6 feet (1.83 m) off the foredeck, and swinging around the forestay as a unit with the twin staysails. We had to resort to handing out photocopies of the original article and waiting for the dropping jaw and intake of breath that signaled the lighting of a bulb in the brain.

The set-up is shown in the accompanying sketches (pages 159–61). Note the two booms, hinged in the middle, whose outer ends are held up by the clews of the twin sails set on one forestay. The hinge where the booms meet is joined on its bottom end to a strop of Dacron line that leads forward to the boat's stem, and at its upper end to a halyard that leads to the top of the mast.

The essential feature of this arrangement is

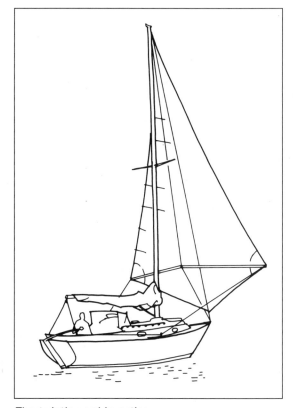

The twistle yard in action

that the total length of the booms is greater than the distance from clew to clew when the sails are stretched flat. An excess of 10 percent is about ideal. In consequence, the yard itself is never able to straighten out, but it is able to exert a powerful spreading force between the clews when the hinge of the yard is forced toward the forestay by the tension in the halyard.

As long as you keep tension on the sheets, the whole unit of sails and yard pivots bodily around the forestay. No guys are needed—the rig can be back-winded with impunity—and even if you lose a sheet while trimming, the only result is that one half of the yard swings against the forestay and recovery is simple.

There are some wonderful advantages to this rig. In heavy weather you can free the sheets,

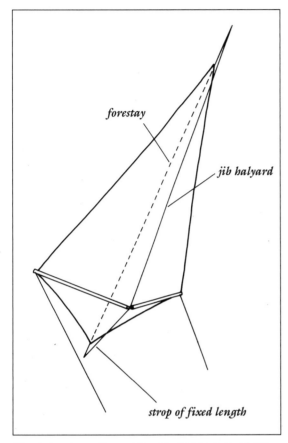

forestay

jib halyard

strop of fixed length

The twin staysails and the hinged booms of the twistle yard form a fairly rigid unit when the sheets are hauled aft and the halyard is tightened against the fixed strop.

the wind at any angle—from slightly forward of the beam to a dead run. You can even beat, if you suddenly need to, by flipping the yard around the forestay and shackling the clew of one sail to the other. In fact, you can spin the yacht in a tight circle without touching a sheet.

Our booms—for a 31-foot (9.4-m), heavy-displacement sloop—were each 13 feet (4 m) long, and made from 2-inch-diameter (50-mm-diameter), heavy-wall anodized aluminum poles. My next set of poles, however, will be of slightly larger diameter but with thinner walls, which will be lighter for the same strength. Each spar had the usual spinnaker pole fitting on the outboard end. The inboard ends were sawn off at right angles and inserted into the hinge.

The stainless steel hinge was custom made for us by a metal shop. It consisted of two cups about 3 inches (75 mm) deep and slightly wider in diameter than the poles. The poles were held in the cups by small stainless steel bolts passing through both cup and spar. Flanges welded to the cups (two on one cup, one on the other) were designed to overlap; and where they did, a hole was drilled to accept a large stainless steel eye bolt. The bolt acted as the hinge pin. A large eye-nut was screwed on the bottom end, and the eyes acted as attachment points for the yard's halyard and the fixed strop to the stem.

tighten the halyard to allow the booms to move even farther forward, and let the sails lie in a deep V. In this position they will exhibit the strong self-steering tendency and the directional stability of a cone dragged behind an aircraft. In that configuration too, much of the force of the wind is spilled. But, even more important, because so much of the area of the sails is now lying fore and aft, the boat's tendency to roll is greatly reduced.

On top of all this, you can slew the whole rig around, merely by tugging on one sheet and releasing the other, so that the sails will work with

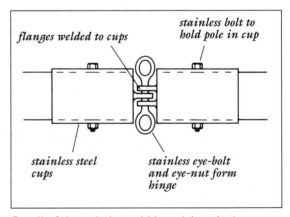

stainless bolt to hold pole in cup

flanges welded to cups

stainless steel cups

stainless eye-bolt and eye-nut form hinge

Detail of the twistle-yard hinge (elevation)

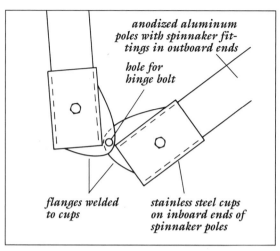

anodized aluminum
poles with spinnaker fit-
tings in outboard ends

hole for
hinge bolt

flanges welded
to cups

stainless steel cups
on inboard ends of
spinnaker poles

Detail of the twistle-yard hinge (plan)

The twin foresails were attached to our single forestay with staggered hanks and one halyard terminating in an eye with two snapshackles. Each sail was about 200 square feet (18 sq m) in area, which we found about right most of the time for a boat 25 feet (7.6 m) on the water that nominally displaces 12,500 pounds (5,670 kg). But there were occasions in the trades when we wished we could have reefed them instead of dropping them altogether. Roller furling and a twin-groove foil would have solved that problem.

The sails were cut fairly flat and had taped leeches that performed efficiently as airfoils as well as stalled wings. The clews were high-cut so that the yard wouldn't dip in the water, even during the worst rolling, and all bolt-ropes were pre-stretched Dacron.

Although there was never any problem about dropping the twins (they came rattling down in any weather), we were leery about lowering the yard from overhead. Without any steadying canvas the boat would suddenly start to roll viciously, and the 30-pound (14-kg) yard would flay back and forth quite ominously.

This problem could be solved quite simply by taking a line from the hinge to a fairlead on the forward edge of the mast. Here, the poles could be secured in the correct position for normal stowage, with their legs alongside the shrouds. Then it would have been merely a question of raising and lowering the feet of the yard, and never having to lower the whole thing to the deck at all.

In the usual rush to get away on a voyage, we didn't have time to try the twistle yard before we left. The very first time we raised it, in fact, was deep in the South Atlantic, on the southern edge of the southeast trade wind belt. It was a fine tribute to Hugh Barkla that it worked perfectly from the beginning.

Incidentally, Barkla was of the opinion that the twins are better set on a single forestay because double forestays would load the mast much more severely and leave an undesirable gap between the sails. In a letter to us, he said he had just tested a Mk II version of the twistle yard. "The one real change was the use of a twin-groove Leistay—opposed grooves, a less common form—so that, with twin halyards in spinnaker fashion, we could hoist and lower the staysails separately. In that way, we could avoid the mass of canvas draped around as we hanked on the sails alternately."

Even with our Mk I version, the center of effort of the sails was so far forward that our Aries wind vane was able to steer us downwind through the trades for thousands of miles without attention, and we regularly reeled off 130 or 140 miles a day.

THINK INVERTED

If your boat turns upside down:

- What parts of your self-steering will fall off or be damaged in a capsize?
- What should you do about it now?

CHAPTER 14

What about You?

A seaworthy, well-found boat is the first requirement for disappearing over the horizon. But what about you? Are you fit to go offshore?

In the flurry of last-minute preparations for an ocean passage, few people give a thought to personal fitness or to the effect a sudden, radical change in lifestyle will have on their bodies and minds.

When you go to sea, your body will be moving—often quite imperceptibly—to keep you balanced and on board, where you belong. Your head will be turned sideways and upwards more, if you look at the sails a lot. Unless you chock yourself into a corner of the cockpit, your torso will be moving back and forth far more than it would on land. In short, you will suddenly find yourself exerting all sorts of muscles that normally had a very easy life on shore. And those muscles might object to being called upon to perform hard work for long stretches without prior warning.

Many years ago, a well-known South African solo racer named Bruce Dalling gave a lecture on celestial navigation in the Point Yacht Club in Durban, during which he continually fiddled with a short length of knotted line. Whenever he wasn't making a gesture, he would pull the line sharply through one clenched hand, and then the other.

One of the club members, overcome by curi-osity, asked Dalling afterward what the line-pulling was all about. He was abashed. "I'm not even aware I'm doing it," he confessed. "I've been at it for weeks."

It turned out that he was preparing for a sin-glehanded transatlantic race, and he was tough-ening the skin on his hands. If you've ever raised blisters on your hands from handling taut, wet lines on your first day at sea, you'll know what a handicap they can be. They're not only painful—but they seem to take forever to heal.

Physical Fitness

Reasonable physical fitness is all you need for cruising. You don't need to go to the athletic extremes that deep-sea racing crews have to resort to for handling coffee grinders, tailing winches, or indulging in high-wire flying from the forestay.

If you have been physically inactive for some time, it would be a good idea to see your doctor for a physical check-up before any major voyage; ask in advance about exercise programs that will get you fit and keep you fit. But if you're under 35, you don't suffer from cardiovascular disease, you have no known primary-risk factors (such as high blood pressure, high cholesterol levels, and smoking) or secondary-risk factors (such as a family history of heart trouble, stroke, obesity, or diabetes), there's probably no need for a check-up.

If you do get advice about exercise programs,

however, make sure your doctor knows you're interested in anaerobic exercises that improve strength. While it is generally thought that aerobic activities such as running, swimming, or cycling make you fitter for every activity, they in fact contribute very little to the needs of a sailor (unless he or she happens to fall into the water a lot). They do, however, improve your general level of fitness, if it has dropped to an unacceptably low level; and they do benefit the heart, lungs, and circulation.

Being reasonably fit means you can tug on a halyard without pulling a muscle and haul up an anchor without straining your back. Your fitness regime should concentrate on strengthening your back, shoulders, arms, and even fingers.

Once you're living on board, at sea or at anchor, you will usually get sufficient exercise to keep you fit. It's amazing how many times a day you find yourself climbing up and down the companionway ladder, for example; and if you're at anchor in port, you'll be getting plenty of good exercise from swimming, walking ashore, trying to get the darned outboard started, and—eventually—having to row ashore. There are, however, certain exercises you can do on board in the unlikely event that your strength and fitness levels are slipping. A specialized workout program for cruisers was featured in *SAIL* magazine in March 1997 in an illustrated article by David Menaker, an amateur sailor and instructor in exercise, martial arts, and self-defense. His method uses only a halyard and two 36-inch (1-m) elastic exercise bands, which are available at any sporting-goods store. (For copies of the article, call *SAIL* magazine at 617-720-8600.)

Mental Fitness

If you're a skipper planning to cross an ocean for the first time, you should acquaint yourself with a basic knowledge of how human beings respond to stressful situations and confined quarters. In fact, in order to avoid unpleasant surprises at sea,

you'd be wise to get hold of a good book dealing with sailing psychology. Two recommendations are Michael Stadler's *Psychology of Sailing* and Michael Martin Cohen's *Dr. Cohen's Healthy Sailor Book*. Cohen's book deals comprehensively with physical as well as mental fitness. Both books are out of print but may be found in libraries and secondhand nautical book services.

"I know of no other activity that so challenges both our mental and physical capabilities as does sailing," Cohen declares. "Enjoyable and successful sailing truly requires a sound mind in a sound body."

Crews often exhibit a variety of individual reactions to being "cabin'd, cribb'd, and confin'd," as Shakespeare put it. Interpersonal friction can arise within days, demonstrated by such signs as irritability, rudeness, and defiance.

"Many crewmembers are surprised to discover how lonely they feel, even though they are surrounded by others with the same experience," says Cohen. "This phenomenon has been aptly dubbed 'the lonely crowd.'"

The author maintains that the first requirement of any skipper is to recognize the stresses that the crew of a small sailboat is likely to experience. They fall into three major categories.

- When you are confined, any environment, even the most glamorous and complicated, becomes boring and monotonous.
- On a boat at sea, many of your usual sources of release and gratification are missing or unavailable to you.
- You are forced to interact socially in crowded and unfavorable conditions. No matter how much you might dislike the others, you have to get on with them for your well-being and the safety of the ship.

COMMON SYMPTOMS

"With so many stresses and so few opportunities for expression and release, it is not surprising that psychosomatic symptoms are common," Cohen observes. He cites difficulties with sleep, headaches, nausea, irritability, depression, and a tendency toward compulsive acts—small annoyances in ordinary circumstances on land, but capable of blowing up into major problems at sea.

So much for the possible problems. What are the answers?

First, make sure everybody understands the goals of the voyage—and even before that, make sure you have a goal for the voyage. Simply sailing off into the blue without a plan, hoping to find the secret to happiness and fulfillment as you head west into the setting sun with a cocktail in your hand and a blond at your side is a recipe for disaster.

Second, make sure everybody understands and accepts the chain of command. The leadership, according to Cohen, should be "formal and defined." The skipper should retain responsibility for making all decisions that affect the safety of the boat and her crew. That doesn't mean she or he can't ask for, and accept, advice, but the final say comes down to the skipper, and that must be plainly understood.

OTHER AREAS

There are many other decisions in which the crew can be involved, and in which their views may predominate, but these areas should also be explicitly defined ahead of time. "The absence of explicit role definition inevitably leads to accusations and recriminations and is the bane of many a sailing cruise," Cohen says.

What can you do that will influence the behavior of your crew for the better? In the first place, you can be very careful about whom you select to go to sea with you. The best crew is a person with previous experience of an ocean crossing, or someone who has been confined with small groups of people for long periods of time (and not committed mayhem).

The three factors to which you should give particular attention are a potential crewmember's like or dislike of work (what motivates him or her to work), emotional stability, and social compatibility. None of this is particularly easy for the layman to establish in a brief meeting, so it would be best to take some time to interview prospective crews over a meal in a restaurant, over a drink in a pub, or with other crewmembers on board your boat.

Because a large part of a skipper's job is to understand human motivation and to recognize certain types of individuals and their likely behavior, you should be able to screen out the most unsuitable applicants this way. That is not to say there won't be any surprises—but just not as many. Incidentally, try to stay well clear of any potential crewmember whose reasons for going to sea with you seem in any way inappropriate. You could be very sorry if you accept someone running away from the law, the Internal Revenue Service, or a spouse.

Singlehanders

Two situations that can put a great strain on the human mind are the inability to go where you want and separation from other human beings.

Shipwreck survivors sitting in rubber liferafts, unable to go anywhere and just waiting to be rescued, die at a much greater rate than those who can do something about getting their lifeboats moving and steering them in the direction of safety—no matter how far away.

And singlehanded sailors, who are deprived of human company and usually short of sleep, face an array of symptoms—both physical and mental—of which they may not be aware.

If you intend to sail alone, you should write down a list of the symptoms to watch out for, then check yourself against the list as objectively as possible. The symptoms of problems arising from social isolation, boredom, lack of sleep, and anxiety are easy to spot if you know what to look for and are willing to admit to them.

For example, quite early on in a trip, you

might suffer a decline in motor skills. Your writing may become irregular—bigger and smaller in the same sentence—or you might write in such haste as to make your efforts illegible. You might find yourself continually oversteering, or missing the winch barrel when you try to drop the turns of a sheet over it.

Your eyes and ears can play many tricks. Sometimes objects will appear smaller or bigger than you think they should be. Sometimes you may hear voices coming from the sea. Forgetfulness is an early sign of fatigue, and you will almost certainly have trouble keeping count of the passage of time. (Most of us have trouble with remembering what day it is, even when we're not singlehanding and while we're still relatively sane; we have to resort to crossing days off a calendar or peeking at the date on the GPS.) You might also find it difficult to concentrate long enough to work out and plot a sextant sight, and you might experience sudden mood swings. If the causes of your problems continue, you will eventually experience hallucinations or illusions. In themselves, these are not usually life-threatening situations or even frightening at the time they occur; but you should try to avoid getting to that stage.

TAKE ACTION

When you first notice the signs of declining performance mentioned above, and any others that might be particular to your circumstances, it's time to take action.

First, you need sleep—deep sleep. Heave-to or lie ahull, if you have searoom and can do so in safety, and try to get at least eight hours of uninterrupted sleep. If your situation is such that you can't afford so much time away from the helm, take as many short naps as you can. Even several naps of 10 minutes each will help.

Second, you need some good, interesting, palate-tickling food. You can anticipate this need by stocking your galley with a favorite, easily pre-pared dish before you set sail. Usually, to get the sensory stimulation you're lacking, it should be a spicy dish—canned vegetable curry, chili con carne, or something similar. Whatever it is, don't be tempted to gobble it straight out of the can. Heat it up, serve it nicely, treat yourself—even if it takes an effort, and it probably will. Follow it up with a tasty dessert and a cup of hot tea or coffee. You'll feel like a new person.

Stimulate your other senses as much as possible. Play some lively, cheerful music; tune your shortwave receiver to the news or to an interesting feature program from the Voice of America or the British Broadcasting Corporation. Read an exciting thriller that moves along nicely and does not make too many demands on the brain. If it's calm, dip a bucket in the water and see how many different slippery, slimy life forms you can find lurking just under the surface.

Sometimes it's impossible to get enough sleep or cook interesting food because you're in a storm, crossing a shipping lane, or approaching land. That's exactly why you should try to identify early symptoms and stock up on sleep and sensory stimulation in advance. Your level of stress will naturally rise when you're nearing land or dodging ships: This is exactly when your level of concentration and performance needs to be at its highest.

Hallucinations and Illusions

Hallucinations caused by fatigue are frequent among sailors undertaking long voyages. Psychologist Dr. Glin Bennet reported that 50 percent of the competitors in the 1972 single-handed race across the North Atlantic experienced one or more illusions or hallucinations.

Probably the best-known example of a hallucination occurs in Joshua Slocum's classic, *Sailing Alone around the World*. Slocum looked out of the companionway and, to his amazement, saw a man at the helm of *Spray*.

"I am the pilot of the *Pinta* come to aid

you," the man said. "Lie quiet, señor captain, and I will guide your ship tonight."

Slocum's hallucination came after he had passed out on the cabin floor, delirious with stomach cramps—so it may have resulted from a toxic reaction rather than from fatigue or sensory deprivation. But this typifies the kind of hallucination commonly experienced. Most hallucinations are imaginary perceptions or sensations of hearing voices or seeing scenes that do not actually exist.

Frank Robb, a South African sailor and author of our acquaintance, tells of the singlehander who encountered four days of rough weather in the Caribbean, during which he got too little sleep. When the storm subsided, he wasn't too sure of his position, but he soon came upon a fishing boat, and near it, an island with a protected harbor.

He sailed in, passing a launch full of sightseers, and found a good anchorage where he dropped the hook before going down below and passing out on the cabin floor. He woke up 12 hours later and went on deck to find that there was no land in sight, no boats, nothing but sea. The anchor was eight fathoms down, however. He concluded that his mind had invented the island and the harbor to relieve him of the anxiety that was stopping him from getting sleep, and his physical actions had been controlled by powerful fatigue hallucinations.

Research indicates that dreams are important for mental health. When you are denied dreams through lack of sleep, you are subject to an alternative in the form of hallucinations—a sort of parade of waking dreams.

Fear

If you are singlehanding, sooner or later you will experience fear. If you understand and accept that fact before you set sail, you will deal with the situation more easily when it arises.

Fear seems to be a natural part of singlehand-

Voices in the Night

As far as illusions go, you will not easily forget the first time you hear a human voice crying for help from a wave breaking astern on a pitch-dark, stormy night. It is a frightening experience, even if you realize there cannot actually be anyone there. Many people hear voices, and probably more hear snatches of music, while alone on watch at night. But in fact this isn't truly an illusion or necessarily the result of mental fatigue. It's a normal and natural occurrence that results from the ability of the ear and the brain to filter out unwanted noise.

The noise of the wind and the sea in stormy weather contains a broad spectrum of almost all possible frequencies in random combinations. Your ear picks up all of them. But in the absence of other instructions, your mind concentrates only on those frequencies that are of significance to human survival—such as those in the range of human speech—and it suppresses the rest.

ed boating, no matter how macho its proponents might seem before or afterward. According to research done by solo sailor David Lewis in collaboration with the Medical Research Council in Great Britain, four out of five contestants in the 1960 singlehanded transatlantic race experienced not only fear, but acute fear.

In general, there are two types of fear. The first is familiar to almost everyone, sailor or not: those generalized tensions and anxieties that occur when we move house, change jobs, commit to a lifetime partner, or sit for an exam. The specifics of what is really worrying us are hard to pin down, but the good thing is that this kind of fear mostly disappears after a couple of days. Once we learn to live with it, it becomes insignificant and we forget about it.

The second type of fear is more specific, such as that caused by an approaching storm, or a collision with a balk of timber, or a sudden squall.

"The sailor need not be embarrassed about feeling afraid," says Michael Stadler in *Psychology of Sailing*. "As long as fear is the response to actual danger, it is a natural and even useful phenomenon . . . fear assists in the avoidance of danger."

FEAR SHARPENS SENSES

Stadler asserts that fear in an ample—though not excessive—degree can mobilize forces that sharpen your senses and improve your capacity to anticipate and assess the risks inherent in certain situations.

Seasoned sailors who experience anxiety before the danger arrives are better placed to meet it or even avoid it. Inexperienced sailors may wander blindly into danger and then become paralyzed with fear when it's too late.

But what if it's your first singlehanded trip? What if you aren't a seasoned sailor? How can you avoid becoming excessively scared and unable to act correctly?

One possibility, says Stadler, is to learn relaxation techniques. Another, the more likely for most of us, is to struggle through anxious situations and thus garner experience.

Interestingly, several investigations into dangerous activities have shown that experienced people feel less fear than inexperienced people—not because the experienced people have become insensitive to fear, but because they do not suffer their anxieties at the same time.

Experienced sailors feel anxious before the danger arrives and can prepare for it—physically for the boat, mentally for themselves. "Even amid the dangers of a storm, these people are only marginally afraid, and are therefore optimally efficient," Stadler explains. But an inexperienced sailor who sails naively into the depths of a storm may be helpless with fear when it arrives.

FORGETTING FEAR

David Lewis adds a fascinating footnote to the subject of fear on small boats. His research among solo sailors unearthed the fact that often the *extent* of the fear is not recalled afterward. Most people recall that they were scared, but they can't remember how bad it was. For some reason, the brain expunges or subdues memories of bad experiences.

Lewis asserts: "Observations noted *at the time* are the only valid ones. I honestly forgot that I had been frightened at all during one gale until I looked up my notes."

In passing, it may come as comfort to anyone who is inexperienced—whether he or she is part of a multiperson crew or a singlehander—to know that gales at sea are no cause for undue concern in a well-found yacht. And gales account for 2 percent or less of your sailing time, on average. The late Eric Hiscock, a very experienced British circumnavigator, learned this lesson relatively late in his cruising life; he had lived for many years with the private fear that really bad weather would overtake *Wanderer III,* his little wooden sloop. Well, eventually it did—and both he and his vessel coped splendidly.

He later wrote, poignantly: "Fortunate indeed is the man who, early in his sailing career, encounters and successfully weathers a hard blow."

POINTS IN THE BOX

The respected American sailor and author Richard Henderson asserts that the best weapon against fear is self-confidence.

"This is best assured by careful preparation, attention to one's health, seeing that the boat is sound and well equipped, learning all one can about the proposed route and weather conditions, preparing for all possible emergencies, and gradually building experience."

All of which sounds like points in the Black Box, of course. In case your memory has failed you (a definite sign of stress or fatigue), Vigor's

A Case of Fright

Fear does not always spring from great drama. My most frightening experience in more than 40 years of sailing came in the quiet of a mid-ocean calm.

We were deep in the South Atlantic, running free: a crew of four in a 33-foot (10-m) homebuilt wooden sloop called *Diana K*. We had blundered too close to the South Atlantic high and it was dead calm. The pinned-in main was slatting and filling noisily. The galley cupboards sang the clink-clank song of all small ships adrift among the southern swells.

My watch mate, having nothing to do, had gone down below to rest. I sat alone in the cockpit marveling at the beauty of the night. There was no moon, but each of a million stars was reflected brightly in the pitch-black ocean and each was connected to its neighbor by a wobbly skein of light. The whole surface of the sea was gently heaving with this magnificent silvery spider's web when I got to wondering how far down into the water the light of a star might penetrate.

I found the deck flashlight and pointed it overboard. The powerful beam stabbed downward forever—twisting and spiraling eerily, boring into the verdant depths.

Suddenly I burst out in a cold sweat. It occurred to me that I had just signaled our presence to every leviathan of the sea within miles.

We all know the size of the tentacled creatures that inhabit the ocean's secret depths. Occasionally some squid the size of an elephant gets washed up on a lonely shore. Enormous whales return to the surface scarred and bleeding after tumultuous fights with squid.

Now I had flashed my light to show the brutes where we were. I had guided them to their prey. And we weren't moving. *Diana K* was a sitting duck. I shivered with fright.

My first impulse was to start the motor and speed away, but we were sailors, not stinkpotters. How would I explain it to the others? They'd think I had taken leave of my senses. I thought of waking the skipper and confessing. But I did nothing. In tense silence I crouched low in the cockpit. After some minutes of near-paralysis, I crept down below to fetch the fireman's ax we kept for emergencies. If any tentacles slid over the gunwale, I wanted to give a good account of myself.

Back on the cockpit floor, ax at the ready, my

Famous Black Box Theory was mentioned briefly in chapter 8, and it is discussed in more detail later in this book (see page 214).

Privacy

The important question of privacy aboard a small sailboat was mentioned in chapter 12, in connection with pilot berths (see page 146); but there is good reason to go into the subject a little more deeply here.

Every crewmember needs a place aboard where he or she is guaranteed privacy. Everybody needs a certain amount of space to himself or herself, a territory for which he or she alone is responsible and into which he or she can withdraw from the rest of the herd. The personal spaces we unconsciously preserve on land—the minimum distance we stay from other people—are simply not available on a small yacht. We have to accept invasion of our personal space for lengthy periods of time, possibly by people we don't particularly like. For this reason, it is very important that we should have places to escape to now and then. And the longer the passage, the greater this need becomes.

A bunk is the most suitable spot: a personal, curtained-off pilot berth can, as we said earlier, be a small piece of heaven. For this reason, experts such as Michael Stadler recommend that the number of people on board for any cruise of

heart racing, I waited five minutes, 10 minutes, who knows how long, on the verge of throwing up. Then I felt a faint breath of air, and I was galvanized.

I ran forward quietly and raised the big genoa. I freed the mainsheet and got her close reaching, full and by, letting her make her own wind. I sucked every ounce of power from every wayward puff.

No Olympic helmsman ever concentrated harder. I sailed like a demon, holding the genoa sheet in my hand, feeling the pulse of each new breath of air, easing and tightening, reading the wind as a clairvoyant reads tea leaves.

After a few minutes, *Diana K* had moved several hundred yards from Ground Zero. My heartbeat slowed down. My grip on the tiller relaxed. No tentacles had appeared over the gunwale. No whale had swallowed us. I wiped my brow. God, we'd been lucky. I smuggled the ax down below again.

I never told the others what I'd done. Even repeating it in my mind made it sound highly melodramatic. But it was very real at the time. In any case, I've never shone a flashlight overboard again during a calm. One fright like that is enough for a lifetime.

more than a week in length should not exceed the number of bunks available. On racing boats, this rule is ignored to keep weight down, of course, and crewmembers practice a regime of hot bunking, or alternating in the same berth after coming off their different watches. But we are not talking about long-distance racing crews here. They are superheroes and not subject to petty fits of jealousy or rage over lack of privacy. What we are talking about here are normal people—crotchety, crabby, prickly people who like their privacy and who will become very nasty if they are deprived of it.

There may well be times when, for various reasons, not everybody can be master or mistress of his or her own bunk domain. Quite often, the main berths in the cabin double as settees; they may be used as sitting-down places by duty crewmembers not needed on deck. This makes them unavailable as private places, of course. In such cases, the skipper should attempt to set some other space aside for the crewmember whose hallowed ground is regularly invaded. A small locker in which to hide your personal supply of chocolate or condensed milk is always very acceptable.

Meals

Food assumes such importance on a long ocean passage that every sailor needs to know at least something about the theory of nutrition, if only to avoid scurvy.

Perhaps because of boredom or the lack of sensory stimuli, members of the crew look forward to mealtimes with ever-increasing anticipation as the voyage progresses—and woe betide the duty cook whose culinary expertise is lacking.

If you have little or no knowledge of cooking, you would be well advised to sort out a few simple, satisfying recipes for the main meal of the day before you disappear over the horizon—even if you are sailing singlehanded. If you are sharing cooking duties with other members of the crew, practice cooking about six different main meals and maybe four different breakfasts.

Don't be tempted to try anything too fancy or exotic. Plain fare, properly presented, tastes like manna to a pack of ravenous wolves newly arrived at the dinner table after a cold, wet spell on deck. As we have already discussed, however, you might include one or two spicy dishes for those times when the jaded taste buds are craving new, exciting sensations. Write down the cooking times and the exact amount of each ingredient when you practice at home, and use the same size pots and the same intensity of heat available on your boat, if possible. And limit your menu choices to dishes that are reasonably quick and easy to prepare in a tiny, wildly lurching galley

A Space Invasion

Be very careful about not invading other people's space accidentally. Don't throw your shirt on someone else's bunk without his or her permission. It may sound petty, but it's not. And respect other people's property rights, down to the last drop of toothpaste in the tube.

Some of us can remember incidents that seem incredibly trivial now, but which assumed dangerous proportions at the time. A small racing boat on which I was navigating and helming fell into a week-long calm in the middle of the South Atlantic. (Until you've experienced a week of calm, you'll never believe what a long time it is.) We were racing, we couldn't start the engine. We just had to sit there—with the sails slatting and swells slamming up under the counter while the four-man crew grew ever more desperate for wind. Inevitably, tensions arose.

One day I came off watch to find my best friend Nick standing down below with a silly wide grin on his face. He had just swallowed a glass of effervescent fruit salts, and he was enjoying the tingle in his mouth after three weeks of drinking nothing but stale, warm, flat water from the ship's tanks.

The only problem was that the fruit salts belonged to me. They were mine. I had paid for them and brought them aboard. They weren't ship's stores, for use by everyone. No, sir. They were mine alone.

I realized immediately that my irritation was out of proportion to the crime. Part of me wanted to accuse him of grand theft and see him hanged (or at least have that silly grin wiped off his face). But the more rational part of me realized that he didn't know the fruit salts were my private property. In a flash, I was appalled at my petty reaction. So I compromised. I would wait until I actually caught him red-handed. Then I would smile and explain to him as nicely and calmly as possible that the bottle of fruit salts belonged to me, and that if he wanted some, he had to ask me first.

I tried to catch Nick for days, gritting my teeth and watching him like a hawk as the level in the bottle went down steadily. But he must have been practicing his thieving ways while I was asleep, for I never saw him near my precious dwindling treasure.

Then one day it happened. He was spooning out some salts when I came below to check the chart. I forgot all about my plan to smile and be nice. I snapped. I screamed at him. I can't remem-

---

tilted 30 degrees to one side. In heavy weather—when you're reduced to cooking the main meal of the day on a special, gimbaled, single-burner stove—choose a recipe such as Commander Martin's Onion Soup (see chapter 11, page 128) or some other dish that involves little more than heating a can of soup.

EASILY FORGIVEN

Midday meals are mostly scratch affairs of sandwiches or salads, while the bread and fresh vegetables last, or some type of canned meat or fish. There's a lot of room to experiment here. Nobody seems to take the midday meal too seriously, and failed experiments are more easily for-

given. It's the evening meal that arouses expectations and warrants serious attention.

Every skipper should know a little about nutrition and keep a good book on board with more information about the basic food groups and their practical application at sea with the stores available aboard a small yacht.

Scurvy is not a threat on most passages, since it takes about four to six months to deplete the body's stores of vitamin C—the lack of which is the prime cause of the disease. But if you ever decide to sail around the world nonstop, or if you happen to live off the ship's stores and never eat ashore if you can help it, you need to watch out for scurvy: It's a killer if left too long. The symp-

ber now exactly what I said, but he stepped back, hurt and alarmed, wide-eyed like a whipped spaniel. As the two other members of the crew poked their heads down the hatch to see what was happening, I caught myself. Suddenly I was drenched in a flood of shame. I apologized profusely. "I'm sorry, Nick," I said, truly aghast at my behavior. "Here, please, you take the rest of the bottle. It's yours. You keep it." I thrust it at him.

But Nick wouldn't take it. He didn't want anything more to do with it, or with me. I naturally wouldn't touch it either, since it was no longer mine. And—as neither of the other two would dare lay a hand on it for fear of provoking another major fit—that bottle of delicious, fizzy, thirst-taming fruit salts sat unused in a galley locker all the way to Rio de Janeiro while we sat out under the hot tropical sun with our tongues hanging out.

Perhaps it was stress or shortage of sleep that induced these wild mood swings and shameful behavior in me; I don't know. It's not my usual style. But it does illustrate the need to make everybody on board aware of what is ship's stores—what is free for everybody to use—and what is private property.

toms of scurvy are weakness, anemia, spongy gums, and bleeding from mucous membranes.

Incidentally, as the British Royal Navy found out the hard way in the late 19th century, preserved lime juice (unlike preserved lemon juice) contains little or no vitamin C. Thus British sailors, or Limeys, suffered outbreaks of scurvy until their Lordships of the Admiralty came to their senses and reinstated the practice of supplying ships' crews with lemon juice for an antiscorbutic in 1918.

OTHER SOURCES

Small sailboats without refrigeration cannot keep vitamin C in the form of fresh produce for long, but there are some excellent alternative sources of the vitamin that will last for reasonable periods if they're kept cool and well ventilated; these include cabbage, carrots, celery, winter squash, garlic, grapefruit, onions, potatoes (cook them in their skins), and oranges. Fruit and vegetables that will ripen on the voyage, such as apples, bananas, and tomatoes, are also excellent sources of nutrition. Still, nothing seems to supply vitamin C in such a concentrated form as lemon juice, fresh or bottled. And if you should run short of foodstuffs containing vitamin C, one multivitamin tablet a day will give you all you need.

Dr. Hannes Lindemann, who made two unusual Atlantic crossings—one in a dug-out canoe, and another in a rubber-and-canvas folding boat—strongly recommends raw onions for the prevention of scurvy. He asserts that garlic also is useful. But perhaps this adventurer's major contribution to the art of small-boat provisioning is his strong recommendation that voyagers should carry plenty of beer to supply them with calories, valuable vitamins, and energy. While this is not a politically correct suggestion in this oddly selective puritanical age, it has long-standing nautical precedents.

In the 17th and 18th centuries, for example, each sailor in the British Royal Navy was allowed one gallon of beer a day, or the equivalent in volume of 13.3 12-ounce cans—a staggering amount, one might say. The quality was admittedly poor, but the sheer volume of beer consumed obviously reduced the demand on the ship's limited supplies of fresh water.

Today's small oceangoing yachts simply do not have the space for a gallon a day of beer per crewmember, and no sane person would suggest it be carried in lieu of fresh water. So Dr. Lindemann's recommendation is largely moot, although a six-pack or two, distributed with discretion to off-duty crew, can add a lot of cheer to those celebrations that mark the special waypoints of a passage.

There is more discussion on the important subject of food at sea in chapter 18, where June Vigor—a sea cook par excellence—gives you the benefit of her practical experience.

Age

As William Shakespeare might have said, there comes a tide in the affairs of men that, taken at the flood, sucks them swiftly away from the sea and boats and strands them for the best part of two decades on the reefs of Marriage, Career, Home, and Bringing Up Kids.

Rusty Shackle

Tom Andersen, a New England cruiser I met in Tortola, British Virgin Islands, tells of a 40-foot (12.2-m) yacht that arrived one day from Venezuela with an elderly couple on board, both in their middle seventies.

Tom watched with fascination while the man wrestled to free the pin of an old and very rusty shackle on his anchor.

"I would have taken a hacksaw to it and replaced it in five minutes with a brand-new, two-dollar shackle," said Tom. "But not him. He was obviously prepared to fight."

Eventually, Tom started to make polite conversation, as cruisers do, and remarked that there always seemed to be something to do on a boat.

"Yes, it's true," said the old-timer, "If this old bitch didn't keep me so busy, I would have died peacefully years ago."

There are many sailors in their sixties and seventies cruising the oceans of the world these days, aided by modern materials and designs that make boathandling easier. Francis Chichester was 66 when he made his famous circumnavigation in the 54-foot (16.5 m) ketch *Gipsy Moth IV*. In fact, people over 60 years old are *racing* around the world, singlehanded.

By the time such men and their partners are free once more to fulfill their adventurous dreams of cruising and voyaging under sail in their own yachts, they are 50-plus and fainthearted.

They no longer have the youthful zeal or the devil-may-care attitude that so many people imagine to be a prerequisite for successful long-distance cruising. Many of them retire and buy motorhomes. Then they search disconsolately in rule-bound RV parks all over the country for the freedom and satisfaction that eludes them.

If you have been wondering how long you can safely leave it, be assured that it *is* possible to start cruising in the golden years of your life. It's never too late to pack up and sail away, from port to port along the coast or clear across the ocean to other lands— provided you're reasonably sane and reasonably healthy.

Contrary to what many people believe, age of itself is not a major barrier to cruising under sail. If you can climb the companionway steps, you're probably fit enough to sail the boat. And there's nothing like living aboard a small yacht to make you fit and keep you fit.

In any case, those whose tread upon the foredeck is no longer catlike, or whose capacity for grinding winches no longer rivals a gorilla's, can make up for it by way of experience and large doses of patience.

JEAN GAU

In Durban, South Africa, I met a famous French-American sailor named Jean Gau. He was compact, crew-cut, wiry, and deeply tanned. He was then in his sixties and racing singlehanded. But he was racing the clock. He had to get back to New York to his job as chef at the Waldorf-Astoria.

His problem was that during his singlehanded circumnavigation aboard his Hanna-designed Tahiti ketch, *Atom,* he had spent far longer than he had anticipated in the South Sea islands. "The girls—in grass skirts, you understand—the girls swim out to your boat and ask if there is anything they can do for you," he told me. "*Anything.*"

Well, naturally, Jean got a little distracted and delayed. To make up time, he sailed an 80-day nonstop passage west-bound, across the Indian Ocean from Australia to South Africa.

During the day, at his mooring within a stone's-throw of the palm-shaded Victoria Embankment and the Point Yacht Club, Jean could often be seen bobbing up and down vertically in the subtropical waters of Durban Bay, demonstrating the latest lifesaving technique, or sitting proudly in the cockpit, displaying the canvasses he had painted. He was, in a word, vital. It would have been hard to imagine him sitting around in an RV park moaning about the heat.

No matter what your age, you'll never want for help when you're in need—as long as there are other cruisers around. Cruisers belong to a select group whose roots go back to the earliest days of civilization. They are a brotherhood of the sea. They're part of a tradition that has its own literature, language, insignia, customs, rituals, rewards, and penalties.

Their team spirit is understandable when you consider this: It takes crews of specialists, all experts in their own fields, to guide large ships from continent to continent across wide oceans. But one or two perfectly ordinary people, aged from their teens through their seventies, can and do navigate small yachts through those same seas, facing exactly the same hazards of the deep.

Seasickness

It is no coincidence that the English word nausea is derived from the Greek work *naus,* for ship, although seasickness is just one form of the motion sickness you can experience in a car, airplane, train, or while riding that lolloping, swaying ship of the desert, the camel.

Even if you have never experienced seasickness while cruising for short periods along a coastline, you should be prepared to recognize

the symptoms and know how to treat them before you decide to disappear over the horizon. While some people are far less affected by motion sickness than others, almost everyone will become seasick if conditions are bad enough.

For example, within the first three days of a normal Atlantic crossing on a large passenger liner, between 25 and 30 percent of the passengers will be sick. On small yachts, the percentage is much higher, and people cast adrift in small inflatable liferafts experience even higher rates of sickness (about 60 percent of them will succumb).

Four Things

It is a joyous feat to bring a small sailing vessel in from deep waters—and one accomplished by comparatively few human beings. In fact, as it was in Biblical days, the passage of a vessel on the ocean beyond the sight of other humans is still imbued with a good deal of mystery.

There is a beautiful passage in the Bible, in Proverbs 30:18-19: "There be three things which are too wonderful for me, yea, four which I know not: The way of an eagle in the air; the way of a serpent upon a rock; the way of a ship in the midst of the sea; and the way of a man with a maid."

Modern science has plucked out the hearts of three of these mysteries. An eagle's prowess at soaring can be explained by simple aerodynamics. The way of a serpent upon a rock is now rather well understood by herpetologists. And any experienced psychologist will tell you that the way of a man with a maid is devilishly devious.

But the way of a ship in the midst of the sea—now there's a real and lasting mystery. No two ships, nor any two seas, were ever the same. That is part of the endless fascination of cruising, a sport that welcomes participants of all ages.

The causes of motion sickness are understood to be a conflict between what the eyes observe and what the balance system of the inner ear "feels." In other words, seasickness is a disorder of the brain, not the stomach, but what is puzzling to most of us is why a troubled balance system should so often result in nausea and vomiting. Science doesn't appear to have a logical explanation for that. To be accurate, though, vomiting is not always present with seasickness, and nausea is just one of many symptoms—some of which make life more miserable than simple vomiting. In fact, a victim often feels a wonderful release from seasickness almost immediately after vomiting, whereas those suffering from other symptoms can expect no relief for hours.

SYMPTOMS IN ORDER

The symptoms of seasickness often occur in the following order:

- frequent yawning and/or sighing
- slight headache
- dry mouth
- unnatural paleness (pallor)
- cold sweat
- nausea
- vomiting

These symptoms, and others, are divided between the head and the stomach like this:

- Head: cold sweats, dizziness, drooling (increased spittle), drowsiness, dry mouth, headache, hyperventilation, pale face, yawning, and sighing
- Stomach: lack of interest in food, nausea, queasiness, and vomiting (or dry heaving)

As far as prevention goes—although many eminent physicians will dispute the notion that what you eat or drink before going to sea has any direct effect on seasickness—many of us believe it is wise to stick to the golden rules:

- Stay away from alcohol and greasy foods for a couple of days before setting sail.

- When you're on board, keep warm and dry.
- If you spot the first symptoms of seasickness, either stay on deck as long as possible—standing upright, legs slightly apart; or lie flat in a bunk down below—face up, eyes closed, as close to the middle of the boat as possible, and with a supply of strong brown paper bags at hand.

WORST POSITION

Beware of sitting crouched and miserable in a corner of the cockpit, or anywhere else for that matter: The sitting position is believed to be the most conducive to seasickness.

If you can volunteer for duty at the helm or as lookout, you will usually find it staves off bouts of seasickness, or at least increases the intervals between them.

Watching the horizon is helpful, too, at least during daytime. Your eyes then confirm the motion that your internal balance system is sensing; when you are down below, nothing moves as far as your eyes are concerned, so conflict arises every time your inner ear senses the boat heaving on a swell.

Another golden rule is to take medications well before sailing or the occurrence of bad weather. The general advice is to take them three hours in advance. If you wait until you start to feel sick, it's too late for the medicine's prophylactic properties to take effect. There are many antiseasickness medicines to choose from, and it's a good idea to consult your doctor before you start experimenting to find which one suits you best (for more information on medications, see page 176).

Try to get advice from a doctor who also sails. Some landlubberly physicians have been known to sing the praises of antimotion-sickness drugs administered in the form of suppositories. But any skipper faced with the prospect of removing thick oilskins and three layers of soggy underclothing from a large crewmember lying recumbent on a lurching bunk, in order to shove a wax bomb into his private parts, knows the whole procedure is so fraught with peril it is unthinkable.

POWERFUL INFLUENCE

Ginger, in soft drinks or cookies, may help prevent sickness. And much as some of us skeptics hate to admit it, some people do seem to find relief from those elastic bands that apply pressure to the *nei-kuan* points on the inner wrist. Perhaps if you truly believe they will work, they will—no matter that there is no good scientific explanation. The mind has a very powerful influence on the body, and this is, after all, a disease of the mind.

In a similar fashion, many people believe anxiety plays a role in causing seasickness. They feel this is borne out by the demonstrable fact that the incidence of bouts of seasickness diminishes as your experience of voyaging on a small boat grows. There is always considerable anxiety present among inexperienced skippers and crews, and very little practical way of reducing it until they meet their first storm and weather it successfully, after which seasickness is not likely to be much of a problem.

The good news is that few people actually die of seasickness, although many wish death upon themselves when the sickness strikes them down—especially those who suffer the longer agony of headache, clammy skin, depression, hopelessness, despair, nausea, and dizziness rather than the relatively quick release of vomiting straight away.

REPLACE ENERGY

After the first onslaught of seasickness has died down, most people find they can swallow dry crackers and hard candy (such as barley sugar), which will provide a little nutrition and replace lost energy. What is more important, at all stages of seasickness, is to replace lost fluids with plain water, orange juice, weak tea, or whatever drink will go down most easily (with the exception of diuretics such as coffee and alcohol).

Anyone who manages to avoid seasickness during the first three days of a trip has usually adapted to the motion and is unlikely to get seasick later during that same trip. There is good reason, therefore, to move aboard the boat for a couple of days before setting off on a trip. A rolly anchorage will probably have you adapted before you get to sea; even the slight movements of the boat in a marina will start the vital adaptation process. Once having adapted, a person is immune to seasickness for six to 10 weeks after stepping ashore, and no readaption will be needed for subsequent cruises during that period.

Incidentally, the after-effects of adaptation—the swaying ground, the rocking bed, and so forth—can be felt for up to three days after a passage.

THE ONLY WAY

Most people will be able to find a medication that enables their mind and their balance system to resolve their apparent conflict fairly quickly, thereby alleviating the symptoms of seasickness or preventing them altogether. For those who don't find the right medicine, the only way to cure seasickness, unfortunately, is to be seasick and wait for the mind to adapt to the new, confusing motion at sea—which it will, eventually. It will adapt faster, though, if you can ignore your symptoms as much as possible; that is, if you can keep busy rather than retreat to your bunk.

There are obvious dangers if you're setting out on your first singlehanded passage without knowing how incapacitated you will become by seasickness. It would be wise to go to sea with a crew first, to find out exactly how you respond when the wind rises, the whitecaps start flashing in the dark, the swell starts heaving, and that dreadful feeling suddenly grips you in the pit of the stomach.

Seasickness Drugs

There are about a dozen drugs on the market for controlling motion sickness.

In the United States, common over-the-counter drugs include:

- Dramamine
- Bonine
- Meclizine
- Marezine

Prescription-only drugs include:

- Antivert
- Phenergan
- Phenergan plus ephedrine
- Transderm-Scopolamine
- Scopolamine HBR plus dextroamphetamine

Transderm-Scopolamine is manufactured in the form of a dime-sized adhesive patch worn behind the ear that releases small amounts of the drug through the skin over a period of 72 hours; after that, you should have adapted to the boat's motion at sea. This has proven extremely effective for many people who were unable to get relief from other drugs.

Even more effective is a combination of scopolamine and dextroamphetamine, which has been prescribed for space-sick astronauts; but its effects last for only about four hours, which means repeated doses are needed.

Phenergan plus ephedrine is only slightly less effective than scopolamine plus dextroamphetamine, and it has the advantage of lasting up to 12 hours, instead of four.

THINK INVERTED

If your boat turns upside down:

- Where will you end up?
- If you are down below, will you be injured by falling against sharp corners?

- If you are in the cockpit and the boat stays upside down for several minutes, will you be able to free yourself from your tether and swim up to the surface?

CHAPTER 15

The Paper Chase

S hip's business involves collecting sheaves of documents to satisfy bureaucratic appetites. It's the last thing you want to be bothered with when you're caught up in the excitement of preparing for an ocean crossing, but it's a necessary prelude to your trip.

You'll be thankful you went to the trouble when you arrive in a foreign port looking forward to peace and quiet, some time to clean up while the boat's not rocking, and a chance to adjust your mind to the hustle and bustle of life on shore. What you'll run into instead are officials. They'll be wanting to see your passport, your crew list, your ship's papers, your visa, your bank balance, your pets, your guns, your return air tickets—and goodness knows what else.

There's no way around it: You have to prepare for the paper chase before you can go, or at least as much of it as you can.

It's not always possible to anticipate all the documents agencies in some countries might want, so like the old-time buccaneers, the modern cruiser sometimes has to play things by ear. If, however, you have a small typewriter and an ink pad and a rubber stamp showing the ship's name, nationality, and hailing port, you can manufacture almost any ship's papers that might be required. Even better, of course, is a computer and a small color printer, with which you can make documents that would put a professional forger to shame.

You can avoid most problems by intelligent anticipation. These are the four major agencies you normally run into abroad.
- Customs
- Immigration
- Health authorities
- Port authorities

When you arrive at a foreign port it is customary to fly the international code flag Q from the starboard spreader. It means your crew is healthy and you are requesting clearance to land. Whether you fetch up at anchor or in a marina, wait for a visit from officials. Try to raise the harbor authorities on the VHF, if you carry one, and do what they tell you. But if you can't make contact and no officials appear after a reasonable time, say two hours, the skipper (and only the skipper) should go ashore with the passports of everybody on board, the ship's papers, the clearance certificate from the last port, and some money for taxis. Chase down the customs, immigration, and port authorities. As a last resort, report to a police station. The crew must not go ashore or let anyone except officials aboard until the boat has been cleared in. And don't let any animals go ashore, either.

CUSTOMS

Customs will ask you the usual things. What cargo are you carrying? Drugs, by any chance? What dutiable items do you have aboard that you plan to sell in this country? Who owns this boat? If you aren't the owner, can you prove you have the right to be in possession of it? Are there any guns aboard? Pets? How much cash and valuables are you carrying? Any alcohol, forbidden fresh fruit or meat, or pornographic literature? (*Playboy* rates pornographic in some countries.)

Customs officials are usually lenient if you tell them you're just a tourist and you are not planning to work or conduct any business deals. They may want to seal your liquor cabinet for the duration of your stay in the country, they may impound your handgun, and your pets may be confined to the boat. But the thoroughness with which they apply the laws of their countries often depends on their individual personalities, the state of their marriages, the phase of the moon, how near it is to quitting time, and the initial impression you make on them. You will find that there is still a certain respect afforded the captain of a ship, no matter how small. It behooves you to dress and behave with reserve and dignity in official circles.

IMMIGRATION

Immigration authorities will want to see proof of the nationality of everyone on board. Passports are the accepted documents for this purpose and will also contain your tourist visas, if they're necessary for the country you intend to visit. You may prove your identity with papers other than passports, of course, but this may result in much inconvenience.

You may have to put down a cash deposit equal to the price of an air ticket to your home country, and it's likely that your movements will be restricted to the immediate dock area until you have satisfied the requirements of their immigration laws. If you arrive with a passport but without a visa, you may also be restricted to the port area, although visas that will let you travel inland are often issued on arrival if you have a good excuse for not having obtained them at your last port of

call. There is often a reasonable excuse because of the amount of time you have been traveling and the fact that the consulates that issue visas are not always represented in every country.

PORT HEALTH

As far as the health authorities are concerned, few countries now require anything special from sailors arriving on yachts. Perhaps they've figured out that after being at sea for three weeks, you'd either be dead or covered in spots if you had anything bad. Or perhaps they've finally realized that amateur sailors represent a very minor health threat compared with the number of air travelers and the speed with which they can spread disease. There may be some countries with special requirements, however, so it would be wise to check with a U.S. consulate whenever possible to learn if any countries require vaccinations or inoculations for yellow fever, typhoid, or whatever disease is causing the latest epidemic.

Check with your doctor or local port health authority before you leave home and carry an internationally recognized health certificate that lists all your shots. Under some circumstances, if you arrive in a country without the required shots, you will simply be sent to the port health authority physician, who will give you what you need. In such a case, however, you may be confined to a quarantine anchorage for some days while the shot takes effect.

PORT CAPTAIN

Port authorities sometimes require foreign yachts to clear in and clear out in the manner of large ships. You will be asked to present clearance papers from your last port. These will prove that you abided by all their rules and don't owe them any money for taxes, ship's stores, or services provided. The port authority, in turn, will issue you with clearance papers when it's time for your departure.

The actual form of clearance varies from a

handwritten receipt to a fancy-looking sheaf of vellum embellished with a red wax seal. Sometimes an exit visa stamped in your passport performs the same function. Sometimes you won't be asked for any form of clearance papers at all.

Always ask if you can pay a courtesy call on the port captain. You usually won't get anywhere near the port captains in the world's larger ports, but you never know. There are some with an interest in small seagoing yachts. They may take the time to see you, and you may benefit from some local knowledge or a better berth.

If you visit ports of entry on the recognized world routes for small yachts, the bureaucratic requirements are often greatly simplified. You will quickly learn the procedure from other cruisers in port, either when you arrive, or by calling them on your VHF radio before you land.

Documentation

U.S. yachts may either be numbered or documented. Registration numbers are issued by the states in which boats are principally used, and they are displayed on each side of the forward half of the vessel. Strictly speaking, registering a vessel with a state provides no proof of its ownership or nationality. But foreign countries seem to accept state papers as evidence of both ownership and U.S. nationality.

Federal documentation provides a form of national registration that legally establishes a boat's nationality and ownership. It also offers her the protection of local U.S. consular officials anywhere in the world.

Your boat must measure at least five tons net in order to be federally documented. Net tonnage in this case is not a weight; it is a volume derived from gross tonnage, which is the total enclosed space or internal capacity of a vessel expressed in units of 100 cubic feet and referred to as tons.

Net tonnage is the gross tonnage minus the volume of interior spaces that will not hold cargo.

In the case of pleasure boats, deductions from gross tonnage would be mainly for engine compartments and control stations.

TONNAGE FORMULA

For the practical purposes of federal documentation of pleasure boats, gross tonnage is measured as half of the overall length, L; times overall breadth, B; times depth, D (the internal measurement of the hull, not the draft); divided by 100; that is: $\frac{1}{2} (L \times B \times D \div 100)$. Net tonnage is taken to be $\frac{9}{10}$ of gross tonnage.

Roughly speaking, 5 tons net corresponds to a moderate-displacement boat about 30 feet in length. A heavy-displacement, long-keeled cruising boat could be shorter overall but still have sufficient volume below decks to qualify for federal documentation.

A documented vessel must be owned by a U.S. citizen. The captain (and any other officer) must be a U.S. citizen as well, although crew members need not be.

Documentation gives you the legal right to fly the special U.S. yacht ensign in home waters, an authority that is not officially granted to other yachts, although many do wear the ensign without authorization, and no action ever appears to be taken against them.

A documented yacht's title also is proof of ownership, since it records the liens, mortgages, and other financial liabilities (if any) that she carries.

Certificate of Competence

There is a growing movement worldwide toward requiring yacht skippers to be qualified. This push for licensing will undoubtedly grow as the number of world-cruising sailboats increases, especially as the number of expensive deep-sea rescues increases. Some countries in Europe already ask for certificates of competence, although they cannot at present require them from skippers of foreign-owned yachts.

If you have a license issued by the U.S. Coast Guard, there can be no argument about your capabilities. If you don't have a license, you would be wise to acquire some kind of written proof of your ability to handle a sailboat. Practical and theoretical examinations are conducted for amateur sailors in many of the world's major sailing countries, and certificates of competence are awarded to those who pass. In the United States, certificates are issued by U.S. Sailing and the American Sailing Association. A sailing school logbook, with your sailing experience duly recorded, could be useful. Some yacht clubs issue letters of competence for their members. Some sailors have even made up their own official-looking documents, operating on the theory that if they have crossed an ocean and arrived safely in a foreign port, who needs any more proof? The chances are that you will never be asked to prove your competence (and if you go to the trouble of establishing your credentials, it will almost *guarantee* that nobody will ever ask you for them). But the act of foreseeing that vague possibility and doing something about it will earn you valuable points for your Black Box.

Firearms Licenses

When you arrive in a foreign port, you must be able to prove the ownership and legality of any firearms you have on board, especially handguns. Don't forget to take those papers with you, and keep them in a place separate from the guns.

Be prepared to have your guns confiscated when you probably need them most (for the duration of your stay in port) and don't be surprised if they are returned to you in less-than-perfect condition after having been left to rust in some damp safe.

Radio Licenses

If you're a U.S. citizen or permanent resident, you don't need a ship radio station license for VHF radios used in United States waters. But as soon as you use a VHF radio in foreign waters, you need a station license and an operator's license, too.

The station license costs about $75, and it covers your single-sideband (SSB) transmissions as well as your radar and VHF. It is good for 10 years. The operator's license is issued free, without an exam, and it entitles you to operate SSB and VHF equipment. Application forms are available at all marine stores.

Ship's Logbook

Nobody asks you for your logbook until you get into trouble. Then you really need it. It doesn't have to be professionally printed and bound in buffalo hide. Some of us use spiral-bound school notebooks and rule our own vertical lines for columns.

The idea of keeping a log is to demonstrate to anyone who needs to know that you run your boat in a seamanlike fashion with due regard to local and international laws.

Entries should be made in a businesslike fashion at least at the end of each watch. You should record the distance traveled during that watch, the reading of the distance log (if you have one), the course made good, wind speed, sea condition, barometer pressure, and the sighting of other ships or important landmarks, with their approximate distances and bearings. At least once a day you should record the ship's position by dead reckoning, celestial fix, or GPS. Log the number of hours you run your engine and your daily consumption of fuel and/or water.

Your log should also record all important radio calls made and received, with a brief resume of their content. International regulations actually call for a separate radio log, but this isn't insisted upon in the case of private yachts.

Make your log a document you could present to a court of law, if necessary, as a record that would demonstrate good seamanship and intelligent anticipation. If you make a mistake in the

TIME	COURSE ORDERED	STEERED	LOG	WIND & WEATHER	BAROM	REMARKS
						SATURDAY MARCH 28
0300	300	270-300	37	ENE - SE 10-15	1010	Wind now back to SE, making 4-5 knots on course.
0600	300	280-300	50	SE.-ENE 3-8	1009	Wind light & switchy, occasional rain
0800	300	280-300	59	ENE 8 mild & overcast	1011	Occasional rain
1200	300	280	75	ESE 5 High cloud, warm	1010	Very slow progress, but flat sea.
1600	315	315	85	ESE 2	1009	Nearly becalmed
1800	315	315	89	SE 5	1009	Making pleasant progress - whale sighted.
2200	315	315	06	SE 5-10 mild & settled	1011	Weather has improved and wind swung to SE. Large ship fine on stbd bow at 1900. Altered course to stbd and she passed us to port about 1 mile off. Making 3-4 knots in light but pleasant conditions.

SOUNDED WATER TANK (MAIN) TODAY. HAVE USED 80L OUT OF 145L. I.E. 6L A DAY. RESERVES: 265L

NOON POSN: 5° 01'S 29° 15'W

DAY'S RUN: 109   BONUS: 121

We used a spiral-bound, hard-cover notebook for the ship's logbook aboard the 31-foot (9.4-m) sloop Freelance en route from the Indian Ocean to Florida via Cape Agulhas with a crew of three. These entries were made in the South Atlantic, two days before we arrived at the island of Fernando de Noronha.

log, don't try to erase it. Simply run a line through the mistake and write a correction nearby.

At the end of each passage, stamp the log with the official ship's stamp and sign it.

Crew Lists

For reasons best known to bureaucrats, foreign officials sometimes ask you for multiple copies of your crew list. So type up a list of all the crew on board (including yourself) with your names, addresses, dates of birth, nationalities, passport numbers, and crew duties. Make some copies and keep them on hand: It could save you some time and trouble in an unfamiliar port.

Ship's Stamp

Have a rubber ship's stamp made up before you leave on a long trip. Give it a plain, bold design and have it read something to this effect: U.S. Vessel CELERITY. 10 Tons Net. Reg. No. 123456.

Buy a red ink pad and use your stamp on anything vaguely official, including the log and your crew lists. Sign it underneath: John Doe, Master. It probably won't overly impress the minor representatives of major foreign powers, but many of us find it does satisfy some deep-seated need to be associated with the ancient rituals and protocols of the sea.

Doctor's Prescriptions

Many yachts carry scheduled drugs in their medicine cabinets for emergencies at sea. These include morphine derivatives and other painkilling drugs of interest to the underworld. They may also create interest among the customs agents who board your boat in a foreign port: Be sure to carry a copy of your doctor's prescription on board, although not in the same place as the drugs. Keep drugstore receipts as well. Certain drugs for seasickness are banned in some countries but not in others, so to be safe you should declare them on arrival and stay legal.

Driver's License

Sooner or later you'll want to rent a car in a foreign country, or take advantage of a friend's offer to lend you one. For this purpose you'll need an international driver's license. Your local automobile association can issue you one, valid for a year, upon producing your legal state driver's license.

Spouse Package

Most long-term cruising boats are crewed by two people, and it often happens that they happily split up the everyday chores between them. As a result, one person knows everything about the engine and the other person knows everything about cooking and food stowage.

While there is inevitably a certain amount of overlapping of these areas of knowledge, it seldom happens that both partners know *everything* about the day-to-day running of the ship. What then, if one partner were taken ill at sea or suffered an incapacitating injury? Wouldn't it be a good idea before going to sea for each partner to sit down and write out a package of instructions for the other partner to use in an emergency? You don't need a full-blown instruction manual—just brief notes to remind you of tasks, or tell you how to perform them.

Here are a few suggestions to get you started. Each boat will have its own systems and its own methods of operating them, so you will need to add to this list as ideas occur to you. A spouse package will add a feeling of security to your sailing, and it will be of special benefit if both partners go through all the steps with each other before sailing.

Anchor: How to lower it and set it. How much scope to give. How to raise it and secure it.

Bilge pumps: Designate which are electric and automatic; which are manual and not automatic. Tell how to use all of them and keep their strainers from clogging; tell how to clear the limber holes so all bilge water drains to the sump.

Compass: How to read a steering compass and hold a course. How to use a hand bearing compass and plot simple position lines on a chart. How to check the accuracy of the steering compass with the hand bearing compass.

Engine: Write, in order of execution, all the steps to be taken to start the engine, to put it into gear, to control its speed, and to stop it. Tell how to gauge the amount of fuel remaining and how to top up the tank from jerry cans; how to keep the starting battery separate from the house battery. If it's a diesel, outline how to bleed air from the fuel lines.

First-aid kit: Where it's kept, what's in it, and where the first-aid manual is kept.

Flares and emergency signals, including EPIRB: Where they are stowed and how to use them.

Furling and reefing: How to furl and release the roller foresail. How to reef the mainsail.

Liferaft: How to deploy it. Where the grab bag is stowed. What's in the raft and how to use it. How to right it after a capsize.

Navigation: A simple example of how to read a GPS position, plot it on a chart, and draw a course from there to safety.

Passports, ship's papers: Tell where they are stowed. Also list the hiding places of cash, traveler's checks, credit cards, and other important documents, including the addresses and phone numbers of family and friends.

Provisions: Tell where all the different food-stuffs are stowed; list what will keep and what won't. List where the recipe books live. Tell how to sound the water tanks.

Radios: Step-by-step instructions on how to work the VHF and SSB transceivers. Include which channels to use, what details rescuers will want to know in an emergency.

Sails: Tell how to raise and lower them, which halyards to use, and where they are cleated. Tell how to know when the luff tension is right, how to tension vangs and preventers, how to place sheet blocks correctly, how to adjust all sheets.

Self-steering gear: Tell how to engage it, how to adjust it, and when not to use it.

Stove and oven: Step-by-step instructions on starting and closing off the stove and oven.

Power of Attorney

Here is the basis of a document that could prove very useful to a couple cruising abroad. It provides a way around the obstacles foreign authorities can throw in your way if your partner becomes incapacitated and you suddenly find you do not have the legal right to move your boat. This simple sworn statement could help bypass some very unpleasant legal tangles at a time of great stress. Have a document like this drawn up by a lawyer before you go cruising. If you insist on drawing up your own document, be sure to have it correctly signed, witnessed, and notarized; try to persuade a U.S. consulate to record it and add their stamp to it.

The following example is based on a suggestion by Lin and Larry Pardey in their book, *The Capable Cruiser.*

POWER OF ATTORNEY

To whom it may concern:

I, Jane Mary Doe, sole legal owner of the vessel *Saucy Sue,* registered in Seattle, Washington, U.S.A., registration number 123456, net tonnage 10.4, do hereby solemnly swear that in the event of my death, incapacitation due to illness, or absence through any cause, determined or undetermined, it is my wish that all my rights and powers as owner and captain of the said vessel shall be ceded unconditionally to John James Doe.

He shall have the right to operate the said vessel and make whatever arrangements he might deem necessary for its normal or abnormal operation, including shipment by road, rail, or sea. He shall be empowered to place the vessel in storage or safekeeping, and/or to leave the vessel and to return at will, without relinquishing any of the powers granted under this document.

He shall have the right to hire another competent captain to carry out his instructions. His signature shall, in the event of my death, incapacitation or absence, be accepted in the place of mine on any legal documents pertaining to the operation, ownership, and movements of the aforementioned vessel, under any and all national and international laws that might apply.

THINK INVERTED

If your boat turns upside down:

• Will your important documents tumble into a flood of seawater and be ruined? Stow your ship's papers and passports in sturdy, sealable plastic bags in a locker that can't accidentally open.

PART 3

Theory and Practice

CHAPTER 16

Surviving Heavy Weather

If you sail a boat that is reasonably seawor-thy—one that fits the theme of this book—you have little to fear from a storm at sea. But you will probably not feel entirely confident during a storm until you've had some heavy-weather experience. And that's the problem. The only way you can gain experience is to go out there without experience and worry your way through a storm or two.

It's true that you could get some practice by going to sea on someone else's boat, with a skip-per who has experience in these conditions. But this would not teach you everything about the behavior of your own boat in a storm, unless it were a sistership and rigged exactly the same way. Every boat behaves differently in heavy weather. To find out how yours prefers to be handled you have to go to sea with all the innocence and con-fidence of an apprentice lion tamer: You have to thrust your head into the jaws of a storm and hope for the best. Interestingly enough, storms are fairly rare if you plan your cruising routes and times correctly—which is why the renowned cir-cumnavigator Eric Hiscock sailed for so many years with a feeling of apprehension. He had never experienced a full-blown storm and he wor-ried about how his little 30-footer would behave.

Accounts from many round-the-world sailors confirm Hiscock's experience, reporting an aver-age of only two sailing days in every 100 when the wind reached 34 knots or higher. These reports are from yachts sailing the traditional trade wind cruising routes, of course, but it explains why many sailors are unprepared when they do finally get caught in a bad storm. When Hiscock got into one, it was a great relief: He found nothing alarming after all, and his appre-hensions were from then on greatly reduced—although, like many good sailors, he never lost them entirely.

The Theory of Heavy Weather

Although the only way to get experience of a storm is to go out and get experience of a storm, you can help things along by teaching yourself the main principles of how a boat behaves in heavy weather. That way, there will not be too many surprises out at sea. To help you toward that end, let's look at some basic theory.

DYNAMIC SYSTEM

The eminent research scientist Tony Marchaj, a champion racing sailor himself, tells us that a boat at sea is part of a dynamic system. The energy expended by the sea in heeling the boat is con-verted into the kinetic energy of rolling motion; but as the yacht rolls from one side to another, the energy is dissipated and returned to the sur-rounding water. The rate at which that energy is returned to the water depends largely on how efficiently the hull and keel are able to damp the rolling.

In short, the large surface area and shape of a traditional, long-keeled underwater hull can damp rolling better than the small surface area of a fin keel can. This difference becomes more marked when the boat is not making way through the water.

When the boat is stationary, after a few rolls the water in which the keel is swinging back and forth becomes filled with random eddies and swirls that offer less resistance to the keel. But if a boat is moving forward, the rolling energy can be dissipated more efficiently into a much greater area of less confused water.

That is why it is usually necessary to keep a fin-keeled yacht running in heavy weather. But a boat with a full-length keel can lie hove-to, or ahull, and still dissipate the wave energy that is trying to roll her over through the greater area and superior damping qualities of her underwater shape.

GREATER SAFEGUARD

Racing boats with fin keels usually carry crews large enough to man the helm at all times in heavy weather, and they can therefore benefit from staying on the move. But shorthanded cruising boats must often stop while crewmembers cook, navigate, or get some rest. A full keel will then be more of a safeguard against being rolled over by wave action than will a fin keel. In other words, a traditional long keel will look after you when the boat is dead in the water; but a fin keel needs to be kept moving.

As Marchaj points out, even a full keel will have more damping action if the boat is kept moving. "In a survival situation, active rather than passive tactics are usually successful," he wrote in an article in *Practical Boat Owner.* "Those who are able to maintain some speed and directional control fare better."

Nevertheless, he pointed out, a situation may arise when the boat simply cannot be sailed at speed. It could be due to rudder failure, exhaus-

tion of the crew, or the extreme severity of the weather. "The seaworthy boat should then be able to defend herself (and the crew) against the sea, and the choice between the type of boat may become a matter of life or death." The seaworthy boat under those challenging circumstances, according to Marchaj, is the one with the same sort of full-length keel found in classic designs of the past.

"To sum up," he said, "we have a picture of a hull being subjected to a continuous input of energy from the power of the sea and wind. In such conditions, it is not the static stiffness of the hull that is important, but its ability to absorb or dissipate the incoming energy without reaching excessive angles of heel. If the hull does not have sufficient damping quality to keep pace with the input of energy, nothing can then prevent a capsize."

GREAT PARADOX

Note that although stability is very important, it is not on its own a measure of seaworthiness. In fact, it is one of the great paradoxes of naval architecture that the more stable the vessel really is (that is, the more resistant she is to being heeled transversely), the more unstable she appears to be in a seaway. Indeed, some of the most seaworthy yacht hulls of the past have been comparatively narrow, and the tendency toward more beam in modern boats is driven by the desire of the racing crew for more form stability, hence more sail area, hence more speed; and by the desire of weekend family sailors for more spacious accommodation. Thus the growth in beam has taken place without regard for its effect on ultimate stability or seaworthiness.

"Stability is not the prime agent that determines a boat's seaworthiness," Marchaj insists. "That is to say, a tendency to dangerous rolling in heavy seas, or ultimately a knock-down, cannot be explained on the basis of stability alone. Seaworthiness is in fact profoundly affected by a number of interacting factors other than mere stability."

It is not the intent of this book to delve too deeply into the many scientific aspects of yacht design, nor to take sides on the issue of fin keels versus full-length keels, since seaworthiness is a combination of so many factors other than hull and keel shape, including the size and fitness of the crew. Some of us must confess to a preference for traditional hull designs, but that is because we prefer to sail shorthanded and like to go below in a gale and leave the boat to look after herself, as long as there is sea room. But we have safely ridden out in a small fin keeler a bad gale that sank a nearby oil-rig supply vessel; and the fact that thousands of fin-keeled boats regularly race across the oceans of the world speaks for itself.

OCEAN RACER

Perhaps the views of K. Adlard Coles, one of the world's best-known long-distance racers and cruisers, will be helpful in this respect. He was one of a small band of fearless ocean racers who roamed the seas in tiny boats just after World War II, but he was unique in that he kept detailed records of all the storms (and there were many) that he nursed his little vessel through.

In his magnum opus, *Heavy Weather Sailing*, Coles allows that the extreme shape of the modern ocean racer's hull—designed to reduce wetted surface with its cutaway fin keel and spade rudder—is fast and efficient. But he points out that the sail area is critical and must be "exactly right" in relation to the strength of the wind, both to preserve balance and to avoid the rudder stalling in the event of excessive heel or a knockdown in a squall.

Coles feels that the motion in fin-keelers is much livelier than it is in older-style boats and steering a fin-keeler requires great concentration. So even when you're cruising, you can't leave the helm for a moment.

Sailboat Motions

Here are the eight motions of a sailboat at sea, as defined by the eminent American naval architect and author Francis S. Kinney.

1. Broaching: accidentally swinging broadside to the wind and sea when running free

2. Heaving: rising and falling as a whole with the seas

3. Pitching: plunging so that the bow and stern rise and fall alternately

4. Pitchpoling: accidentally tumbling stern-over-bow in a half-forward somersault

5. Rolling: inclining rhythmically from side to side

6. Surging: being accelerated and decelerated by overtaking swells

7. Swaying: moving bodily sideways

8. Yawing: lurching and changing direction to either side of the proper course

---

Steering, he says, is at its worst when running in strong winds and gales, particularly with the wind on the quarter. Such a boat would need a constant supply of rested crew at the helm; but its quicker motion would throw the crew under greater strain than a "conventional" boat would, and it would make the crew more prone to seasickness.

Another disadvantage that can surface in exceptionally rough going is that the spade rudder is more vulnerable to damage, whether it is attached to a skeg or not.

Coles used to be an enthusiastic fan of light-displacement yachts, but he was later converted to heavier-displacement racing boats of the same overall length. He found these to be better sea boats, with "immeasurably improved windward performance in really heavy weather" because of their ability to carry more sail.

Seamanship

When we talk about seaworthiness in a boat, we have at the back of our minds a picture of her in a storm. We wonder how she will lie among the waves, and whether she would be safer with or without sail. We wonder, too, how she would behave if she were engulfed by a plunging breaker, or thrown upside down by pitching herself at full speed into the back of the swell ahead.

But an important component of seaworthiness is the experience of her crew. Seamanship is largely a matter of keeping the boat under firm control all the time. Seamanship consists of being in charge of the boat, rather than letting the boat take charge of you.

Let's have a look at how this works in practice. Let's assume we're aboard a medium-to-heavy displacement cruising sloop of about 25 feet (7.6 m) on the waterline, 31 feet (9.4 m) overall. Let's call her *Kate*. She has a traditional underwater shape, except that her long keel is cut away for almost a third of her length at the forward end in the modern fashion. *Kate* has a transom stern with an outboard rudder that hangs off the end of the keel, and she is steered with a tiller. She has a fairly tall mast with a sturdy masthead rig and one set of spreaders. She carries a crew of two. We are 150 miles offshore at the beginning of an ocean passage when the wind goes forward of the beam and starts to rise.

Now, the question most frequently asked by beginners is: "How do you know when to reef? Do I need a wind-speed indicator?"

No, you don't need an instrument to tell you when to reef. When you're beating to windward it's easy to tell. Things start getting unpleasant very quickly. Small white horses appear on wavelets and start sending spray over the bow. *Kate* begins to heel excessively in the gusts, and she needs a harder pull on the tiller to keep her on course. When the gunwale is persistently under water, rather than just dipping occasionally, it's time to reduce sail.

WHEN TO REEF DOWNWIND

If the rising wind were abaft the beam, it would be much more difficult to recognize the need to reef. If *Kate* were reaching or running, the extra pressure of the wind in her sails would be urging her forward (rather than sideways), and the gusts would translate into more speed instead of more heeling. It's an exhilarating experience to feel the boat surging down the swells, responding instantly to your command; but the euphoric feeling of control is deceptive and dangerous. The rule of thumb is that you should never carry more sail downwind than you would if you were beating in the same force of wind. Racing boats break this rule all the time, but they are manned with hefty crews trained to deal with the consequences. Shorthanded cruisers would do well to heed it.

How, then, will we know when *Kate* is reaching or running too fast and in danger of getting out of control? The wave that *Kate* digs for herself as she plows through the water at top speed starts at the bow, dips down to its lowest point amidships, and rears up to a crest again near the stern, where it threatens to break into the cockpit. That's a sign that it's time to slow her down by reducing sail.

The swells approaching from astern gradually lengthen and gain speed and steepness as the wind rises. *Kate* will eventually start to surf on breaking crests. The tiller will go slack and feel floppy for a second or two as the mass of swirling, broken water passes under her stern and affords the rudder no grip. You will experience the sensation that the stern wants to slew around sideways and overtake the bow. The boat is starting to wrest control from you. It's time to slow her down. You don't want her to match the speed of the oncoming waves and be stuck for long periods with her rudder in a mass of swirling foam. You want the waves to pass under her quickly, so that the rudder, lying in solid water, can do its important work of controlling *Kate*'s forward direction.

WHICH SAIL DO I REEF FIRST?

This is the next decision, deciding which sail to reef first.

In theory you should reduce sail by compatible amounts fore and aft: that is, in front of and behind the boat's turning axis, her center of lateral resistance (CLR). In practice, most displacement boats tend to gripe as the wind increases, and that makes them want to head into the wind; so you have to apply weather helm to keep them sailing on course. Thus, to maintain control without excessive weather helm, it is customary to reef the mainsail first: This relieves some of the force that is trying to turn the boat into the wind. The full working foresail is left to do its job of pulling the bow away from the wind.

Kate has a moderate beam and a sweet hull whose immersed areas fore and aft are roughly the same when she heels, so she does not become hard-headed as she lies over. Nevertheless, the pressure on her tiller increases when she gets her rail down, simply because the center of effort of her sails is now farther outboard, so the power that drives her forward is coming more from the side. As we reef, she will come more upright and her weather helm will become almost unnoticeable again.

STEPS TO TAKE

The rising wind that affected *Kate* was coming from ahead of the beam. But whether you're beating, reaching, or running, these are the steps to take when you reef.

1. Reef the mainsail. If you're inexperienced, and the wind seems to be rising quite suddenly, take in two reefs. It's easy to shake a reef out, but often more difficult to tuck a second reef in when the weather is deteriorating badly and you have delayed too long.

2. If you have a furling foresail, furl it while the going is good and set a hanked working jib on your inner forestay.

3. If the gunwale is still persistently under water, or if you are running too fast, strike the working jib and hoist a storm jib.

4. Most seagoing boats under a double-reefed mainsail and storm jib will be under good control until the wind reaches about 27 or 30 knots, after which they will become overwhelmed in the gusts. Your action then depends on whether your destination lies upwind or downwind.

5. If your course lies downwind, and you are being overwhelmed under a double-reefed mainsail and storm jib, strike the mainsail. A hollow-cut cruising mainsail will come down on the run, but you may have to round up temporarily, and with great care, to lower the mainsail if it has battens that could hang up on the shrouds. Once the mainsail is secured, resume your course, running under your storm jib only.

6. If your course is to windward—or if you wish to avoid being blown too fast toward dangers to leeward—and you are being overwhelmed under a double-reefed mainsail and storm jib, you should heave to.

Heaving To

As *Kate*'s destination lies to windward, we will heave to by pulling the sheet of the storm jib to weather until the sail is slightly backed. We will heave to on the starboard tack for two reasons. First, it gives us legal right of way over almost all other vessels, including sailing vessels. Second, it places our galley down to leeward, which makes cooking a lot less hazardous. You will naturally choose for yourself which tack to lie on, also taking into consideration the need to avoid land or other obstructions.

We may have to experiment a bit to establish just how far the storm jib should be brought to weather of the mast. We'll slack the mainsail off slightly, and lash the tiller to leeward with shock cord or thin nylon line to absorb shocks from the rudder.

The difference in *Kate*'s behavior is astounding. Just a moment ago she was standing on her head, bashing and crashing to windward, heeled far over, and shipping seas green. Now she lies quietly like a duck with her head under her wing, 50 to 60 degrees off the wind, so that her bow is facing the waves at an angle. But as her forward speed is so low, the waves seem to slide under her bow, and only the occasional dollop of heavy spray comes flying aft. *Kate* is, in fact, moving slowly through the water at right angles to the wind direction, leaving a tumbling, swirling slick of water to windward. She can safely be left to look after herself for a few hours if the wind doesn't increase appreciably, and we can get some sleep or cook a meal.

The wind direction often changes in the gusts, but because of her long keel, *Kate* cannot quickly change her course in response, and by the time she is ready to do so, the wind has gone back to its original direction.

CONSTANT ATTENTION

If *Kate* were a fin-keeler, things would be different. Each switching gust would have her spinning on her axis, possibly forcing the bow through the eye of the wind and causing her to run off and jibe (a very dangerous maneuver in these conditions) unless someone were paying constant attention to the helm. With her fin keel stalled, she would make a great deal of leeway—hastening her progress toward a hazardous lee shore. There would be no rest for a shorthanded crew, and the boat would demand constant attention.

As the wind continues to rise to 30 or 35 knots, we find we have to lash *Kate*'s tiller farther and farther to leeward to keep her facing toward the oncoming waves. She has a cutaway forefoot. Without any sail up at all, her natural inclination would be to lie with her bow slightly downwind, since the mast, which constitutes most of her windage, lies forward of the CLR. The raised cabintop aft of the CLR does compensate somewhat,

it's true, but the mast and its rigging wires are tall, and they exert a surprisingly powerful force in a heavy wind.

So as the wind gets even stronger, *Kate*'s bow sags farther to leeward until she is lying broadside-on to the waves instead of facing them at an angle. It's time to drop the storm jib.

Under her double-reefed mainsail alone, with her tiller lashed slightly to leeward (so that if she moves forward too fast, she will be slowed down by heading into the wind), *Kate* now lies at a good angle to the waves again; she takes them on the shoulder of her bow. The wind, incidentally, is blowing a full gale—Force 8 on the Beaufort Scale, or 34 to 40 knots; the swells are 12 to 20 feet (3.6 to 6 m) high, but a long way apart. Each wave forms a spilling breaker about 12 or 18 inches (300 or 450 mm) high, and while spilling breakers don't pack the force of plunging breakers, one will occasionally strike the bow with a surprisingly solid thump—feeling as if you had run into a concrete block and sending a shiver back through the boat.

But *Kate* was built to take this. She is in no trouble. Gales, after all, are a normal part of life on the sea.

HOWLING WIND

Kate's crew, however, might not be faring as well as she is. It's not only the frightening thump of solid water hitting the hull. It's the howl of the wind in the rigging. It is loud, very loud. Even down below you can't escape from the maddening thrumming and tapping of wires and halyards and the deep moan of a blast that seems to take the boat by her throat and shake her. In the background, the banshee wail of approaching gusts never stops for a moment.

At first, the noise is terrifying and exhausting. But after a few hours, you learn to live with it. The noise will not lose its menace; but when you realize that it has not destroyed you yet, you will come to terms with it—perhaps even snatch a few winks now and then.

We have already mentioned the slick that *Kate*'s deep keel leaves to windward as she drifts slowly along at 1 or 1½ knots. You would get the same effect by dragging a barn door through the water—huge eddies and flat-topped swirls of water would mark its wake. It has often been observed that this unstable mass of water has the beneficial effect of causing an oncoming wave to break prematurely. If we could prevent *Kate* from moving forward, she would lie directly to leeward of her slick, thus causing waves to expend their energy before they reached her. But how can we achieve this beneficial state of affairs?

PROTECTIVE SLICK

The Pardeys say we could do it with a parachute anchor. Lin and Larry Pardey lay hove-to this way, behind a protective slick, in their 24-foot cutter *Seraffyn* in a Force 10 storm. They stayed behind the slick for 30 hours, in 50- to 55-knot winds, some 400 miles west of England.

"By the second day, the waves had built until they had long overhanging crests which were breaking dangerously on either side of our slick," said Larry. "Yet in the afternoon our foredeck was only damp from the spray and the side decks had actually dried off in the September sun."

No green seas had broken against their hull, and broken white foam only occasionally skidded across the slick to slap ineffectively against *Seraffyn*'s bow.

Now don't be confused. *Seraffyn* was not lying bow-on to the seas behind a sea anchor. She would never be able to do that, any more than *Kate* or any other displacement boat could. These boats' natural tendency in heavy winds is to lie beam-on to the seas, or slightly down-wind—no matter what kind of sea anchor is streamed from the bows. *Seraffyn* was riding to a parachute anchor streamed from slightly forward of amidships: The idea was simply to stop her from moving forward and out of the protective slick. This was accomplished by setting the para-

Seraffyn hove-to under a triple-reefed mainsail. The 8-foot-diameter (2.4-m) parachute anchor stops her forereaching and keeps her dead downwind of her protective slick.

anchor from the bow, and then clapping on a line, led to a turning block well aft, to form a bridle. In addition to her para-anchor, *Seraffyn* lay to a triple-reefed mainsail, equivalent in area to a storm trysail.

CARGO CHUTE

Seraffyn's para-anchor was a surplus U.S. Navy cargo chute of a type used extensively by the fishing fleet in Southern California. It measured 8 feet (2.4 m) in diameter and was made of coarsely woven nylon. *Seraffyn*'s inclination to forereach could be controlled by adjusting the length

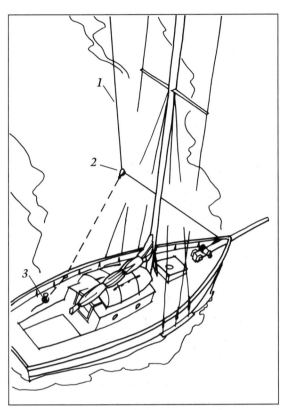

Detail of Seraffyn's *para-anchor line (storm trysail not shown for clarity): (1) Line from para-anchor to bow. (2) Snatch block, with line leading to aft sheet winch. (3) Adjusting the line on the winch brings the bow up into the wind, or lets it fall off.*

of the arms of the bridle. Adjustment was quick and simple, because the aft line led from a turning block to a winch.

Those of us who have never had to use an 8-foot-diameter (2.4-m-diameter) para-anchor in storm conditions have to wonder how easy it would be to set it and recover it without getting the anchor—or its many lines—wrapped around any underwater appendages or trapped in the rigging. We wonder too why the boat—being driven by a reefed mainsail—doesn't simply sail forward and out of the protective slick, in an arc

whose center is marked by the sea anchor. But the Pardeys insist the set-up works perfectly and is easily managed by a small crew.

Those of us who have been forced to move out of the way of freighters while lying ahull (and almost invisible) in a storm also wonder how a boat tethered to the spot by a para-anchor would survive. It is something to think about before you try it.

Meanwhile, *Kate* has no para-anchor to experiment with. In the calmer patches between seas she continues to lie with her head toward the wind. But the wind is still rising and the breakers on the wave crests are starting to plunge now. Every time one hits her bow, she gets thrown broadside on. After being knocked about by big seas a few times, we decide that something must be done. It's time to lie ahull.

Unstable Moments

A boat hove to in steep seas is probably at a greater risk of being capsized when she is on top of a wave than at any other time.

When she is hove upward and then quickly abandoned by a passing wave, she momentarily experiences a feeling of weightlessness (or partial weightlessness). At that moment, with a large area of her hull out of the water, she has practically no form stability at all.

In theory, the slightest puff in her sails could blow her over 90 degrees. In practice, the inertia of her mast and rig slows down her response: Before she can heel too much, she is once again being supported by water all around and experiencing an excess of buoyancy and righting moment by being pressed down into the sea.

Nevertheless, it is a fascinating exercise to sense those moments of instability when you're sailing on a beam reach in a lively sea, especially on a light-displacement yacht.

Lying Ahull

The wind has risen to a steady 45 knots, gusting to 50 or more, and it's no easy task to strike the reefed mainsail or trysail. As we take in the canvas, *Kate* starts to roll mercilessly, and it's almost all we can do to hang on. Then, as she falls broadside on to the wind, things steady up a bit. The force of the wind on the mast and rigging alone is now enough to heel her over 15 degrees or so and prevent excessive rolling.

Without the sail, her drift to leeward has slowed, and she feels more under control. We'll lash the helm down to leeward a little with shock cord, as we did before. That way if she does gather way for some reason, she will round up into the wind and stall before she can go about.

Although she's heeled over, *Kate* is in no danger of tripping on her leeward side deck and rolling over because she has plenty of freeboard. And the great advantage of being slightly tilted to leeward is that she presents a strong egg-shaped portion of her hull to the breaking waves.

Occasionally, a wave breaking against the hull will slop over into the cockpit. Luckily, *Kate*'s cockpit is watertight, and her seat lockers are tightly sealed. She has four 1½-inch (40-mm) cockpit drains, but they work slowly, despite the fact that we've carefully kept them free of rope ends and debris. If necessary, we can bail the cockpit with a bucket that's kept handy in a seat locker; but at the moment, the swells are far enough apart that the water drains away before another wave can be threatening. It's very unlikely that she would retain a cockpit full of water anyway. She rolls to leeward when the waves hit, and that would spill out at least half of the water.

REDUCE WINDAGE

We have folded the dodger down flat against the cabintop to reduce windage. If we had weather cloths made fast to the lifelines around the cockpit, we'd take those in too because a heavy wave breaking into them might rip out the stanchions and lifelines.

Kate can lie passively like this in very heavy weather, and you might wonder why we don't lie ahull as soon as heavy weather strikes, instead of going through the routine of reefing and heaving to. The fact is, *Kate* needs some sail up to steady her until the wind has reached more than full-gale force. Without sail, she would roll so excessively that you probably wouldn't be able to move around; and her jerking and heaving would put an overpowering strain on her rigging. But when it's blowing 50 knots or so, the wind force on the mast alone is enough to steady her.

Francis Chichester lay ahull in his 40-foot sloop *Gipsy Moth III* with winds gusting to 100 mph during the 1960 singlehanded transatlantic race; he was able to go below, cook a meal of fried potatoes, onions, and eggs and fall asleep reading (appropriately enough) *The Tempest*.

Alec Rose used the same tactic during his circumnavigation, in 1967–68, in *Lively Lady*, and he insisted that it was safer to lie ahull—"that is, to strip off all sails and let the yacht go with the sea and take up her own position." *Lively Lady* lay with the wind just ahead of abeam, moving forward very slowly, and heeling slightly to leeward. Rose admitted that the boat was thrown about "unmercifully." But he felt that the motion would have been the same whatever he'd done, and he said he'd be prepared to lie ahull in the "very fiercest storms."

HURRICANE CARRIE

Those of us who knew the famous round-the-worlder Jean Gau during his wanderings in his 30-foot Tahiti ketch, *Atom*, in the late 1950s were often told how fond he, too, was of lying ahull. In fact, *Atom* rode out Hurricane Carrie, which sank the nearby bark *Pamir* with the loss of 80 lives. Gau said he lashed *Atom*'s tiller to leeward and left her to her own devices in 120-knot winds while he shut himself below.

Atom was comparatively shallow-drafted, and thus able to slip bodily to leeward when huge seas hit her. But boats with deep draft might trip over their keels, dig a side deck in the water, and flip over. So any boat that lies ahull needs to be able to withstand a 180-degree capsize.

How would a fin-keeler fare under the same conditions while lying ahull? Probably better than she would hove to. The ease with which a wave can swivel a fin-keeled boat horizontally means she would be very unstable when hove to—alternately pointing too high and falling down too low. Constant manning of the helm would ease that problem; but this is not a remedy available to a shorthanded crew.

When a fin-keeler is set to lie ahull in really heavy weather, however, she seems to do about as well as a boat with a full keel. Because the area of her keel is small, she slips to leeward easily under a blow from a wave, and she is less likely to trip over her keel. Overall, she is still more likely to be capsized by a plunging breaker than a full-keeled boat, however, for reasons we have already discussed. She also needs plenty of sea room, because she will drift downwind faster than a full-keeled yacht will.

John Guzzwell's famous *Trekka* was a 21-foot (6.4-m) fin-keeler, a light-displacement yawl with a separated, skeg-mounted rudder. Those of us who saw her hauled out of the water at Point Yacht Club in Durban, South Africa, could hardly believe a boat so small could come through a hurricane unscathed. But that's precisely what she did.

A few months before she was hauled out, Guzzwell had run into a six-day tropical cyclone off the coast of Australia, in June 1958. He furled the sails, lashed the helm down, and left her to drift to leeward, beam to the seas, at the rate of about 1 knot.

WORSE SEAS
Meanwhile, back aboard *Kate,* things are beginning to get uncomfortable. The wind has not risen much more—perhaps a steady 50 knots now, gusting to 55—but the seas seem to have worsened considerably. Perhaps we are encountering a current running contrary to the wind. That would explain why the seas seem so much closer together now—and so much steeper.

One huge sea, approaching at a slight angle to the rest, rides up and across the back of another and towers over *Kate*. As it breaks, *Kate* is hurled bodily to leeward and her side decks and cabintop are buried. Luckily, although we had only one set of storm windows on board, we fitted them to the leeward portlights—because that's where the damage always occurs in these conditions. The windward ports are well tilted over and are not very susceptible to damage, but when a ship is thrown sideways off a wave, she lands with great force: The leeward cabin side and portlights take much of the strain.

Kate recovers quickly. We weren't damaged that time, but we don't want to risk it again in this exceptional storm. It's time to run off before the wind.

Running Off

When a boat runs dead before the wind, her course is perpendicular to the track of the waves. She is much less likely to be capsized in this position, because it takes much more energy to tilt her head over heels, or mast over keel, than it does to roll her over sideways. That is not to say that longitudinal rolling, or pitchpoling, never occurs. It does, and quite frequently—but always in very exceptional circumstances.

We plan to raise a small storm jib on *Kate*, pull her head off the wind, and get her moving forward so we can steer her. But in fact, the windage of one of us on the foredeck is just enough to do the trick, and there is no need to raise the sail.

Kate pays off slowly and then gathers speed and runs downwind under bare poles. We can steer her 20 or 30 degrees to port or starboard and still keep her moving. Now we can keep an eye on what's happening astern. Having figured out which sea is likely to break where, we can weave a path through the heaving swells so as to miss the worst of the plunging breakers.

The first problem is that somebody has to steer her. It's not physically challenging, but it is mentally very wearying to sit exposed on deck in a bad storm. You never know when a wave is going to break over the stern and fill the cockpit, but you're very aware that it's up to you to keep the boat out of trouble. One minute of distraction, and a rogue wave can be rearing up astern.

RUNNING FAST

The second problem is that *Kate* seems to be running too fast, just as she was at the very beginning of this exercise. Even without the tiniest scrap of sail, she's surging down the backs of swells at nearly 7 knots, which is more than her hull speed. The steering is feeling sloppy again when swells pass under the stern.

There are two dangers here. The first is that she will broach to, that is, her stern will slew around until she is broadside-on at the bottom of a trough, at which point her considerable momentum will roll her over. The second con-

The Sandefjord *Shock*

In Chapter 9, we mentioned the *Sandefjord* in our discussion on barometers (page 97). For many years, this boat was regarded as a famous example of what can happen if you keep a sailboat running too fast for too long in bad weather.

Sandefjord was a 47-foot (14.3-m) gaff ketch designed and built by Colin Archer. She was a type of vessel often regarded as the perfect ocean cruiser: deep, strong, and very beamy.

Her Norwegian owner, Erling Tambs, sailed her to Cape Town, South Africa, in 1935, but *Sandefjord* encountered a storm en route. She was run off before it under her double-reefed mainsail only.

The seas were so heavy that she needed two men at the helm to control her. They had, in fact, already complained that they could not hold her when an extra-steep sea lifted her stern high in the air. Her bow then dived deeply into the back of the swell ahead, and *Sandefjord* turned end over end—losing one man and her mizzen mast.

Her mishap caused consternation in the yachting fraternity, and led to a re-evaluation of the theories of yacht design and handling, ultimately leading to yachts of somewhat lighter displacement with more of the keel area cut away at the forefoot, and recommendations that drogues or warps be towed to slow down a boat running in a seaway and thus avoid the dangers associated with uncontrolled surfing. The real message is this: Although no boat is totally immune to capsizing, intelligent handling can reduce the risk considerably.

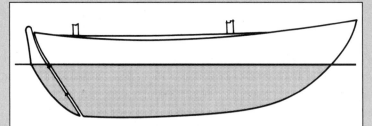

Sandefjord's *underwater body profile was a typical Colin Archer design: deep, beamy, and long-keeled. Her full forefoot enabled her to heave to well. Modern cruising yachts have a cutaway forefoot that enables them to run downwind with less of a tendency to broach to in heavy weather.*

cern is that as she surges down one swell, she often plunges her bow into the back of the swell ahead. You can feel her brake suddenly as the bow tries to stop, and you wonder if the stern is

---

Jordan's Drogue

After the Fastnet Race tragedy of 1979, much attention was focused on the question of preventing capsize. Studies undertaken by the inventor of the series drogue, Donald Jordan, in conjunction with the U.S. Coast Guard, indicated that the following characteristics of small sailboats discouraged capsizing.

- Heavy displacement
- Low center of gravity
- Moderate freeboard
- Narrow beam
- Tall, heavy mast

Jordan subsequently devised a new type of drogue to help boats ride out storms. As we mentioned in chapter 8 (see page 88), it consists of many 5-inch-diameter (127-mm-diameter), cone-shaped sea anchors made of sailcloth and spaced along an anchor rode, one every 20 inches (508 mm).

By this means, a continual tension is maintained on all parts of the rode, so that the boat's stern is held up to the seas more constantly, thus avoiding the dangerous tendency of an ordinary drogue to tumble or collapse with the passage of a breaking sea, and to be swept quickly forward. If the boat hesitates in a trough, the weight at the end of the drogue sinks and removes the slack immediately.

Interestingly, one manufacturer of the drogue, Ace Sailmakers, of New London, Connecticut, estimates that a boat displacing 10,000 pounds (4,536 kg) needs 100 cones, or droguelets—but a boat displacing twice as much needs only 16 more, and a 30,000-pound (13,608-kg) boat needs only 132 cones. So a series drogue is particularly good value for larger boats.

---

going to fly up and over your head. That is a classic pitchpole.

ROUND AND BUOYANT

Luckily, *Kate*'s keel is cut away under her bow, so she is not as likely to trip over it (as she would if she had a deep forefoot). Her bow is round and buoyant too, so she rises quickly from the back of the swell. Nevertheless, you still need to slow her down.

One thing you are grateful for is the fact that *Kate* does not require a great deal of sawing at the tiller to keep her going straight. There are currents moving in different directions on the backs and fronts of waves; and on a fin-keeled boat, the sudden change in direction physically pushes the bow around and puts the boat in danger of broaching to. The rudder must be turned quickly to straighten her up again. This continual movement of the tiller is very tiring. One lapse in concentration could spell disaster, so spells at the helm must be short, and the crew must stay fresh.

Kate's long keel stops her from reacting too quickly. By the time she is starting to respond to the current on the front of a wave, the crest has passed and a current in the opposite direction is tending to cancel out any tendency for her to deviate from her course. Nevertheless, as we said, it's still time to slow her down.

We are in the early stages of a very bad storm now, one approaching hurricane force. It's blowing too hard and the seas are too steep and confused for us to heave to, lie ahull, or run off under a bare pole. But we still have some survival tricks up our sleeves. The first is to keep *Kate* on her downwind course, but to slow her down by towing warps or drogues.

Towing Drogues

Before we stream our drogue, let's make sure we understand the difference between drogues and sea anchors.

A *drogue* is something that is dragged through the water at a speed of a knot or two. A *sea anchor* offers much more resistance—so much so that it acts more like an anchor dug into the bottom of the sea. A drogue is normally streamed from the stern, and a sea anchor is set from the bow.

A drogue can consist of almost anything that will cause a drag in the water. Some people use old car tires on the end of a long line, weighted down with the ship's anchor. Others use planks of wood bolted on to steel angle iron. Still others use thick, long hawsers—streamed in a bight, with each end made fast to the boat. One advantage claimed for the bight is that it offers the same kind of protection from oncoming waves as the protective slick the keel makes when you're hove to: It causes dangerous waves astern to break prematurely and expend their energy before they hit you. This might be true for a bight that can be weighted and kept a little way under the surface. But it is likely that a bight floating on the surface would be hurled a long way forward by a breaker, and it would suddenly relieve the boat of much of its drag at the exact time when she needs it most. Perhaps the most scientifically designed drogue is the series drogue, invented by Donald Jordan.

PACKED WITH CARE

A sea anchor looks like a parachute. It has fewer strings and is made of much tougher material than a regular parachute used on an aircraft. But a sea anchor has to be packed with almost as much care, because it can be the devil to set in a storm. If a corner escapes prematurely, it can be plastered in the rigging or lifelines and out of control in a second or two.

A sea anchor is set on the end of a stretchy nylon line that absorbs the shock of the boat's sudden movement when a breaking crest strikes it; the sea anchor is always set from the bow. But there is hardly a sailboat of any design that will lie quietly bow-on to the seas in a storm behind a sea

anchor. Because the windage on the mast is so far forward, and because the center of lateral resistance is usually fairly far aft, almost any monohull sailboat will tend to lie broadside on to the wind and seas in a storm—or nearly so.

It may be hard to believe that the bow of a yacht firmly tethered to a sea anchor could blow away downwind to such an extent, but it is true. On the other hand, nearly every monohulled sailboat afloat would lie quietly if she were tethered by the stern; but that would leave her very vulnerable to the seas. Experience has proved time and time again that extreme wind pressure in storm conditions will turn a sailboat until she lies along the axis of the troughs—despite the tugging of a sea anchor.

There are, however, some craft with deep forefeet and shallower sterns (or canoe-bodied craft of almost equal depth from bow to stern) that will lie quietly, bow to the seas, behind a sea anchor. Powered fishing boats will often do so, depending on the relative heights of their superstructures fore and aft. Monohull sailboats with canoe bodies, centerboards, and shallow stub keels will do so, too. In fact, John Voss invented a folding, cone-shaped sea anchor and then sailed around the world in his small Nootkan canoe, *Tilikum,* to prove the anchor worked. Multihulls will also lie peacefully to an unyielding sea anchor.

STEEP AND CONFUSED

But enough talking. Let's get back to *Kate*. We left her in near-hurricane-force winds, with steep and confused seas. She has no canvas showing, but she is running downwind too fast, surfing down the faces of waves and starting to bury her bows in the back of the wave ahead.

Luckily, we have a Jordan series drogue on board. We nearly didn't have it, because the price for 42 fathoms (77 m) of $5/8$-inch (16-mm) nylon line and 107 nylon cones seemed expensive—especially for something we never really expected to have to use anyway. We bought it ready-made

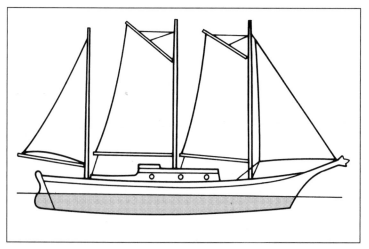

Captain John Voss's famous Tilikum *had a shallow-drafted canoe body that enabled her to lie quietly to a sea anchor streamed from the bow.*

from Ace Sailmakers, of New London, Connecticut, for the price of 312 beers. But now we're very glad we've got it.

First we take three turns around a cockpit winch with the inboard end of the line and then cleat it securely. Then we shackle a length of chain weighing about 15 pounds (7 kg) to the outboard end of the line and feed it over the stern, letting it pull the nylon line after it. The cones, the wide end facing toward us, fill with water and we can feel the drag. Soon the line and cones are flying out of their box at great speed. We keep our hands well clear and hope like hell there won't be a tangle—because there's no stopping this little lot. We wonder, in fact, if it's going to jerk the winch out by the roots when it comes to the end, but we are happy to note that there is no noticeable shock—probably because of the stretch in the nylon. Nevertheless, the line is now under great strain; within a minute our speed has dropped from more than 6 knots to a little over 1 knot. We clap another line onto the drogue line to form a bridle with 10-foot (3-m) legs, lead them through the aft chocks, and pad them well against chafe with duct tape.

STEADY PULL

The difference is remarkable. *Kate* is behaving like a real lady. That out-of-control, headlong rush has disappeared. She lies stern-on to the waves with almost no help from the helm at all. In fact, we could lash the tiller amidships and she would look after herself.

With an ordinary drogue, there is regular slacking in the line as the drogue encounters foam instead of solid water, or it is thrown forward by a breaking crest. And every time the line goes slack, the stern is quickly slewed around by the wind and waves, putting the boat in a vulnerable broadside-on position. But this drogue exerts a steady pull all along its length, and it is not afflicted with periods of dangerous slackening.

We find we can steer *Kate* 20 or 30 degrees away from dead downwind, if we want to. This would be useful if there were reefs or islands ahead. For the moment, however, we have plenty of sea room, and we mostly leave *Kate* to her own devices, her tiller lashed amidships with several lengths of strong shock cord to absorb the kick of the rudder when a wave passes beneath the stern. We are surprised at the way so many fierce-looking waves seem to slip under her stern without crashing into the cockpit, and we wonder if those scores of nylon cones dragging astern are forming some kind of protective slick. It's impossible to tell. With flying spindrift, we can hardly see more than a few yards astern—except when we rise to the top of a large swell. It actually stings our faces when we look aft.

THREATENING WAVES

Kate rides this way for more than half a day. One crewmember rests down below while the other sits in the cockpit on a short tether, keeping as good a lookout as possible and occasionally steering clear of a set of waves that looks more threatening than usual.

This wind is very worrying. It is showing no signs of abating. On the contrary, the whole surface of the sea is now white with flying spume. The swells have lengthened and the size of the plunging breakers has grown. There seem to be fewer than before, but they are far more menacing, leaving behind them when they break an area of churning foam that looks the size of a football field. One or two plunging crests break near *Kate,* and we find it impossible to escape their path because our speed is so slow. It is time to start scudding.

High-Speed Scudding

Luckily, we know about Bernard Moitessier's technique of high-speed scudding, the one he used to save *Joshua* during his "ultimate storm" in the southern Pacific. We have been a fan of Moitessier ever since we met him, broke and friendless, in an Indian Ocean port way back in the 1950s, and we have kept up with his writings.

We remember, too, that C. A. Marchaj also recommends high-speed scudding in long, fast-moving seas. In short seas, like those *Kate* was experiencing at first, Marchaj feels it is better to stream a drogue that will hold the stern up when the boat is on a crest and the rudder is inefficient. But when the seas lengthen and speed up, it's time to scud.

Moitessier found himself in exactly the same conditions we are now experiencing, and he, too, found that his drogues were hampering his steering in those huge seas: *Joshua* was being held fast while massive breakers boarded her aft and rampaged over her decks.

We haven't reached that stage yet with *Kate*—and we don't want to either. She has a watertight cockpit and a strong bridge deck at the forward end of it to stop water going down below. She has strong drop slides in the compan-

ionway instead of weak doors, and the construction of her transom and rudder is about as strong as it gets. But we don't want to be swamped and trampled by the tons of solid water bearing down on us. So we'll do what Moitessier did.

GOOD-BYE DROGUE
We cut the drogue free. It has no trip line. The inventor doesn't recommend one, because it complicates the gear and may lead to fouling. So it's good-bye to 312 beers; but there is no way we can recover the drogue under these conditions. If the wind were dying, we could winch it in carefully, or even clap hauling lines on it with rolling hitches and recover a few feet at a time. But that process would take a half-hour or so, and we don't have the time, the energy, or the willpower. The drogue has, in any case, done its job. It was only one of a long series of defensive moves we've made. Now we're ready to move on to the next.

We free *Kate* from her shackles and let her flee downwind under bare poles, as she did before. This time, however, the swells are much bigger and farther apart. They're like small mountains, and at their peaks long lines of surf avalanche down their steep faces. We keep *Kate* running dead downwind until a steep following sea rears up close astern. Just before it strikes, we turn her 15 to 20 degrees to one side and try to maintain that course as the sea breaks under her and passes by. If the helm pulls when the wave is underneath, we release the tiller completely for a few seconds until the pressure is released. (It's important not to fight the sea at this critical period.) Then we put the helm up again to bring her back on course. When *Kate* settles back into the trough we turn her dead downwind again. We find that taking the seas at a slight angle like this prevents her from getting out of control by surfing too fast and plowing into the sea ahead. The oncoming sea also heels her to leeward quite a lot; if she does dig into the back of sea, her rounded bow tends to scoop her out of it.

OUT OF CONTROL

Moitessier says he got the idea for this method of high-speed scudding from Vito Dumas, who sailed around the world in the roaring forties during World War II in *Lehg II*. Dumas found that his boat could get out of control in the troughs of big seas, where she was blanketed from the wind, if she was running too slowly.

There is little doubt in our minds that fast scudding gives us the best control of the boat now, active control rather than passive, for it allows us to cover a lot of ground quickly and weave among the waves to avoid the most dangerous seas. We don't kid ourselves that we can avoid all of them all the time. We are mentally prepared for a capsize. But we believe we can improve the odds this way.

Scudding is also less punishing on the boat. When *Kate* was lying to her drogue, her flat transom was beginning to take a heavy pounding from the seas. Had she been a double-ender, or even if she had had a short counter stern, we might have left her on the drogue and simply shut ourselves down below, but the strikes against the flat transom were becoming very worrying.

Kate is now doing fine, considering the circumstances, but she needs constant attention. An hour at the helm seems too long, even though the crew below complains that an hour is not long enough for a decent sleep (or rest, rather, because sleep is impossible). Everything below is soaking wet; we pump the bilges for five minutes every half hour before we hear the welcome sucking noise that indicates they're dry again. The water squirts through the cracks in the dropboards and we guess the seat lockers are letting some in, too.

After four hours, the wind begins to veer slightly and drop in velocity. After another hour and much more veering, it's down to 30 knots, but the sea is misbehaving badly, with lumpy waves running in all directions. We raise the double-reefed mainsail, lash the helm to leeward, and leave *Kate* safely hove to on the starboard tack. She gets shoved off course frequently, but never enough to make her go about. We lie down on our bunks, still in our wet foul-weather gear, and pass out.

STEPS TAKEN

You will probably never experience the kind of weather we've just been through with the mythical *Kate*, unless you're planning to round Cape Horn, or unless you get caught up in a hurricane. All the same, we cannot emphasize too strongly the importance of gathering the best and latest weather forecasts, either by single-sideband radio or from ham nets.

Few round-the-world sailors, sticking to the trade wind routes and avoiding hurricane seasons, run into winds of more than 40 knots; so it's unlikely that you'd need to cut away your drogue, as we had to on *Kate*. But now, at least, you know the order of things: You know what to do when the wind begins to pipe up. To recap:

1. Reef the mainsail
2. Furl the foresail and set a hanked working jib on the inner forestay
3. Strike the working jib and hoist a storm jib
4. Heave to
5. Lie ahull
6. Run off
7. Tow a drogue
8. Scud at high speed

Dangerous Currents

Finally, a word or two about currents. If you come across seas that seem unreasonably steep and close together for the force of the wind, you're probably experiencing one of the most dangerous sea states that any vessel can encounter: wind versus current.

A current is an invisible river in the sea. And a wind blowing against a current has the effect of rippling up the water, just as if it were a rug being pushed from one end.

Steep seas that are close together are unstable, and their tops have a tendency to topple over, plunging down their faces with great force in the same way that swells turn into surf as they encounter shallows.

The temporary currents we call tidal streams will often create dangerous local races and overfalls. But the real monsters—the freak waves—are created where fast-running ocean currents meet swells generated by winds unhindered by contact with land for hundreds of miles.

A fresh Norther blowing contrary to the fast-flowing Gulf Stream can create very dangerous conditions for small craft, but when that vast river of warm water called the Agulhas Current meets gales spawned in the roaring forties at the southern tip of Africa, even large passenger liners run into trouble.

Jean Gau's *Atom,* Tom Steele's *Adios,* and dozens of other small sailboats have been capsized off the coast of South Africa between Durban and Cape Town in fierce seas kicked up by southwesterly gales blowing against the Agulhas Current. In light of their experiences, however, a plan has evolved for rounding the Cape more safely.

Round-the-world cruisers heading south and west from Richards Bay or Durban are now given detailed instructions on how to avoid the worst of the storm-generated seas along the route. And what it boils down to is avoiding areas where the wind and the current are at cross-purposes—usually by moving away from the particularly dangerous area of the 100-fathom line, where the 4-knot current runs up against the continental shelf, and staying within a mile of the coast in a gentle counter-current.

WITHOUT TRACE

For big ships, the freak waves off South Africa often come as a surprise. The passenger liner *Waratah,* en route from Australia to Britain, was lost without trace off the Wild Coast, southwest of Durban, in July 1909.

More recently, in August 1964, the Union-Castle liner *Edinburgh Castle* fell into a deep trough that opened in the sea very near the spot where the *Waratah* was lost.

The liner was 750 feet long and displaced 28,600 tons gross. She was heading southwest into a strong southwesterly wind and a heavy southwest swell in the vicinity of the 100-fathom line off Port St. Johns. Her master, Commodore W. S. Byles, had a healthy respect for this coast, having completed hundreds of voyages between Durban and East London, so he decided to take a knot off her speed and close with the coast.

"The distance from one wave top to the next was about 150 feet [45 m]," Commodore Byles reported later. "The ship was pitching and scending about 10 to 15 degrees to the horizontal. And then it happened. Suddenly, having scended normally, the wave length appeared to be double the normal, about 300 feet [91 m], so that when she pitched she charged, as it were, into a hole in the ocean at an angle of 30 degrees or more, shoveling the next wave on board to a height of 15 or 20 feet [4.5 to 6 m] before she could recover, as she was 'out of step.'"

The wall of water that coursed over the foredeck swept away rails and ladders, and a great quantity of water flooded into the passenger accommodation.

A British naval cruiser hit a "hole" in the same area and shipped a sea that came green over her gun turrets and broke over the bridge.

WAVE TRAINS

Freak waves are as common as freak holes, but neither condition is really "freakish" because sea systems are composed of many different wave trains, each with its own speed and height.

At random intervals, the wave trains can fall in step with one another, literally riding on one another's backs, to form an exceptionally high wave. It doesn't need to be blowing a gale for this to happen. But if the weather is indeed stormy, and if there is a contrary current to steepen the face of the giant wave, it will topple over and release its energy in the form of a plunging breaker large enough to overwhelm any small sailboat.

It is no old wive's tale that every fifth, or seventh, or ninth wave is larger than the others. It is the result of interacting wave trains.

According to Laurence Draper, of the National Institute of Oceanography, the probability of occurrence of any such wave is finite and can be predicted. He asserts that one wave in 23 is over twice the height of the average wave. One in 1,175 is more than three times the average height. One in 300,000 exceeds four times the average height. There is an equal chance, he adds, of an unusually low trough occurring.

CHAPTER 17

Anchoring in Practice

The theory of anchoring is one thing. The practice is quite another.

Most authorities recommend a 7 to 1 scope for safety under average conditions; that is, the length of your anchor rode should be seven times the depth of the water. Note that the depth of the water in this calculation includes the extra length between water level and the bow chock or roller. In other words, depth of water really means the distance from your bow roller straight down to the sea floor. The difference between this measurement and the actual depth of the water becomes significant in shallow anchorages.

The idea is that such a long anchor line will exert a pull on the anchor that is more horizontal than vertical, so the anchor can dig in better.

But if you anchor in water 30 feet (9.1 m) deep, and you let out 210 feet (64 m) of anchor line, your boat may range back and forth over a circle with a diameter of more than 400 feet (122 m)—or longer than a football field.

That might be fine in a deserted roadstead; but in a popular anchorage, there simply isn't room for everybody to wander around on the end of 200-foot-long (61-m-long) tethers.

One practical answer in settled weather is a 3 to 1 scope of all-chain rode. Drop your hook half a boatlength behind the boat ahead, pay out a 5 to 1 scope, dig the anchor in well by putting the engine into reverse, and then shorten the scope to 3 to 1.

Most anchors will break out of the ground if the angle of pull on them is greater than 8 degrees from the horizontal. But the weight of chain gives it a curve, known as the catenary, that holds it low against the bottom. For this reason—combined with the fact that chain is far more resistant to damage from coral, rocks, underwater obstructions, and passing outboard engine propellers—most cruising boats carry all-chain rodes. Chain is also self-stowing and doesn't often tangle.

STRIKING A COMPROMISE

The weight of an all-chain rode so close to the bows can be very detrimental to performance on a small boat, so a compromise is usually struck. The part of the rode that is in contact with the ocean floor is made up of chain, and the rest comprises stretchy, three-strand nylon. How long should the chain be? As long as you can bear it to be, but at least as long as your boat.

An all-chain rode is so much to be preferred for cruising purposes that even a small boat should try to carry at least one rode of chain—even at the inconvenience of having to stow it lower and farther aft.

One idea that has worked well for some boats is to move the windlass to a position just forward of the mast. You can also have a chain gipsy installed on a winch mounted on the mast, with a chain pipe leading to a locker in or near the bilge at the foot of the mast. On other boats, a long, sloping chain pipe, usually of plastic, guides the chain to a locker farther aft than normal in the forepeak. However you arrange it, the idea is to get that weight closer to the middle of the boat and as low down as possible—and to make sure it will not come spilling out in the event of a capsize.

Your boat's tendency to wander around in a large circle at the end of its rode can also be reduced by dropping a second anchor underfoot from the bow, preferably on a chain rode. Give it a bit of slack in the rode, but not too much. The anchor won't be able to set itself properly, of course, but its drag will drastically cut down on the amount of aimless wandering caused by random puffs of wind and stray licks of current. At the same time, this anchor won't prevent the boat from taking up her proper position in the event of a permanent change of wind or current.

Anchoring by the Stern

It's often useful to be able to toss an anchor over the stern, particularly if you are under sail in a small boat or if you have no engine with which to

set the anchor. A nylon rode and anchor will usually fit neatly in a cockpit locker or on a special reel on the stern.

When you sail into a crowded anchorage, you can simply strike your mainsail when you're all the way to windward. Then sail downwind gently under a foresail—or under bare poles if the wind is blowing hard—and ease the anchor over the stern in your chosen spot. Let out a scope of at least 5 to 1 as fast as you can so that no pull will come on to the anchor until you're ready to snub it.

As the anchor digs in, you can raise a foresail (or sheet it in, if it's already flying) to set the anchor firmly. Then, at your leisure, take a line from the bow roller, run it aft outside all the rigging and lifelines, and clap it on the anchor line with a rolling hitch. Ease away on the stern anchor line, and your boat will be lying to her anchor by the bow like everybody else.

Incidentally, if you're ever troubled by your boat's excessive hunting from side to side in a crowded anchorage, you'll usually find she will be far more docile if you anchor her by the stern. This works only in protected anchorages, of course, because most anchored boats are uncomfortable with large waves smacking up against the stern, but it can be a handy trick to know.

If you have a ketch or a yawl, you can also cut down on wandering at anchor by leaving the mizzen set and sheeted well home, though it does add to the wear and tear on the sail if you're planning to do it for weeks at a time.

Some boats will wander less if you lash the helm amidships; others seem to be more discouraged from hunting by leaving the rudder free to swing. A boat's behavior depends on the amount of windage, where it has most effect, and the shape of the immersed hull. Experiment with your boat to see how she behaves best.

Snubbing

If the waves get up, your all-chain rode may start to snatch and jerk at the foredeck bitts or cleat. You can then hitch a 20-foot (6-m) length of three-strand nylon to the anchor chain, where you can conveniently reach it from the foredeck, and make the bitter end fast to some strong fitting. Then veer about 24 feet (7.3 m) of chain and make it fast again, leaving the nylon to take the snubbing strain with the chain hanging in a loop beneath it.

Dragging

If your anchor drags, let out more line immediately. If that doesn't do the trick, and you have the room and the time, send out another anchor in the dinghy and set it at the bow at an angle of about 45 degrees to the other one.

If you don't have time, or if the water is deepening too quickly, you'll have to start the engine or make sail, get the anchor up, and drop it again closer in.

If it looks as though you're in for a really bad blow, but the anchorage is protected from large seas, shackle the kedge to the crown of your bower with about 10 feet (3 m) of chain. Then lower them both overboard on one line. Nothing is more secure than that.

If the anchorage is open to large seas, make haste to get out of there while you still can. You'll be safer at sea.

There are times, particularly at night, when it's difficult to tell if your anchor is dragging. As the water level drops with the outgoing tide, for example, your scope will increase and your boat will lie farther back: and at night, land masses and other boats always look nearer than they do during the day.

After you have set your anchor and are lying back to the full length of the rode, try to find two objects in line ashore abeam of you (or nearly so). The crown of a nearby pine tree might be in line with a distant mountain peak, for example. This transit will open quickly if you start dragging and you'll get a quick warning when the tree no longer lines up with the mountain.

If you can't find two objects in line abeam, take a beam bearing of a conspicuous object with your handheld compass and write it down. If the bearing changes substantially, you're dragging. At night, unless the moon is very bright, you'll need to find a light to take a bearing on.

Watch your depthfinder, of course. If you have an alarm, set it so it warns you when you're moving into shallower water. Some Loran-C and DGPS sets can also be programmed to sound alarms if you start to wander.

If you're uncertain about whether you're dragging or not, feel your anchor line in the bow, just forward of the roller or chock. Most dragging anchors will jiggle and jostle the rode. It feels almost like a fishing line when you've hooked a really small but lively one. All-chain rodes will often produce a rumble from the sounding box of the forepeak, particularly if there's rock down there.

Finally, don't be confused if the boat at anchor behind you starts moving slowly upwind toward you in a blow. It can be a deceptive phenomenon, but as some of us have belatedly discovered, it doesn't pay to stand there too long trying to solve the puzzle. You're dragging. Do something about it, quickly.

Mooring

Technically speaking, mooring is anchoring with more than one anchor. Some insurance policies mention it, so be sure you understand the term.

If you're planning to leave your boat unattended for a while in an anchorage, both you and she will be happier if she's moored.

The usual way to moor is to set out your bower anchor in the direction of the prevailing wind (or the direction of the strongest expected wind) and to drop the kedge in a straight line aft. Then make the end of the kedge line (usually nylon) fast to the bower rode (usually chain) and ease away the bower rode until the kedge warp is well under water and will not be fouled by the

yacht's keel as she swings over it. This is often called a Bahamian moor.

Don't attempt to make a taut, straight line of your rodes between the two anchors. Leave some slack, so that if the wind blows from abeam, the rodes will lie to windward in a V shape and relieve the anchors of a great deal of strain.

You can use an adequately sized swivel to join the kedge warp to the bower rode to avoid ending up with a fouled hawse from the boat's swinging around the clock. But this is not totally necessary—although you might need some

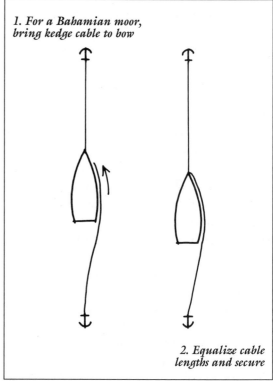

1. For a Bahamian moor, bring kedge cable to bow

2. Equalize cable lengths and secure

The Bahamian moor places anchors fore and aft in the direction of the strongest current or wind, but the aft rode is taken to the bow (1), secured to the forward rode, and lowered beneath the water (2). This way the keel will not foul the rodes as the boat swings.

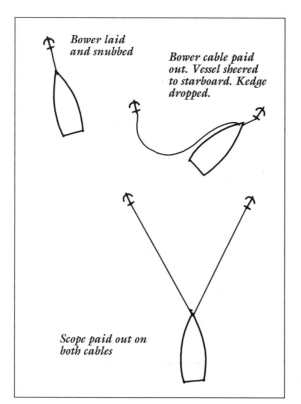

Bower laid and snubbed

Bower cable paid out. Vessel sheered to starboard. Kedge dropped.

Scope paid out on both cables

The fork moor. Two anchors laid out to windward in a wide V restrict your boat's swinging circle and add greatly to the holding power.

patience to unpick the tangle of two unswiveled rodes when you're ready to leave.

Terrain

Take note of the terrain around your chosen anchorage. It gives you a good idea of how quickly the water will deepen. A steep beach is likely to continue that way under water, and a gently sloping mud bank will probably signal shallows a long way out from the shoreline.

Coral

Sooner or later you'll come to anchorages whose floors are dotted with coral. It's not good to anchor among heads of coral because coral comprises living creatures and is easily damaged by chain. But coral also slices through nylon line, just as if it were butter.

Whether it's good or not, there will be times when you'll have to anchor on a sandy bottom dotted with coral heads. In this case, the best plan is to use chain, but to buoy it about two-thirds of the way along its length from the boat so it rises from the anchor at a fairly steep angle. You may need more than one buoy. This will prevent the line from fouling underwater coral as the boat swings, dangerously shortening the scope. If the wind pipes up, however, the boat will lie back to its full scope and drag the buoys under water. And there will be the chance of fouling the coral again.

When your boat has circled a coral head once or twice, there is only one way to free your chain and recover your anchor: Dive for it. Be sure to keep a snorkeling mask on board.

If you can find a suitable clear patch, you can lay out anchors from the bow and stern to stop the boat from swinging around, but beware of winds or currents that come at you from the side. They put an extraordinary strain on the anchor lines, and you are likely to drag. Giving more scope to one or the other, preferably the bow line, will bring the strain back to normal, but the boat will take up a new position that might or might not be free of coral just below the surface.

Some experienced cruisers prefer to anchor in water 90 to 120 feet (27 to 36 m) deep when possible, because coral heads are far less common in deeper water, but they have to carry an awfully long anchor line.

Safe Anchorage

When you're seeking a safe anchorage, bear in mind these four basic requirements.
- Shelter from wind and waves
- Room to swing around
- Sufficient depth of water at low tide
- Good holding ground

Anchoring Rights

In the ancient tradition of the sea, the first boat in an anchorage claims the right to ask others for room to swing freely. Not only that; she can also claim a clear exit to the harbor mouth, without having her maneuvering room hindered by another boat, should she wish to leave.

This custom was codified in the U.S. Admiralty Court's decision 124-5861 of 1956. This stated, *inter alia*, that "A vessel shall be found at fault if it . . . anchors so close to another vessel as to foul her when swinging . . . (and/or) fails to shift anchorage when dragging dangerously close to another anchored vessel. Furthermore, the vessel that anchored first shall warn the one who anchored last that the berth chosen will foul the former's berth."

CHAPTER 18

Gastro-Navigation

J U N E   V I G O R

I found no fault with the cook, and it was the rule of the voyage that the cook found no fault with me. There was never a ship's crew so well agreed.

—Joshua Slocum, *Sailing Alone Around the World*

It was a moment of pure triumph for the cook. We had crossed the equator, a major seamark on a passage from South Africa to Florida. The little Brazilian island of Fernando de Noronha—with its schools of dolphin, fleets of frigate birds, and magnificent white beaches—was behind us. Bequia and the turquoise waters of the West Indies lay ahead.

Neptune had chosen to "whoosh" us over the line with some hectic weather. The motion was violent and there was a double reef in the mainsail. When the two able seamen aboard—my husband John and our 17-year-old son Kevin—had to go forward, they went with lifelines clipped on.

Nevertheless, I proudly served a special three-course meal in honor of the occasion. It began with Equatorial Tomato Bisque, served with fresh-baked bread. The main course was a fine dish of Shrimp Fried Rice à la Neptune. And for dessert we had New World Fruit Cocktail, a heady mixture of litchis, mandarin orange slices, and chopped nuts marinated in orange liqueur and topped with whipped cream. Coffee and after-dinner mints followed, of course.

The meal earned the high honor of a special mention in John's usually terse log. Never mind that it depended heavily on tinned food; never mind that on dry land I have cooked up far more impressive dinners for far more people. Our crossing-the-line feast made me feel I had finally mastered the intricacies of gastro-navigation and earned my stripes as a sea cook.

"On-the-Job" Training

There were times when I thought I'd never make it. When we set off on our six-month voyage, I had no idea a sudden roll could leave you holding a hot frying pan with your elbow jammed between the towel rack and the bulkhead. I hadn't learned the basic fact that one hand for the boat and one hand for the can means no hand for the can opener. I didn't know every object I set down would become a malicious unguided missile.

What I did know was that the galley in our compact 31-footer was Spartan enough to delight those religious orders that go in for mortification of the flesh. It had a single stainless steel sink with two cold-water pumps, one for fresh, one for salt; a two-burner kerosene stove; an icebox, which served no purpose at sea once the ice had melted; and several lockers and shelves. There was no oven, but the pressure cooker did double duty.

We lived aboard for two months before we set sail, so I had plenty of time to get used to the equipment, such as it was. I had tried out lots of recipes and read all the books I could get my hands on. I had talked to experienced sea cooks and attended a seminar or two, so I was full of confidence.

I was going to make my own yogurt and cream cheese. Soups and stews would be made from scratch, with good dried beans and such. We'd have scones, bread, or pancakes every day. Breakfast would always be hot. Dinner would always include dessert. I even toyed with the idea of a barrel of salt pork.

None of this seemed ambitious while we were happily bobbing at the mooring; none of it seemed impossible while we were conducting fair-weather sea trials. But when our real voyage started, things were different.

On the second day out we hit the first of the seven gales we would encounter between Durban and Cape Town. Very suddenly, trying to fix food was as frustrating as trying to put your elbow in your ear. Nothing I had read and no one I had talked to had prepared me for the problems of a seasick cook trying to work on a wildly erratic platform that never stopped lurching.

So I learned the six essential rules for the survival of a sea cook the hard way. But I learned fast.

SIX ESSENTIALS
1. You have to eat.
Even a seasick cook has to provide food and drink and see to it that everybody eats, at least a little. It's an important morale booster and it's also a safety factor. A weak and dispirited crew endangers the safety of the ship. Think of yourself as the welfare officer, as well as the cook.

It's a good idea to have some food prepared in advance for the first day or two. I did that, but I made the wrong choices. I put milky cream of potato soup into a thermos and it soured before I could persuade anyone to try it. A light broth would have been much better. I took fried chicken—one of our favorite finger foods—but it was too greasy for queasy tummies.

Bland, fresh food in small pieces got the warmest welcome. Trail mix, carrot sticks, hard-boiled eggs, chicken broth, dry crackers, and fresh fruit (peeled and sliced) were all acceptable. The fried chicken was appreciated after I removed the skin and cut the white meat into dainty cubes. Fruit juice went down well, too. Don't expect thanks or enthusiasm. Don't get upset if the crew glares at the mere mention of food. Just be glad if they get something down.

2. Find everything before you start cooking.
Get out all the ingredients and all the implements you will need before you start to prepare a meal. Rehearse the steps in your mind, so you can be sure you have everything. Once you start the mixing and cooking process, interruptions are awkward. This was particularly true in our galley, since the lids of the icebox and the dry stores locker formed the working surface. Once I started stirring things up, it was a major job to get into either one. The shelves where I kept cutlery and condiments were behind the stove and it was dangerous to reach over it when things were cooking. (We didn't design the galley, and as a first-timer, I couldn't tell what was wrong with it until we were at sea.)

Once you've got everything out, you need a safe place to stow it all. I wedged a square plastic basin into a corner where it couldn't shift and put everything to be used for a meal into that. Of course, the corner was in front of the pan locker, so first I had to be sure I got out all the pans I needed.

3. Always have a plan before you pick up a pan.
Once you start mixing and cooking, be sure you know where you will put the things you've finished with. My small sink quickly filled up, so I

put a plastic bucket in the locker space under it. Dirty dishes and utensils went into the bucket as I finished with them.

If I could, I just turned off the heat and left the pans on the stove until after the meal. If I needed to put something else on to cook, hot pans went into the steel sink. There is no worse feeling than finding yourself holding a hot, heavy pan in a rough sea, with nowhere to put it down.

Cooking on two burners inevitably involves some switching. Your meat sauce is coming along nicely on one burner. The spaghetti is ready to come off the second burner, and the vegetables are ready to go on. You pick up the spaghetti pan, put the vegetable pan on the burner—and then what? If the sink's not empty, you're in trouble. Always figure out where the hot pans go before you pick one up.

4. Don't hit the skids.
Purpose-designed mugs and dishes for boats have skid-proof rubber rings set in the bottoms, and these work well. We used a cheaper method: I painted the bottoms of dishes, plates, and mugs with thick layers of rubber cement. It stuck to the dishes well and dried to a good firm nonskid finish.

Damp cloths, sponge cloths, or paper wipes spread on working surfaces makes them nonskid, too. Our Formica surfaces looked nice, but they were as smooth as glass; before I figured out the wet cloth trick, I had to make some pretty fancy catches. Even with the cloths, I learned never, ever to put an open container of liquid on an ungimbaled surface. Even in the calmest sea, it's an invitation to disaster—such as zig-zag trails of evaporated milk all over the cabin.

5. Play it safe.
If you can, sit while you work. If you can't sit, wedge yourself into as secure a position as possible. Some sea cooks use a waist strap in the galley

to brace against, but I was always afraid of hot spills and preferred to be able to escape—fast. I worked sitting on the companionway steps a lot of the time, which meant that no one could go in or out when a meal was in progress, but it went a lot faster when I could use two hands.

The cook should not wear only a teeny-weeny bikini. Spills happen, burns are serious. Cover up with a plastic apron or at least a shirt, even when it's sweltering, and be careful of bare feet. When the weather was really rough, I cooked in my rubber boots and oilskins: not my most elegant hostess attire, but it saved me from burns a couple of times.

Use a mug or a ladle to dish up hot foods: Don't try to pour from the pan. When you have to pour, from a kettle for instance, be sure the direction of the spout is fore or aft, rather than athwartships. Hold the kettle in one hand and the mug or dish you are pouring into in the other. That way you can move them in sync. Since this is a two-handed operation, do it in a well-braced, secure position. Never try to pour into a stationary container: The cup will move with the boat and you'll find yourself pouring in the place where it used to be.

Make sure your gimbaled stove is balanced correctly for the weight of your heaviest pan and its contents. If the balance is wrong, the pan can fall off the stove. Test your pan guards to make sure they don't slip.

6. Save your sanity—keep it simple.
I soon learned to serve one-dish meals as often as possible and to avoid anything that had to cook for longer than 20 or 30 minutes.

I set sail with a waterproof folder stuffed with interesting recipes for chocolate fondue, English muffins, curried egg dip, and other such delicacies. The dishes were easy enough to cook, but making them meant reading the recipe. I would not have believed that could be too much trouble; but a lot of the time it was. My recipe folder spent most of the voyage wedged in the pan locker to stop rattles, and I cheerfully invented as I went along.

It's amazing how much effort it takes to work on a constantly moving platform. Preparing a meal can be exhausting, particularly when the weather is bad. It isn't old age getting a grip. It's just that you are using a lot of physical energy to keep your balance and juggle everything—so make it easy on yourself whenever you can and don't feel guilty. Go for convenience foods when the going gets rough. Good food is important, but it can also be easy food.

The best time and place for elaborate creations is in port. Then you can take your time, turn out a feast, and talk till dawn about the trials and triumphs of cooking on the crest of a wave.

Sea-Tested Tips

On an ocean passage, the first thing to suffer from a sea-change is usually the crew's appetite. Suddenly they won't touch foods they've always loved; suddenly they'll crave things they've never eaten in their lives. They'll eat all day and all night or they won't eat at all. So, if you want them to kiss the cook, even after months of cruising, try these sea-tested tips.

- Variety is everything. Once you're out of sight of land, food is entertainment as well as nourishment. Take as many different snack foods as possible.
- Don't depend too much on any one item, no matter how popular it was before you cast off. If the crew suddenly decides that muesli is yucky, it won't matter that you brought 15 packets because it's always been their favorite. They still won't eat it.
- When you crave something fresh, something crisp is almost as good: pickles, nuts, crackers, chips, pretzels, trail mix, sunflower seeds, coconut strips, banana chips, ginger snaps, freshly made popcorn. Anything crunchy will do the trick.

- Apples, oranges, pineapples, coconuts, carrots, onions, cabbage, and potatoes keep better than other fruits and vegetables and make welcome snacks and salads. Ration them, if necessary, because you'll miss them when they're gone.
- You'll always have something fresh if you sprout seeds. In warm weather, sprouts are quick and easy to grow. Take a couple of quart-size wide-mouthed glass jars; cheese cloth, cut in 8-inch (200-mm) squares; wide rubber bands; and a variety of fresh, natural seeds. Seeds for sprouting can be bought at health-food stores. Alfalfa and mung beans taste great and sprout quickly. Adzuki, soy, garbanzo, kidney, pinto beans, sunflower seeds, lentils, peas, and wheat are good, too. Put a handful of seeds in a jar, cover with lukewarm water and soak for eight hours. Cover the mouth of the jar with cheese cloth, held in place by a rubber band.

  After soaking, drain off the liquid through the cheesecloth and rinse the seeds with lukewarm water. Put the jar at a 45-degree angle, mouth down, to drain. (I propped the jar in the sink with sponges.) Cover loosely with a cloth to keep out light but allow for ventilation. Rinse two or three times a day with a small amount of water to keep the seeds moist and drain well each time. In warm weather, sprouts will be ready in two to three days. Uncover the jar on the last day and the sprouts will turn green.
- Fake fresh, by creating salads out of tins. Try sweet corn, lima beans, baked beans, new potatoes, artichokes, sliced beets, asparagus, peas, pineapple, olives, and mixed pickles, served with mayonnaise or other salad dressings. Sprinkle with sprouts or chopped hard-boiled egg to complete the illusion.
- Fried food almost never loses its appeal.

You can fry almost anything in pancake or fritter batter.

- Fresh bread makes up for everything. Make rolls or small loaves to cut down on baking time.
- Take twice as much canned fruit and fruit juice as you think you will need.
- Take half as much canned meat as you think you will need.
- Provide a snack bag and a vacuum flask of cocoa, coffee, or fruit juice for night watches. Vary the snacks from night to night. Granola bars, beef sticks, cookies, candy, nuts, crackers, hard-boiled eggs, cheese wedges, and dried fruit are good choices.
- Keep a secret store of luxury items, such as glacé fruit, exotic tinned fruit, mints or chocolates, canned fruit cake, candied ginger, rum baba, special jams or preserves, a bottle of good port, or an exotic liqueur. A surprise treat is a great morale booster. Be sure you have something unexpected hidden away for special occasions such as birthdays, the half-way mark, and your first sighting of the Southern Cross.

CHAPTER 19

The Black Box Theory

V igor's Black Box Theory explains why fate treats some boats differently from others, why some boats and their crew survive storms that others don't.

But before I expound on the Black Box Theory, let me take you back many years to a day when an American scientist first planted the seeds of the theory in my mind.

I was a brand-new cub reporter on a large metropolitan daily newspaper in Durban, a large seaport on the Indian Ocean coast of South Africa. One of my very first jobs was to cover the luncheon speech at the local Rotary Club.

The speaker that day happened to be Dr. Earle Reynolds, an American anthropologist who was a member of the Atomic Bomb Casualty Commission. He had been studying the effects of the atomic explosions on the Japanese populace. But he hadn't come to Durban to discuss nuclear fallout with Rotarians. He had come to talk about his passion—sailing.

Reynolds had sailed from Japan to Durban on his 50-foot (15.2-m) ketch *Phoenix* with his wife Barbara, his daughter Jessica, and a Japanese crew. The title of his talk that day was "The Fifth Essential for Successful Yacht Voyages."

FIRST FOUR

He quickly listed the first four essentials.
- A well-found ship
- A good crew

- Adequate preparation and maintenance
- Seamanship, "What we Americans call know-how"

But never once during the course of his half-hour speech did he name the Fifth Essential. "I am not superstitious," he said, "but I am not going to name it. I'll leave that to you to work out."

Although he wouldn't name the Fifth Essential, he was quite happy to describe its effects on famous small-boat sailors such as Joshua Slocum, Alain Gerbault, and Harry Pigeon—all lone voyagers who needed more of the Fifth Essential than anyone else.

Slocum almost drained his reserves of the Fifth Essential when he set out in 1898 to be the first person to sail solo around the world. Off the coast of Morocco, Reynolds told the Rotarians, Slocum's sloop *Spray* was chased by a pirate vessel. Slocum cracked on all the sail he could carry, but the pirates were still gaining on him. So, determined to give a good account of himself, he ducked down below for his rifle. But *Spray* was suddenly hit by a powerful squall. In the flurry and turmoil of lowering sail again and making everything shipshape, he had little time to worry about his pursuers.

It was not until some time later that he was able to look back for them. Then he saw that the same squall that has caused him so much trouble had dismasted the other vessel, which then stood wallowing dangerously in the wreckage of her spars.

TURNED AROUND

Without further ado, Slocum decided to cross the Atlantic again and sail around the world the other way—tackling the notorious southern tip of South America from east to west, against the prevailing winds.

Spray was a most remarkable vessel in that she would sail herself on a dead run, or nearly so, with the mainsail set; Slocum boasted that his world-circling voyage was a good chance for him to catch up on his reading. From that date to the present, Reynolds said, no other boat had been able to do this—not even an exact replica of *Spray*. Was that pure Fifth Essential, or what?

And then there was Harry Pigeon, who sailed around the world twice on his own. After he had left Cape Town on the homeward leg of one of his circumnavigations, a change of wind direction set his yawl *Islander* sailing toward the coast while he slept below.

She actually ran aground in the only sandy bay in a stretch of coastline composed of nothing but rocks for tens of miles on either side. And that wasn't all. To reach the soft sand, the yawl had to pass over a rocky ledge at the entrance to the bay. Had it been low tide at the time she came along, *Islander*'s wanderings would have ended right there.

Pigeon was able to get his boat to sea again with the assistance of some craft from Cape Town. After refitting there, he set off again for America.

NO DOUBTS

Reynolds gave his audience several other examples of the Fifth Essential in action. Pretty soon, not even the dimmest Rotarian had any doubt about what it was.

I certainly knew what he was talking about, having met as a schoolkid some of the single-handed trailblazers of that early era, including Jean Gau, Bernard Moitessier, and Marcel Bardiaux.

Wizened little Gau arrived in Durban unheralded after an 87-day nonstop voyage from Christmas Island in the Indian Ocean in his 30-foot Tahiti ketch, *Atom*.

He was about to close with the shore off Durban with just three gallons of drinking water left when a northeasterly gale sprang up. He was driven 50 miles off course, pushed south along a very inhospitable shore with no ports of shelter. To make things worse, when the gale died down he would either have to claw his way back to Durban against the wind and the 4-knot Mozambique Current or carry on farther south for another 250 miles to East London. He wanted to get into port as soon as possible because he didn't think *Atom* could stand much beating to windward: One of his forestay fittings had pulled out of the stem, and all the strain was being taken by the jibstay that ran to the end of the bowsprit.

He didn't have to agonize over a decision for very long. Just as the northeasterly gale died down, a southwesterly "Buster" came roaring up the coast—and he high-tailed it all the way back to Durban in no time. "Pouf! I am 'ere!" he grinned. "And still I have two gallons of water; Look!"

LOST A SHROUD

And talking about northeasters and the Fifth Essential, there was a lovely Australian cutter, a 50-footer called *Active*, that lost one of her main shrouds on the way from Madagascar. She was being singlehanded by her owner, Jack Tomkin, who immediately put her onto the starboard tack and kept her there. Repairs at sea in the stormy Mozambique Channel were impossible, so whenever the wind backed around to the west, he hove to. But strangely enough, he encountered enough northeasters to allow him to reach Durban without ever having to go onto port tack.

When Bernard Moitessier arrived from Mauritius in his second boat, *Marie-Therese II,* he told me, "You have to try hard to get killed on a yacht at sea." Perhaps he was pushing his Fifth Essential a bit, because he lost the first *Marie-Therese* on a Mauritian reef when he went to sleep; he was later to lose the second one in similar fashion. But he didn't lose his life on either occasion, and that was a distinct possibility.

Yukio Hasebe, a Japanese singlehander I met while he was rounding the Cape in his sloop *Pink Maru Maru,* told me he had almost run out of the Fifth Essential on his previous yacht near Australia's Barrier Reef.

He fell overboard and was dragged alongside by his harness while the boat sailed at full speed under the control of the vane steering gear. He couldn't climb aboard because the boat was heeled over, and he was getting ripped to pieces by barnacles on the hull. Weak, exhausted, bleeding profusely, and hardy able to breathe, he was able to drag himself to safety when the boat ran full-pelt up onto the reef. He lost the boat, but he didn't die. At least, not on that occasion. A few years later, though, his Fifth Essential must have run out at last. Hasebe and *Pink Maru Maru* sadly disappeared on a passage from San Diego, California, to Japan.

So much for the Fifth Essential. I wondered for years why some people have it, and some people like Yukio have it some of the time, but not all of the time. Did it go with the boat? Did it go with the owner? And then the rationale occurred to me: the Black Box Theory.

INVISIBLE BOX

Vigor's Black Box Theory states that there is an invisible Black Box aboard every boat. Whenever you take the trouble to consult the chart, inspect the diesel filters, go forward on a cold and rainy night to check the running lights, or take any other seamanlike precaution, you earn a point that goes into the Black Box.

When things start to go wrong in bad weather, when you get to the stage where you can accomplish nothing more through your own skill and physical effort, the points are cashed in as protection. You don't have any control over their withdrawal: They withdraw themselves, as appropriate.

If you have no points in the Black Box, you will suffer the fate the sea decides. You may be one of those later described as unlucky.

If you have sufficient points to spend, you'll survive the storm—but you'll have to begin replenishing your savings immediately because the sea offers no credit.

Your initial deposit in the Black Box is the result of *thinking* about safety before you ever go to sea. More points come when you actually acquire some safety equipment, and even more when you learn how to operate it under emergency conditions. After that, it's a question of listening to your conscience telling you to get on with those necessary little acts of seamanship, and continually topping up your balance.

Your Black Box is probably the most valuable safety aid you can own. If you've only just discovered you've got one, don't hesitate. Start filling it with points straight away.

Overture's Atlantic Adventure

W hat happens when you set out to cross an ocean shorthanded during the wrong season in an unsuitable boat: a small, light-displacement fin-keeler with a detached rudder and a racing rig? Well, you survive, it seems. But only just.

For over 20 years, I have kept a letter that tells the tale of a remarkable voyage from Cape Town, South Africa, to Brest, France. The letter was written to a Durban resident named David Lewis, from whom I once bought a 28-foot (8.5-m) sloop called *Trapper.* The boat was a Canadian design off the boards of the Cuthbert and Cassian design team. She was built in England, then exported to South Africa to serve as a mold for a fiberglass production run for a boatbuilder near Johannesburg.

She was as pretty as a picture, one of the early IOR designs, with an elegant sheerline, a low cabintop, and a reverse counter stern of just the right proportions. Her good looks stopped the traffic wherever she went. In fact, we were out sailing on Durban Bay one summer's day when a schooner motored by with people all over her decks: They actually crowded the rail and clapped us. My wife June and I were caught totally off guard and quite nonplussed. We considered standing and bowing gravely. But in the end, as the schooner was pulling away, we settled for that little royal wave with which Queen Elizabeth greets the peasants.

Trapper was designed to take an outboard motor in a well. But by the time I acquired her, the well had been glassed in and a small Farymann diesel had been installed.

Even with the heavy engine and a propeller, she was fast. She would blast her way to windward through the white caps of a summer northeaster off the Durban beachfront and leave the competition wallowing far behind and to leeward. But, of course, she had precious little in the way of accommodation, and certainly nothing approaching standing headroom.

As a racing boat, she was not particularly heavily built. I recall an engineer friend's astonishment at the way her sides panted with the vibrations of the idling diesel, sending continuous ripples of waves away from the hull in calm water.

She was demanding on the helm, too, on any course other than a beat. You couldn't take your hand off the tiller for a second. If you did, she'd be haring off on some new course of her own choosing. I wouldn't have dreamed of crossing an ocean in her—even with a full crew.

But a man named David Parsons bought a sistership built from *Trapper's* mold. He called her *Overture* and sailed her all the way up the two Atlantic Oceans, north and south, with his wife Jean, in the 1970s. They had some extraordinary adventures that tested their adaptability and bravery to the limits.

I never knew David or Jean Parsons. I know they used to live in Newton Abbott, Devonshire, England, more than 20 years ago. But my recent efforts to trace them have failed. If anyone reading this knows of their present whereabouts, I would be grateful to receive their address in care of the publisher of this book, whose address appears at the front of this book.

In any case, at the end of their epic voyage, David Parsons wrote a letter to David Lewis, thinking Lewis would be interested to know how *Trapper*'s sistership had got on. Lewis passed on to me the copy of Parsons' letter, which is reproduced here.

It's a thoroughly British letter—laconic and self-deprecating—in which it is difficult to appreciate the seriousness of the problems they overcame, unless you have been to sea in bad weather in a small yacht yourself. Suffice it to say that medals for seamanship have been awarded for much less.

Here, in David Parsons's own words, is the story of *Overture*'s Atlantic adventure.

Dear Dave:

Hi there! This is a condensed version of the story of the journey of *Trapper* number two, *Overture*, from Cape Town to England—involving the loss of a rudder 600 miles south of St. Helena and a dismasting in a bad storm in the Bay of Biscay, and paying due respect to the extremely good design of the Trapper Class and to the soundness and strength of the hull and deck, which enabled said vessel to survive in spite of a severe beating which included three knock-downs in waves that were reported by the French navy afterwards to have reached 12 meters in height.

After the boat was delivered to Cape Town, a journey which had many incidents, we launched. It was then early June, I think. We set sail on the 14th of that month with a plentiful supply of food and water, but with a minimal knowledge of celestial navigation (we being my wife Jean, and myself).

Three days out of Cape Town, having headed 330 degrees magnetic all the time, we were rather lost. My sun sights put us in a variety of places ranging between the Skeleton Coast and mid-Atlantic. However, the errors were soon located and after the first week we had mastered the art and never again had any trouble in this field, the sextant becoming our most reliable method of position determining; even coastal navigation benefited from the occasional sun sight.

RUDDER LOST

A bit of a blow resulted in a largish following sea and this was too much for the rudder, which was constructed of a 25-mm stainless steel tube with 3-mm wall thickness, instead of a solid 25-mm stock as called for in the specifications. It probably saved the builder a few bob but it could have cost us a lot more. However, using a bookshelf and galley cupboard door and a few bolts, we made a jury rudder which lasted us to St. Helena. We arrived there after 23 days at sea, the jury rudder having taken us 600 miles.

St. Helena is an interesting place. Time stopped in the 1800s there, probably with the death of Napoleon. We found a carpenter who constructed a new rudder for us out of teak—4-inch by 4-inch stuff, very strong and with pintles of $1/2$-inch mild steel.

We departed after a three-week stay in St. Helena, and a passage of nine days saw us at anchor in Ascension. We only stayed there 24 hours—they don't encourage visitors, being a military base. We took on water and supplies.

The next haul was nearly 3,500 miles non-stop to Horta in the Azores. All trade wind sailing is a beautiful experience; day after day of warm sunshine, good following (or, in the northeast trades, opposing) breezes that are predictable. In the northeast trades we were on the starboard tack for nearly two weeks nonstop at one point. She steered herself merely by lashing the helm and trimming the sails, a fact which came as a pleasant surprise. We sighted a sperm whale, many porpoises and dolphins, and flying fish, which land on deck and are good to eat—but not too often! This part of the journey actually made us lazy and lethargic.

RESTFUL TRADES

The doldrums, which we had encountered after Ascension, kept us on our toes with squalls and calms, but the trades were restful.

We reached the Horse Latitudes, where the trades run out, after 36 days, and it took us a further eight days to finish the last 400 miles—continuous dead calms and light airs being the reason. The foresail had worn its piston hanks right through, but the sails (10-ounce) had stood up well to the continuous use they got.

Horta is a very friendly and likeable place. We were not allowed to buy drinks at all the first day in the yacht club. The members paid for everything for us, and we dined well also. We saw the famous "wall" where yachtsmen through the years have painted murals of their yachts and signed them. I did one of *Overture* not far from *Gipsy Moth IV* (Francis Chichester) and beside *Ondine*—so we are in good company. We set off early in October for Plymouth, and the first week went well—we covered over half the 1,300 miles.

The trouble started with a severe gale, forecast by the British Broadcasting Corporation (BBC) as Force 8 rising to Force 9, and by jingo that's what we got. Even under bare poles she was surfing. So, to stop her tendency to broach, we had to trail warps and a water container. This slowed her, but killed the steering quite a lot. We were pooped several times. Everything was soaked, including the bedding, and we were driven quite a way to the southeast, since the gale had been a westerly, veering northwest as the center of the depression passed to the north of us.

NO LIGHTS

The lighting systems (a gas lamp and a Coleman paraffin lamp) were smashed, which left us without effective navigation lamps. I have no real idea of either the wind speed or the wave heights of this gale, but they were severe, and I don't think an open-cockpit yacht should have been out in them.

By this time, after nearly a week of bad weather, we had reached sea area Finisterre (west of Biscay) when we heard the BBC broadcast a Force 9 to Storm Force 10 warning for our area. There was nothing we could do except push on, and that evening, even though it was a dead calm almost, the barometer fell 19 millibars in a few hours. So I put up the storm jib at the end of my watch, and everything was lashed down. When the storm started it blew like crazy, heeling the yacht about 45 degrees under just the storm jib. The seas did not build up until later, but I was forced to take down the storm jib (which is only 12 square feet in area). Not that it helped much. We had great difficulty in steering her; perhaps because of the new rudder. But it seemed that when she heeled right over she would steer on her keel, attempting to get up into the wind.

She started to surf again and out went the drags or warps, tied to the winches rather than the aft cleats to leave the stern free to rise to the waves.

KNOCK-DOWN

We experienced our first knock-down about this time and it did a lot of damage. The contents of the galley cupboards (being on the port side) ended up along the starboard side—coffee, salt, tea, tomato sauce, rice, everything you can think of. Some of the things were even found on the starboard cabin roof, so we must have been over at least 90 degrees. The car battery, which ran the chronometer, "walked" quite a way. It took time to find it, there was such a mess.

The cockpit had half filled, and there was a fair amount of water down inside. The bilge pump then packed up because a ball-point pen had been sucked into the inlet pipe and jammed open the valves—no strum boxes!!

The galley sink had also come out of its base and added to the jolly mess. (Worse—my only bottle of brandy got smashed.) We fixed the pump and arranged to do two hours on and two hours off, lashed into the cockpit during the storm. We found that the cyclone produced a cross-sea as the wind veered, and in this sea too much warp dragging behind was dangerous—we had to be able to steer her quickly to get her stern-to the biggest waves. Yet too little drag resulted in surfing, which was just as dangerous.

MAST OVERBOARD

A second knock-down cost us our mast. It broke below the lower shrouds where cuts had been made for internal lower shroud fastenings, and both halves went over the side.

By using bolt cutters to sever the two forestays, and because the mast had broken cleanly, we were able to get both halves back on board and lash them down. Perhaps the fact that the internal halyards kept them above water also helped—I don't know. Our radios were also knocked out by now due to salt water.

We didn't know it at the time, but the French navy later told us that a short way from where we were, an oil tanker had gone down in the same gale with a loss of 24 lives. A larger yacht with a crew of four also broke up and sank not far away.

Being just a "hulk," we found steering much easier, as fewer warps had to be dragged, but we sustained a third knock-down before we were through.

Next day, having half erected a jury mast out of the top half of my normal mast, we were surprised to see several ships bearing down on us. We later found out that the yacht that sank had sent out an SOS, and these ships naturally thought we had radioed the Mayday. We had no transmitter, of course—too expensive. One of them came alongside, in spite of my frantic waving to try to get him to go away. There is no international signal meaning "I am not in distress." Consequently, with the heavy seas that were running, our jury mast came down. All the port side stanchions were smashed in; I also sustained a bad gash in my left hand.

DOING HIS DUTY

By now, the skipper of the vessel was aware of the situation and left us. He can't be blamed—the "brotherhood of the sea" is a wonderful thing and he was doing his duty as he saw it. No less than eight other ships came close to ensure we were OK.

During the following hours we got the jury mast up and sailed to Brest, France, arriving two days later.

Ushant is a rocky area to the north of the river that leads to Brest and there were some sticky moments with a 2-knot, north-going tide. We were south of the rocks! However, we made contact with a French minesweeper once we were in the river and we were their guests aboard once we had "docked" at the naval base.

The meal was good, and showers et cetera were made available for us. The next day they gave us a lunch of fresh salmon, quail, champagne, two excellent wines, and an exotic patisserie. Gentlemen and seamen—great hospitality.

Overture is now out of the water and laid up in Brest. We returned the last 90 miles to Plymouth by car ferry. We will return in the spring and finish the journey.

All the best,
Dave and Jean Parsons

Beefing Up a Catalina 27

T his book has covered in theory what you need to do to make a boat seaworthy. In this appendix, we will take a closer look at what one man did in practice to make a circumnavigation safer in a Catalina 27—a boat that just scrapes through the seaworthiness test in chapter 2.

The Catalina 27 is one of the most popular small sailboats in the United States. *Practical Sailor* magazine describes her as the Volkswagen of the boat market: "It's basic, but it will get you where you want to go." The fact that she's cheap, roomy, fast, and readily available makes her a prime target for would-be ocean cruisers. Many neophyte sailors will be tempted by her. But beware: She needs a little help.

"Despite the fact that the Catalina 27 was designed and built as a coastal cruiser-racer," said *Practical Sailor* magazine, "several have actually made circumnavigations. We don't recommend using the boat this way, but it goes to show that good preparation and seamanship may be more important than your boat when it comes to successful offshore voyaging."

Patrick Childress of Newport, Rhode Island, was one of those circumnavigators. In the 1980s, he bought a secondhand Catalina 27 and sailed her around the world alone. Childress, now a Coast Guard-licensed skipper, agrees with *Practical Sailor*: He doesn't recommend that you jump into a standard Catalina 27 and try to sail around the world in three years, as he did. He feels that she needs beefing up first, in the manner described in

The Boating Beetle

T he Catalina 27, designed and built by Southern Californian Frank Butler, has been in production since 1971 and well over 6,000 have been built.

The boat is a fin-keeler with a raked, detached rudder well aft and a masthead sloop rig. But she was never designed for sea work. Early boats lacked backing plates on deck hardware, stanchions, and rails so that the gelcoat flexed and cracked quickly. Through-hull fittings were simply gate valves screwed onto pipe nipples glassed into the hull. Spreader sockets were made of cast aluminum, which fractures when overstressed. And the list goes on.

On the other hand, this boat has more headroom and interior space than almost any other 27-footer (8.2-m boat) on the market. In fact, she has about the maximum amount of interior room you could possibly cram into a 27-footer (8.2-m boat); the trick that made it all work was that she didn't look boxy or ugly. And—the cherry on the top—the owners didn't have to pay BMW prices for their Catalina 27s. They perceived them to be good value for the money, suited to the job this boat was expected to do: family racing and cruising, with a short coastal passage thrown in now and then.

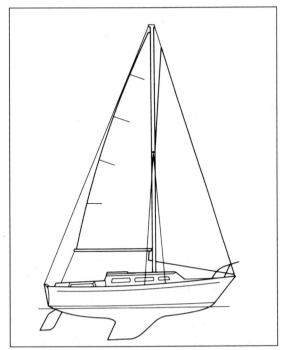

The Catalina 27 is 26 feet, 10 inches (8.2 m) long and has a waterline length of 21 feet, 9 inches (6.6 m). Beam is 8 feet, 10 inches (2.7 m), and draft is 3 feet, 5 inches (1.04 m) (shoal) to 4 feet, 0 inches (1.2 m) (standard). Design displacement is 7,300 pounds (3,311 kg), of which 3,150 pounds (1,429 kg) is carried as ballast.

this appendix. Even then, she needs careful handling. He chose a Catalina 27, he says, only because she was cheap and had ample accommodations.

Childress grew up on the water in southern Florida and was no stranger to boats. He knew this Catalina design was not an ideal round-the-world boat, especially for a singlehander. But he also knew her weak points, and he knew how to fix them.

His boat, *Juggernaut*, was a shoal-draft 1973 model that drew about 3 feet (914 mm), instead of the normal 4 feet (1.2 mm). She had the traditional interior plan and the standard rig. "There is no advantage to the shoal-draft model except

that the boat runs aground in shallower water," Childress admitted. "The keel weights on the earlier Catalina 27s were the same for the 3-foot (914-mm) and 4-foot (1.2-m) drafts. The lack of one foot (300 mm) of keel made for a tender sailing boat and a very uncomfortable one at anchor. She not only ranged around from side to side; she also did a lot of rolling."

FEW PROBLEMS

In his book *Singlehanded Sailing*, 2nd Edition (International Marine, 1992) the well-known sailor and author Richard Henderson says:

"Frankly, the Catalina 27 would not be my choice for extended offshore work, but Patrick Childress made a solo circumnavigation in his

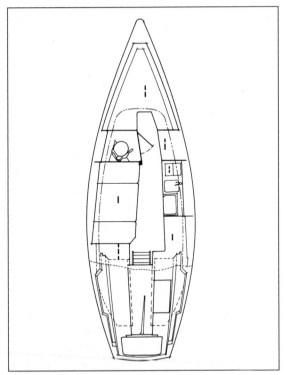

This version of the Catalina 27 interior features a midships galley and dinette. The alternative, which most owners prefer, is an aft galley layout that provides more storage and makes better use of space.

Juggernaut with very few problems. I am including the boat here because it is quite easy to singlehand, is readily available, and offers more boat for the money than almost any other I know. Designed by Frank Butler in 1970, the Catalina 27 is an inexpensive craft but one that is attractive-looking and sails very well. Advantages for coastal singlehanding are a buoyant hull with moderately high freeboard, a fairly long fin keel, swept forefoot, good hull balance, maneuverability, and a simple rig. Disadvantages include light construction, an accommodation arrangement that is best for harbor living, and a raked spade rudder that makes the helm a bit too quick for singlehanding. The boat can be beefed up and modified, of course, and the first thing I would do is replace the cast-aluminum spreader sockets with those made of stainless steel."

Henderson was right to have his doubts. Few people with any seagoing experience would hold up a standard Catalina 27 as a sterling example of a seaworthy cruiser. But the design certainly does have its merits. In fact, in the April 1998 issue of the magazine *Cruising World,* mechanical engineer John Holtrop did research into the "ideal cruiser," and the Catalina 27 rated *second best* in the 22-foot to 28-foot range.

VITAL STATISTICS

Holtrop made his choice mathematically, comparing the vital statistics of hundreds of boats in a computer, and using a software concept called "fuzzy logic" to judge those most seaworthy.

This seems to prove two things: computers are landlubbers, and fuzzy logic is no substitute for common sense. There are, as Patrick Childress points out, many boats the size of the Catalina 27 that are more seaworthy. Nevertheless, after suitable beefing up and fitting out, the Catalina 27 has proved that she is capable of sailing around the world—if she is used in the right places at the right times.

Henderson was right about the weakness of

the Catalina's aluminum spreader sockets, too. *Juggernaut*'s did break, as a matter of fact, and Childress had to install new stainless steel ones. He worked all day every day for three months to prepare *Juggernaut* for her voyage. And even then there was more to do.

After setting sail from Miami in 1979, he kept strengthening her and improving her seaworthiness as he went along. "It wasn't until I got to Australia," he said, "that I felt I had done as much as I could."

Juggernaut's route for her three-year circumnavigation took her from Miami to St. Thomas, U.S. Virgin Islands, then through the Panama Canal, across the Pacific to Australia, across the Indian Ocean to South Africa, around Cape Agulhas, and north through the Atlantic to tie the knot at St. Thomas again.

FEW LUXURIES

Juggernaut had no inboard engine; she had an outboard motor mounted to one side of the transom. And this boat was short on luxuries: She didn't even have a spray dodger. But Childress was young and enjoyed the Spartan life.

"I deliberately kept her as light as I could," he said. "I figured making her light and buoyant would help her seaworthiness."

To this end, he never carried more stores than were necessary to last him to his next landfall. On occasion, he even ran out of fresh water and had to catch rainwater.

His strategy paid off. Keeping her light relieved the hull and rig of much of the extra stress of ocean voyaging, and *Juggernaut* averaged 120 miles a day during her passages.

STORM STRATEGY

The worst weather Childress experienced was in the temperamental Indian Ocean. "We were several thousand miles from nowhere when the storm hit. Even from down below I could hear huge breakers out in the distance."

Childress's storm strategy was unusual. He stripped *Juggernaut* of all sail except a storm jib, which he sheeted in. Then he set his Navik windvane self-steering gear to keep *Juggernaut* close on the wind. With the tiny jib pulling the light hull to windward slowly, *Juggernaut* lay pointing about 45 degrees off the wind, taking the brunt of the waves on one side of her bow.

"She got lifted up, carried sideways, and dumped down three times," Childress said. "I began to wonder if it was time to run off before the wind; but despite the bouncing around, she seemed to be handling things OK, so I left her to it." The storm lasted about a day, but—thanks to Childress's careful preparation—it did no major damage.

KEEP MOVING
Even though Childress's method of handling the storm was unorthodox, the fact that he kept *Juggernaut* plugging away to windward supports C. A. Marchaj's theory that fin keels should be kept moving through the water to enable them better to dissipate the capsizing energy of the waves. Had *Juggernaut* been hove to or left to lie ahull, her shallow fin might not have been sufficient to prevent a roll-over.

Incidentally, his Navik vane gear served him well, steering for tens of thousands of miles in all conditions. "The only problem I had was with the welding," he said. "It just wasn't strong enough. I had to have it welded up in Australia, and then again in South Africa. After that, there was no problem."

Given the choice, Childress wouldn't do the trip again in a Catalina 27. "People occasionally ask me what they should do to beef up their Catalina 27s for an ocean passage and I tell them: 'Buy a different kind of boat. There are plenty of more seaworthy boats out there.'"

The trouble, of course, is that the more seaworthy boats are more expensive, so the Catalina 27 will always attract the budget-conscious cruiser.

"If they choose to do it in a Catalina 27, however, I strongly advise them to install extra cockpit drains the way I did," Childress added. "There were times in the Indian Ocean when the cockpit was more than half full."

Would he choose a traditional boat with a long keel next time? "Absolutely. I only went with *Juggernaut* because she was what I had at the time." And that brings us full circle, back to Eric Hiscock's statement, included in the introduction to this book, that remarkably few vessels used for ocean voyages were actually built for that purpose: The boats people voyaged in were the ones they happened to possess, "at the time they decided to cross an ocean or two."

The fact that Childress was successful also points to the fact that when it comes to seaworthiness, the knowledge and experience of the skipper count for at least as much as the fitness of the boat.

List of Alterations
For the record, here is Patrick Childress's list of the alterations he made to *Juggernaut*. Any comments in parentheses are mine.

1. Boarded over outboard engine well to mount a self-steering vane gear.
2. Strengthened starboard side of transom with 1-inch-thick mahogany plank on the inside, to accept an outboard engine bracket.
3. Installed four large cockpit drains horizontally through the aft end of cockpit and piped them through to transom. (Childress did this by installing through-hull fittings in the aft cockpit bulkhead and, lower down, in the transom. He joined them with hoses in the usual way.)
4. Made shelf in large cockpit compartment, extending the full length of the compartment, to hold gallon-sized containers and to utilize the top half of the otherwise wasted space in the compartment.

5. Installed ¾-inch (19-mm) wood frames around base of fuel tanks in the lazarette and installed tie-downs. These were regular steel 6-gallon (23-liter) outboard motor fuel tanks; the frames were simply to stop them sliding around.

6. Reworked the companionway entrance. Raised threshold wood to 2½ inches (63 mm) above the fiberglass threshold to force water running down slats into cockpit. Made overhang on hatch ¾ inch (19 mm) thicker to overhang companionway slats. (The threshold wood he raised is a vertical lip attached to the inside of the bridge deck. The original wasn't high enough to stop water running back inside the boat. The slats he refers to are the companionway drop-boards, or slides.)

7. Made new hatch runners, for a tighter fit. Installed plastic tabs on the front of the hatch to reduce spray entering hatch runners and dripping into cabin.

8. Cut fiberglass section from rear of quarter berth to open a new storage compartment.

9. Bulkheaded all storage compartments beneath berths. (By doing this, he not only divided the stowage into more conveniently sized compartments; he stiffened the hull panels with a series of mini-bulkheads.)

10. Moved electrical switch box to a position high inside the quarter berth. (Originally, the boat's electrical panel was on the face of the port quarter berth and vulnerable to spray and bilge water.)

11. Opened fiberglass panels behind the port and starboard bunk backrests, for added stowage.

12. Installed sliding doors for starboard shelf over the bunk.

13. Drilled drain holes from all storage compartments under the bunks to drain water onto the main saloon floor and into the bilge.

14. Installed a Whale foot pump for salt water at the galley sink.

15. Made a splash border around the sink (to stop water from slopping onto the cabin floor).

16. Installed chainplates for aft lower shrouds in place of deck plates. I first tried installing deck plates twice as large and thick as the originals, but that only threatened to pull a larger chuck of side decking out of the boat. (Childress added: "I used to watch the side decks flexing, and it was scary." He bolted the new chainplates through the hull. This interfered with the sheeting angle of the fore-sail somewhat. "But I felt it was more important to keep the mast up," he said.)

17. Installed a chart rack, dish rack, radio racks, and a medicine cabinet.

18. Made a door for the hanging locker.

19. Made a door for the small locker over the head.

20. Cut new access panel for storage under the V-berth, on the port side of the walk-in area.

21. Made a front vertical panel for the walk-in section of V-berth so this otherwise useless area could be used for storage.

22. Changed stove burners from alcohol to kerosene. The threads are the same, so it is a simple matter of unscrewing the old burner and screwing in the new one. Still, propane would be the best stove fuel.

23. Installed double headstays.

24. Installed heavier upper shrouds and aft lower shrouds. The forward shrouds stayed the same.

25. Installed open-faced, stronger turnbuckles.

26. Installed double backstays, with a backstay adjuster.

27. Removed the forward bolt on the rudder bracket going through the tiller and replaced it with two stainless steel hose clamps. A hole through a nonlaminated tiller of solid wood creates a weak spot at this point where the tiller can—and did—snap under stress.

28. Installed a ½-inch (12-mm) bolt through the

rudder-post cap, where the cap attaches to the rudder stock. Original bolt was too small in diameter and eventually wore an oblong hole.

29. Moved the lifelines aft from the foredeck, where they interfered with the anchor line.

30. Installed handrails and grabrails inside the cabin and on deck.

31. Made inboard guides for the companionway dropboards wider than the outboard guides, to facilitate installation of the boards in a choppy sea.

32. Made three companionway dropboards instead of four. The top board could then be inserted in a louvered position to deflect rain over the other boards, keeping the cabin dry and allowing ventilation.

33. Caulked around the water tank filler cap on deck to stop leaks.

34. Caulked all bolts going through the deck to stop leaks.

35. Replaced the corroded aluminum backing-plate for the main anchor cleat with a large, 3/4-inch (19-mm) block of teak.

36. Installed a galley harness to free both hands for cooking in a seaway.

37. Installed straps to hold a scuba tank to the top of quarter berth.

38. Installed cam cleats for the jib sheets.

39. Rerouted the icebox drain hose from the sink through-hull and let it drain into the bilge instead. Seawater was backing up into the icebox from the through-hull.

40. Installed medium-duty electric bilge pump in the bilge, fitted with float switch and manual override. Installed a large-capacity electric pump with float switch in a protected area under the cockpit for extreme emergencies in case the cabin became flooded. (Childress had only one solar panel to charge his battery, aided occasionally by a small-capacity genera-tor on his outboard motor.)

41. Caulked the hull-deck joint with 3M-5200 sealant to fill the void behind the rubrail, which was leaking.

Bibliography

Bauer, Bruce. *The Sextant Handbook,* 2nd. Camden, Maine: International Marine, 1995.

Blewitt, Mary. *Celestial Navigation for Yachtsmen,* 4th ed. Camden, Maine: International Marine, 1996.

Brodgon, Bill. *Boat Navigation for the Rest of Us.* Camden, Maine: International Marine, 1995.

Burch, David. *Emergency Navigation.* Camden, Maine: International Marine, 1990.

Casey, Don. *This Old Boat.* Camden, Maine: International Marine, 1991.

Coles, K. Adlard. *Heavy Weather Sailing,* 4th. Camden, Maine: International Marine, 1995.

Cohen, Michael Martin. *Dr. Cohen's Healthy Sailor Book.* Camden, Maine: International Marine, 1983.

Eyges, Leonard. *Practical Pilot.* Camden, Maine: International Marine, 1989.

Henderson, Richard. *Singlehanded Sailing,* 2nd. Camden, Maine: International Marine, 1992.

Herbulot, Florence. *Cooking Afloat.* Lymington, England: Nautical Publishing Company, 1970.

Letcher, John. *Self-Steering for Sailing Craft.* Camden, Maine: International Marine, 1974.

Slocum, Joshua. *Sailing Alone around the World.* New York: W.W. Norton & Company, 1984.

Spurr, Daniel. *Spurr's Boatbook: Upgrading the Cruising Sailboat,* 2nd. Camden, Maine: International Marine, 1991.

Stadler, Michael. *Psychology of Sailing.* Camden, Maine: International Marine, 1987.

Woas, Lee. *Self-Steering without a Windvane.* Newport, Rhode Island: Seven Seas Press, 1982.

Index

Page numbers in **bold** refer to pages with illustrations.

A

abandoning ship, 81
abandon-ship bag, 80–82, 86, 95
accommodations, 20, 145–46
Ace Sailmakers, 89, 197, 198–99
age, 172–73
air-conditioning, 139–40
alarms, 110, 206
alcohol: as cooking fuel, 121, 123; drinks, 122, 127, 171
alternators: engine-driven, 115–16; smart, 118
American Boat and Yacht Council (ABYC), 54, 93
AM radio, 111
anchor, 43–54; bitter end, 52; Bruce, **46;** buoying, 52; casting, 204–8; CQR, **45;** Danforth, **46**–47; Delta, **45**–46; dragging, 206; fisherman types, **44**–45; Fortress, 47; Herreshoff, **44**–45; holding power, 44, 47; lightweight pivoting flukes, **46**–47; Luke, **44**–45; parachute, **192**–93; plow types, **45**–46; Performance, 47; rollers, **51;** sea, 88–89, 198; sizing, 47–48; stowing, 51–52
anchor line, **43;** chafe, 48; chain stoppers, **49;** chain vs. nylon, 49–50; length, 51, 204; semantics, 205; sizing, 48, 54
Andersen, Tom, 172
anxiety, 166, 175. *See also* fear
Auto-Helm system, **156**
autopilots, **154**–55

B

backstays, running, 41
baggywrinkle, 32

Baker's Position Line Chart, 110
Bardiaux, Marcel, 81
Barkla, Hugh, 159, 161
barometer, 97–98
battens, 87
batteries: number of, 114–15; recharging, 115–17
beam: ratio to waterline length, 6–7; test of seaworthiness, 17; width, 5–8
beer, 171; bread recipe, 135; fiscal, vi
Bermudian rig, 12
beverages, 143–44. 171; punch recipes, 122, 127
bilge, hard vs. soft, **9**
bilge pump, 57, 219, 226
Bimini tops, 55–56, **60,** 140
biocides, fuel, 67, 68
bitter end, anchor, 52
Black Box Theory, 75, 214–16
bleach, 136–37
bleeding, engine, 69
Blewitt, Mary, 97
blistering. *See* osmosis
boarding ladder, **56,** 63
boom: brakes, 32, **33;** dimensions, 32; gallows, 32–33, 140; preventers, 33, 94; topping lifts, 33; vangs, 33, 93–94
bower, 43, 44
brass, 93
bread, 213; recipes, 133, 135
British Thermal Unit (Btu), 142
broaching, 188
bronze, 93
Bruce anchor, **46;** roller for, **51**
bulkheads: defects, **26;** fitting into hull, **25;** inspection of, 25–26; mini, 225
bulwarks, 61
bunk, 20, 92, 140–41; dimensions, **140;** pilot berths,

146–47; privacy concerns, 168–69, 170
buoy, anchor, 52
butane, as cooking fuel, 125

C

cabin trunk, 56; design, 8
calculator, navigation, 108
capsize, 3–4; causes, 6, 9; prevention, 197; and self-righting, 4–8. *See also* Think Inverted
carbon monoxide detector, 75, **76**
Carol cruisers, 12
Casey, Don, 36, 63, 142
Catalina 27, 7, 221–24, **222;** alterations to, 224–26
Catalina 30, **3**
celestial navigation, 97, 98, 108–9; idiot sheets for, **107, 108;** learning, 218
centerboard, 11
center of lateral resistance (CLR), 151
certificate of competence, 179–80
chain: advantages, 204; locker pipe, 56; stoppers, **49;** types, **50**
chainplates, 33, 225; sizing, 34
chart, 99; Baker's Position Line, 110; electronic, 103–4; plotting, 110; scale differences, **100**–101; storage, 99; types, 101
chart table, 20, 98–99
Chichester, Francis, 172, 194
Childress, Patrick, 221–26
chlorine treatment, 136–37
chronometer, 99
clearance papers, 178–79
cleats, 49
clothing, waterproof, 95, 146

CLR (center of lateral resistance), 151
CNG (compressed natural gas), 126
coastal vs. ocean cruiser, 2
cockpit: cushions, 142–43; design, 8; drains, 57–**58**, 194, 224; inspection, 27–28, 55; lockers, 58; requirements, 59; size, 59; test, 19
Cohen, Michael Martin, 163–64
Coles, K. Adlard, 188
collision mat, 76–77
colregs (International Regulations for Preventing Collisions at Sea), 36–37
compasses, 99–102
compressed natural gas (CNG), 126
cooking, 121, 169–70; fuels, 121, 123–26; practical advice, 209–13; safety, 130. *See also* recipes
cooking stove, **126,** 131; gimbals, 123, 211; placement, 122
cooling, 139–40, 143
coral, 208
cost, system for estimating, vi
CQR anchor, **45**
cracks: gelcoat, 27; keel, 29, 30; star, 24
cravings, food, 143–44
crew: fitness, 162–71; lists, 181; selection, 164
crew overboard pole, 59
Cullen, Barry and Patrick, 97–98
cupboards, 127
currents, dangerous, 201–3
cushions, cockpit, 142–43
customs, 177–78
cutter rig, 14

D
Dalling, Bruce, 162
Danforth anchor, **46**–47
dead reckoning, 102–3, 112
deck: inspection, 26–27, 55, 56, 61–63; skidproofing, 63; test of seaworthiness, 18
delamination, 27, 29
Delta anchor, **45**–46

depth markers, 50–51
depth sounders, 112–13
design: and seaworthiness, 3, 5–15; trade-offs in, 4
diesel: as cooking fuel, 124; engines, 65, **66**–68, 71–72
Differential Global Positioning System (DGPS), 105, 108
dinghies: vs. liferafts, 85; rubber, 87
dining table, 127
distance logs, 103
documentation, ship's, 179
dodger, 55, 59, **60, 147**–48, 194
Dorade boxes, 59–60, **61**, 63, 150
drain: cockpit, 57–**58**, 194, 224; shower, 148
drain holes, blockage of, 27–28
Draper, Laurence, 203
driver's license, 182
drogue, 86, 88–89; cutting, 200; Jordan series, 89, **90**, 197, 198–99; vs. sea anchors, 197–98
drop slides, 60–61, 225–26
drugs, 182
dry mat, **25**
Dumas, Vito, 201

E
electricity, 114–20
emergency: flotation, 81; navigation, 104–5; steering, 77
emergency position-indicating radio beacon (EPIRB), 77–78
engine, 65–74; gas vs. diesel, 65, **66**–67, 68; life expectancy, 66–67; maintenance, 69; mounts, **67;** outboard, 65–66; power, 69–70; runaway diesels, 71–72; spare parts, 72; starter motor, 114, 115; test, 19
engine-driven alternators, 115–16
EPIRB (emergency position-indicating radio beacon), 77–78
escape hatches, 78
exhaust, waterlift, **74**

extinguishers, fire 78–79, 127–28

F
fans, cooling, 143
fatigue, 92, 165–66
faucets, 128
fear, 166–69. *See also* anxiety
fiberglass, 23; edges, **28;** stiffening, **23;** thickness, **24;** types, **22**
filter: fuel, 67–68; raw water, 71, **72**
firearms, 79; licenses for, 180
fire extinguishers, 78–79, 127–28
fitness: mental, 163–69, 170–71; physical, 162–63
flare, freeboard, 9
flares, 79–80
flexing, 24, 27
flotation, emergency, 81
food, 143–44, 165, 169–72; variety, 212–13; weight, 124. *See also* recipes
foredeck wells, 49
foresail: safety features, 88; twin, 159–61
forestay, inner, 34–35
Fortress anchor, 47
Franklin, Nick, 157
freeboard: design, 9; test, 16
freshwater still, **80**
fuel: consumption, 68; cooking, 121, 123–26; filters, 67–68; tanks, 73, 224
furling systems, **39, 88**

G
gaff rig, 12
galley, 121–38
galley straps, 130, 226
gasoline: engines, 65, 66–67, 68; generators, 117
Gau, Jean, 172–73, 194–95, 215
generators, 115–17, 226
Global Positioning System (GPS), 103–4, 105–6; Magellan Nav 6000, **104;** vs. sextant, 111–12

gouges, in lead keel, 29, 30
grab bag, 80–82, 86, 95
griping, 15
gunwales, 61
Guzzwell, John, 195

H
habitability, 3, 4
hallucinations, 165–66
halyards, led aft, 33–34
ham radio, 82; time signals, 107
harness. *See* safety harness
hatch: design, 9; escape, 78
head (toilet), 144–**45**
headroom, 20, 145–46
health authorities, 178
heating: cabin, **141**–42; water, 130–31
heaving to, 190–93
heavy weather: Childress's strategy in, 223–24; experience in, 218–20; seamanship in, 189–201; theory of, 186–88
heliographs, 90–92, **91**
Henderson, Richard, 167, 222–23
Herreshoff anchor, 44–45
high-frequency (HF) transceivers, 82; time signals, 107
Hiscock, Eric, v, 49, 70, 167, 186, 224
Hiscock, Susan, 70
hobbyhorsing, 10
hour meter, engine, 68–**69**
hull: desirable features, 23–24; fixing, 24–25; hole fittings, 92–93; inspection, 22–23; shape, 9; test, 16–18; thickness, **24**
hydrodynamic lift, 10

I
idiot sheets (celestial navigation worksheets), **107, 108**
immigration, 178
inertia, 9–10
International Regulations for Preventing Collisions at Sea (colregs), 36–37
inverters, 117–18

J
jacklines, 82–**83**
Juggernaut, 222–26

K
keel: centerboard combinations, 11; depth and shape, 10–11; evolution, **10;** inspection, 29–30; length, 152, 187–88, 191, 195; test, 17; weight, 5–8
kerosene, 123–24, 225
ketch rig, 14
knife, 83–84, 94

L
Lacey, John, 5
ladder, boarding, **56,** 63
laminations, separated, 24, 25
lanyards. *See* tethers
leaks, cockpit, 27, 28, 55
lee helm, 153, 158
Lewis, David, 166, 167
life jackets, 84
lifelines, 62, 84–85
liferafts, 80, 81, 85–86; navigation of, 104–5
lights: masthead, 36; navigation, 36–38; reading, 147; strobe, 86–87
Lindemann, Hannes, 171
liquid petroleum gas (LPG), 125–26; delivery, **125**
lockers, cockpit, 58
logs, 103, 112, 180–**81**
Loran, 103, 108
Luke anchor, 44–45
LWL (length at waterline), 6–7, 14
lying ahull, 194–95

M
mainsail: battenless, 87; furling systems, **39;** triple-reefed, **192**
Marchaj, C. A. (Tony), v, 9, 186, 187, 200, 224
Marconi rig, 12
Marelon, 93
Mary T, 55
mast: boots, 35; breaking, 219; dimensions, 35; and inertia, 9–10; keel-stepped, **35;** noise

inside, 35–36; raking of, 153; steps, 36; vibration, 36; wedges, 36
masthead lights, 36
masthead VHF antenna, 36
Matthiesen, Peter, 157
meals. *See* food
mirrors, signal, 90–92, **91**
mizzen sail, 14
Moitessier, Bernard, 200, 201, 216
monohulls, and self-righting, 5
mooring, **207**–8
mooring bitts, 49
mounts, engine, **67**
mugs, **122**
multihulls: escape hatches, 78; and self-righting, 4–5

N
nautical almanacs, 98, 108, 109
navigation: emergency, 104–5; gear, 97–113; tools, **106**
Nicholson 31, **3**
noise: engine, suppression of, 69; mast, 35–36; wind, 191
noon sun sights, 108–9

O
ocean cruiser, 2
off-course alarm, 110
Offshore Racing Council, 84, 88
oilcanning, 24
osmosis, 24; fixing, 25
ovens, 131
overhangs, 16; design, 11, **12**
Overture, 217–20

P
panting (oilcanning), 24
paper towels, 132, 149
paperwork, 177–83
parachute anchor, **192**–93
Pardey, Larry and Lin, 25, 54, 70, 89, 142, 192
Parsons, David and Jean, 217–20
passports, 178
Pearson Triton 28, **6,** 7
Performance anchor, 47
Pigeon, Harry, 215

pilot berths, **146**–47
pitchpoling, 188, 195
plotting charts, 110
port authorities, 177–79
portlights, 56, 62
position fix, 102, 105, 111, 218
power of attorney, 183
pressure cookers, 132–33
pressurized water systems, 133–**34**
preventers, boom, 33, 94
privacy, 146–47, 168–71
propane, for cooking, 125, 225
propeller(s), 65, **70**–71; odometer attached to, 103
propeller shaft(s), 70; locks, 71; stuffing boxes, 72–**73**
psychology, sailing, 163–71
pulpits, 62–63

R
radar, 108
radio, 82, 94, 95, 110–11; licenses for, 180
radio direction finders (RDF), 110–11
rainwater, catching, 137
range under power, 71
rations, survival, 137
raw water filter, 71, **72**
RDF (radio direction finders), 110–11
recipes: appetizers, 130, 131; bread, 133, 135; punch, 122, 127; soup, 128
reefing, 38–40; slab, **38**–**39**; storm, 189–90
refrigeration, 121–22, 128–30; holding-plate kit, **129**
Reynolds, Earle, 214–15
rig, types: Bermudian, 12; gaff, 12; ketch, 14; schooner, 14; sloop, 12; yawl, 14
rigging, 14; inspection, 32–42; test, 19; wires, 40–41
righting moment, 6
roach, 87
Robb, Frank, 166
rode. *See* anchor line
rollers, anchor, **51**
rope clutches, 41

Rose, Alec, 194
rudder: inspection, 28–29; shape and fastening, 11–12; test, 17; types, **13**
rum punch, 122, 127
running off, 195–97

S
safety, 216; equipment, 75–95; test, 19–20
safety harness, 88; clip-on points, 61–62
sails: flattening of, 153; foresail, 88, 159–61; mainsail, **39**, 87, **192;** plans, 12–14; safety features, 87–88; steering with, 158–61; storm jib, 87–88, 219
Sampson post, 49
Sandefjord, 98, 196
schooner rig, 14
scudding, high-speed, 200–201
scurvy, 170–71
sea anchors, 88–89, 198
seacocks, 93
seasickness, 173–76
seaworthiness, v–vi; and boat design, 3, 5–15; and self-righting, 3–5; and stability, 187–88; test, 16–21
self-righting capabilities: and boat design, 5–8; and seaworthiness, 3–5
self-steering: deactivating, 90, **91;** gear for, 151–61
servo-pendulum gears, 155, **156**–58
sextant, 106, 111–12; index error, 108
ship's log, 112, 180–**81**
showers, 130–31, 148–**49**
shrouds, 40
signal mirrors, 90–92, **91**
singlehanders, 92, 136; mental strain on, 164–68
sinks, 135, 219, 225
skidproofing, 63
skipper: experience, 20, 224; leadership, 164; licensing, 179–80
slab reefing: single-line, **39;** traditional, **38**

sleep, 92, 165. *See also* bunk
slick, protective, 192, 198
Slocum, Joshua, 158, 165–66, 214–15
sloop rig, 12
smart regulators, 118
smoke detectors, 92
solar panels, 116
solar still, **80**
sounding, 112–13
Southern Cross 31, **6,** 7
spars, inspection of, 32–34
spouse package, 182–83
spreaders, 41–**42**
sprouts, 132, 212
Spurr, Dan, 61
stability: directional, 152; initial, 5; and seaworthiness, 187–88; ultimate, 5
Stadler, Michael, 167
stamp, ship's, 181
stanchions, **62,** 84–85
star cracks, 24
stays, 34–35, 40, 41
steering: cable-quadrant system, 77; emergency, 77; with sails, 158–61. *See also* self-steering
stern: anchoring by, 205–6; shape of, 14
storm. *See* heavy weather
storm covers, 56, **57,** 62
storm jib, 87–88, 219
stove. *See* cooking stove
strobe lights, personal, 86–87
stuffing boxes, 72–**73**
sun sights, 108–9, 218
superstructure, 55

T
table: chart, 20, 98–99; dining, 127
Taleisin, 70
tangs, 33; sizing of, 34
tank: fuel, 73, 224; water, 137–38, 226
test of seaworthiness, 16–21
tethers, 88
Think Inverted, 5, 30, 42, 54, 64, 74, 96, 113, 120, 138, 150, 161, 176, 183
through-hull fittings, 92–93, 224

Tilikum, 198, **199**
tiller, emergency, 77
time signals, 107
Tomkin, Jack, 215–16
tonnage, formula for, 179
Trapper, 217
trim-tab gear, 155–56
trip line, **43,** 52
tumblehome, 9
turnbuckles, 42
twistle yard, **159**–61; hinge, **160, 161**

U
utensils, 122, 135, 211; washing, 135–36

V
vacuum flasks, 135
Valiant 40, 7
vane gears. *See* wind-vane gears
vangs, boom, 33, 93–94
vegetables, 132, 144, 212

Vendée Globe 60-footers, 7–8
ventilation, **63**–64, 68, 149–50
ventilator, **61;** waterproofing, 59–60
VHF radio, 82, 94; license for, 180; masthead antenna, 36
visas, 178
vitamin C, sources of, 171
Voss, John, 198

W
Wanderer III, 14, 70, 167
washboards, 60–61
watches, 92
water: delivery systems, 133–35, **134;** fresh, floating atop salt water, 137; generators, 116; heating, 130–31; impeller, 73; needs, 137; purification, 136–37; tanks, 137–38, 226
waterlift exhaust, **74**
waterline length, 6–7, 14
watermakers, 80, 94–95, 137

wave: freak, 202–3; plunging breaker, **4;** and protective slick, 192, 198; threatening, 199–200
weather cloths, 150, 194
weather helm, 15, 152, 153
weather information, 95, 201
West Marine, 154
wind: vs. current, 201–2; howling, 191
windage, 54; reducing, 194
wind generators, 116, **117**
windlasses, 52–**53,** 204
wind-vane gears, 155–58, **156, 157,** 216, 224
wires, rigging, 40–41
wiring, 118–20

Y
yawl rig, 14
Yukio Hasebe, 62, 216